Fall Girl

Fall Girl

My Life as a Western Stunt Double

MARTHA CRAWFORD CANTARINI
and CHRYSTOPHER J. SPICER

McFarland & Company, Inc., Publishers
Jefferson, North Carolina, and London

Unless credited otherwise photographs belong to the Martha Crawford Collection.

LIBRARY OF CONGRESS CATALOGUING-IN-PUBLICATION DATA

Cantarini, Martha Crawford, 1928–
    Fall girl : my life as a western stunt double / by Martha Crawford Cantarini and Chrystopher J. Spicer.
      p.   cm.
    Includes index.

    ISBN 978-0-7864-4753-4
    softcover : 50# alkaline paper ∞

    1. Cantarini, Martha Crawford, 1928– 2. Stunt performers — United States — Biography. 3. Women stunt performers — United States — Biography. 4. Show riders — United States — Biography. I. Spicer, Chrystopher J. II. Title.
PN1998.3.C3557A3   2010
791.430′28092 — dc22 [B]   2010013525

British Library cataloguing data are available

On the cover: Martha and her horse Jim during a promotional shoot for *The Big Country* in 1958 (photograph © Martha Crawford Collection); background ©2009 Shutterstock

Manufactured in the United States of America

McFarland & Company, Inc., Publishers
  Box 611, Jefferson, North Carolina 28640
  www.mcfarlandpub.com

To my friend Beverly King who encouraged me
when I was discouraged and would not
let me give up writing this story.

Acknowledgments

There is a select group of people out there without whom this book would not have taken the shape it has.

Many years ago the Australian writer John Baxter wrote a book called *Stunt*, now long out of print, about the history of stunts and stunt people in the movies, and his book and his encouragement remained an inspiration to us during this project.

Sometimes memory needs just a little prompt and some back-up, and so we would like to thank Michelle Plotnik from the town of Murphys, California, who very kindly organized some memory-gathering of her own amongst people she knew, including Don Boos and Bill Riedel, about the shooting of *Texas Lady* in and around that town.

Photographs for this book came from many sources, apart from our own collections, and so we owe thanks to the following people and organizations for their assistance. At the various studios, we would like to thank Jeremy Lott at MGM Worldwide Digital Media, Brian Palagallo at Paramount Digital Entertainment, Julie Heath at Warner Bros. Entertainment and Trinh Dang at Twentieth Century-Fox Clip Licensing. For contributions from their own collections, we would like to thank Jerry Schneider, Doug Hansen and Kirsten Andersen at Hansen Wagon and Wheel Shop, Carol and Tom Wood, and Bill Orvis at Snow Ranch. We would also like to thank Priscilla Finley and Su Kim Chung at the University of Nevada Las Vegas Library for their endeavors in locating information and photographs.

Special thanks to the producer and committee of the Golden Boot Awards of 2005 for allowing us to have another look at the memories, and to those who watched from the wings and cheered us on, especially our respective marriage partners John and Marcella.

Table of Contents

Prologue

When Chicago's first swimming pool for horses was built in 1965, my jockey husband John Cantarini and I were invited to the opening. It was such a big event that reporters and photographers from *The Chicago Tribune* and other papers were there to cover it. The trainer had an exercise rider and his gentlest race horse standing by to take the first swim. When the big moment came, however, that horse would not go into the pool.

After a few awkward moments, the embarrassed trainer grabbed the shank and began to fight with the horse, whose eyes grew wide with fear. The man jerked so hard on the chain in the horse's mouth that the poor animal reared and fell over backwards with a bloody froth on his lips. This particular trainer had an ego as big as his reputation, and at that time a woman didn't interrupt a man with his kind of standing. So, I had to watch in misery for the horse until the trainer ran out of ideas and was so red-faced that he looked ready for a heart attack. Only then could I step up and quietly ask:

"Bill, would you like me to put the horse in the pool for you?"

Completely at a loss as to what to do next, and so frustrated and humiliated he couldn't speak, Bill just nodded.

"Okay," I said. "Give me a rope and twenty minutes."

Their curiosity piqued, Bill and the gathered press contingent agreed to wait. So, I led the horse over a little hill, out of sight of the pool and the people. Did that poor animal ever need a friend right then! When we were alone, I took the length of rope and put a hitch called a "come-here rope" on him. It's a war bridle of sorts and takes skilled hands to work it correctly, but I knew what I was doing. Then we proceeded to get to know each other.

After about fifteen minutes, I had taught him to come to me and put his head on my shoulder when I clucked to him. He learned quickly, eagerly, because he understood what he was being asked to do and was anx-

1

ious to please. I rewarded him and soothed him and finally led him back to
the pool. The murmuring crowd fell silent as I kept walking right on down
the ramp into the pool in my expensive dress, meanwhile clucking to the
horse. To their surprise, that horse followed me right on in and put his head
on my shoulder. Next thing, he was swimming around the pool. I handed
the shank to the exercise boy, who was already in the water, and then they
both swam around as the crowd applauded and cameras flashed. I thought
I saw the horse eyeing the ramp, so I told the trainer to wave his hands as
he passed by. Pretty soon, we were all waving every time they came around.

"By the way," I asked the trainer, "what is that horse's name?"

"Keep Waving," he replied.

"I am," I said, "but what's his name?"

Believe it or not, that horse's name actually was Keep Waving. The
ensuing story and the pictures earned a spread in *The Chicago Tribune*.

A few years later, John was riding in Canada and we were having dinner with his agent, a former trainer himself. We were swapping stories
about horses we had known when the agent commented about a very sweet
horse he had once met that, "did the darnedest thing. Every time I cleaned
out his stall, I would cluck to ask him to move over. Instead, he would
come over to me and put his head on my shoulder."

I couldn't believe what I was hearing! I glanced at John, and then I
asked the agent, "Was his name Keep Waving?" It was.

That story always brings tears to my eyes. I had no idea at the time
that those few moments I spent with Keep Waving made an impression
on him that lasted the rest of his life. I have always thought that what
occurred between us all those years best exemplifies my attitude about my
career as a stunt rider and trainer. The horses always came first with me,
not the actors or directors or even heads of studios. Now, I can look back
on a body of work of which I'm very proud, knowing that each of my stunts
was performed as a team effort between this rider and a horse that understood exactly what I wanted and did it willingly.

I had an adventurous life, but I didn't seek that out for the sake of
it. Sometimes, such as with Keep Waving, I was honored to be a horse's
healer and guide. Sometimes, they were both healer and guide for me.
Mostly, I just followed the scent of the horses.

Preface

Of the many stories I have lived to tell, two of them stand out first and foremost in my memory. One was of a little horse that captured my heart and made it his own, and the other was the story of my movie work when I was getting paid to do what I most enjoyed doing. It was my husband John who eventually reminded me that all the stories in my heart were really just the one story.

I seem to have been bursting at the seams for so many years with an unquenchable desire to share the story of my horse with all the horse lovers of the world and at the same time answer the myriad of questions about my movie stunt work. People over the years have been fascinated by what goes on behind the camera, even though it seems more has been written about what goes on in front of it. I've never seemed to match many people's preconceived idea of what a stunt girl should look like, so I've constantly been asked, "How did you become a stunt girl?" In truth, I really did step out of a stereotype and reach for a dream.

When I was working in the movies, there were only about twelve women that did stunts with horses. However, unlike most who were trick riders at rodeos, my career had started years before when my father hand-polished my riding as my mother sent me to modeling school and groomed me for a social life that was more to her liking. Obviously, my father won!

For a long time, I thought these stories would never be told. I tried a number of times, but none were successful. Then, one day I received an email from an author who had seen a photo of me standing with Clark Gable and who was interested in the story behind that photograph. When he heard me talk about my life, and of the difficulties I had encountered, Chrystopher Spicer said that he would help me in any way he could, and so he has. To this day we have never actually met, but somehow he has managed to look inside my heart and help me write this story.

3

While indeed the past might be another country, I've no idea who governs it. So, I would ask you to bear in mind while reading that it is many years since these events took place and, although we have endeavored to place events within the context of recorded history as accurately as possible, this story is after all based on my all-too-human memory and personal perception of that time.

Now, I see a dust cloud in the distance and I can hear hoofbeats, so I think it's time to roll that camera.

Martha Crawford, British Columbia.

1

Riding to Hollywood

If we can start out there and end up here, then where can't we go?
— *Seabiscuit*

The moment my horse Jim left the ground, I knew the stunt had gone wrong. The wagon we were jumping was wide, and I could feel that Jim simply hadn't achieved enough traction in the sandy ground to carry us over. At the crest of the jump, his front legs hit the straw bales atop the wagon, slowing our momentum. I could see that we were going to collide with the wagon wheel on the far side and collide hard.

Making a split-second decision, I stepped out of the saddle in mid-air and, grabbing the saddle-horn, I pulled Jim toward me just as his legs were about to go into the spokes of the wheel. It was enough; he missed it. Letting go, I dropped backwards, unable to break my fall. I hit the ground on my rear, feeling the jolt all the way up my spine, and quickly did a back roll. Jim was still falling and I wanted to avoid his thrashing hooves if he tumbled my way. Through a cloud of sand, I saw him land with his front legs crumpled under him, then jump to his feet. I groaned as I saw that one of his shod hooves had carved an eight-inch gash in his chest. The skin was torn on his shins. While knowing it could have been much worse, I hated that my horse was hurt at all. Glancing around, I noticed that everyone had frozen in place, speechless.

Scrambling to my feet, I walked up to his head, stroking his neck and speaking softly in his ear. There was a collective sigh as everyone saw that both of us had survived and were standing on all legs. The wranglers rushed forward and led Jim away to tend to his injuries. Fortunately, his cuts turned out to be superficial and, with careful doctoring and a long rest, he eventually healed without scars. I was dusting myself off when the still photographer approached me.

"Believe it or not," he said slowly, "I'm pretty sure I got that shot. I've never seen anything quite like that. I'm still amazed I didn't freeze with everyone else when you hit the straw bales."

I gave him a slightly dazed grin and replied emphatically: "Good, because we're not doing it again."

At that, everyone started laughing and the tension of the moment was broken.

It was originally supposed to be just another simple photo shoot. I was doubling both Jean Simmons and Caroll Baker in the United Artists feature *The Big Country*, and actor-producer Gregory Peck had asked me to set up some action stills to be used for publicity. I had arranged for the photographer to meet me at the ranch of Fat Jones, a well-known live-stock contractor for Western films, where I stabled Jim. I allowed Jim to be used in other movies, and the actors and stunt people all liked him. In *The Mating Game* he jumped a moving car, and in *The True Story of Jesse James* he jumped through a plate glass window. Well, it was really just sheet candy that shattered into pieces on contact, but the jump looked spectacular and was still a lot to ask of a horse. I had ridden him when I doubled Debra Paget in *Love Me Tender*, Elvis Presley's first movie. Jim was a smart, easy going horse who would do anything for you as long as he understood what was being asked of him.

Jumping that wagon should not have been a difficult task for Jim. We had schooled him over it on a long line to let him see how wide it was before he had to jump it with me in the saddle, but I had my misgivings about the deep footing. In retrospect, I should have listened to my gut and taken more precautions, such as laying a pole in front of the wagon as a ground line. That wagon shot came to epitomize a rule of stunt work I learned early in my career: *Always know what you are going to do if what you have planned doesn't work.* On this occasion, what I did was based on just pure instinct, rather than on anything I had planned. Looking at that photograph later, horse trainer Clyde Kennedy said it was the most spectacular shot he had ever seen, and he promptly hung a print of it in his stable office. Walter "Chappy" Chapman, who trained Cass Ole, the Arabian star of *The Black Stallion*, just shook his head when he saw it and exclaimed: "My God!" He pointed out that, even in the heat of the moment, I had held the reins lightly in my fingers so that I would not interfere with Jim's mouth.

My step father Carl would have been proud. I owed my gentle hands to him. In fact I owed everything to him, including the chance to live my

Martha, almost three here, was not happy that her first ride with Carl was over.

dream as a movie stunt rider. I was only six months old when my father died as a result of complications from gall bladder surgery. Owner of the largest auto finance company south of the Mason-Dixon Line, he had been so impressed by a particularly smart, independent and beautiful young lady that he had married my mother when she was only nineteen. A self-educated woman who was at home in any surroundings, she received frequent mentions in the society columns for her perfectly arranged and catered dinner parties, yet only six months before her marriage she had been expelled from high school for smoking. Then, to make matters worse, she had promptly run away from her home in the small rural town of Durant, Oklahoma, to search for a better life in Dallas, Texas, where she rented sleeping space on someone's kitchen floor until she found herself a job.

After my father's death, my mother and I had spent some time with his family in Springfield, Illinois, and we were returning home to San Antonio by train when a handsome stranger sat down beside my mother. He looked at me for awhile and then said to her, "You know, I would just love to have a little girl like that."

Two years later that handsome stranger became my step father. Carl Crawford was a dashing professional polo player and one of the kindest men I have ever known. Naturally, one of his first ambitions was to teach his new daughter to ride. I will never forget my first time on a horse. In fact, I remember it like it was yesterday. I was almost three years old and Carl put me on the saddle in front of him after a polo game. I screamed and yelled and cried. He rode off and then he told me we were going to make a goal. Holding me tight to him, he cantered through the two white wicker goal posts.

Suddenly, the warmth and the smell of that horse's body enveloped me so completely that I can still recall them now. I remember how utterly secure I felt with Carl's leather-gloved hand spread out over my small chest as he held me close to him. Those gloves were soft and worn, and they fit just above his wrist on the right hand that held me. I felt as one with this master horseman, and right then I stopped hollering. At least, I stopped until he brought me back to my mother and started to lift me down. Then I started all over again, because now I wanted the ride to last forever. When my feet touched the ground, I immediately wrapped my arms around the horse's front leg and held on to it like a tick, pouring out my heart to him for being taken off.

After that day, my life changed. By the time I was four, I was allowed to walk the polo horses after their games to cool them off. I never did have any formal riding lessons; I absorbed what I learned from being with Carl and watching him. Only once did I give him a scare, when one of the horses ran off with me towards the stable. It did not scare me at all, but a steel cable that was strung as a picket line for the practice games was looming up as we approached at a dazzling speed. I just flattened out over the pommel of the saddle and that day, perhaps, laid the foundation for my career as a stunt girl as we ran under the low-hanging cable. Eventually, it became a routine for Carl to school the horses and for me to sit around on them, sometimes all day, to let them totally relax. Later, I came to realize that this was their reward time.

Now that I was the "polo assistant," I traveled that year with my parents from San Antonio to New York for the polo season, and at the Blind Brook Polo Club I was entered in my first horse show at the grand old age of four. It was a devastating experience for a seasoned rider like me to find that I had been entered in the lead line class for which my mother would lead my horse. Her capable, four-year-old daughter could not have felt more embarrassed! Being awarded my first red ribbon as the club president's wife and child took the blue was my introduction to horse politics. After all, that kid really needed a lead line! However, not only did I have to bear the insult of my second place, I did it wearing little-girl Mary Janes with my jodhpurs because my feet were quite narrow and no boots my size could be found in time. Before long, though, I was wearing boots made by the famed Lucchese (pronounced Lu-case-e) Boot Company in San Antonio, Texas, makers of elegant western boots for millionaire ranchers and celebrities, who had made their first pair of English polo boots for Carl.

Despite that initial embarrassment, I came to like the Blind Brook Polo Club. Located near White Plains, it was not too far from West Point and Carl would often drive us by there. I became fascinated with the elite military school, although the military wasn't a new concept for me. San Antonio was predominately a military town and Carl's stables were located across a creek from Fort Sam Houston Army Post. They played a great deal of polo at Sam Houston and had a beautiful field that eventually became a parade ground. I have a picture of me at aged four being carefully set down in Carl's polo boots with his helmet on, holding a polo mallet that was way taller than I. Even though my feet didn't touch the bottom of those boots, I managed to balance precariously until they took the picture that I had insisted on, and then I promptly fell over backwards and needed help getting up and out of the big boots. But, I was happy!

A four-year-old Martha stepping into Carl's boots at his stables in San Antonio.

After that, following in the steps of those boots became my dream. Carl's stables and the memories I have from there will always have a special place in my heart. Years later, the extraordinary horse trainer Walter "Chappy" Chapman, now a legend in his own horseshoes, purchased those stables, and my beloved horse Frosty would be born there.

While my mother willingly supported our horse activities, as a confirmed city slicker she would never have voluntarily walked across a street to see a horse. If you were very lucky, once in a blue moon you might just happen to hear her admit to liking a certain horse from a distance. In reality, horses for my mother were not living, breathing, rideable creatures but were four-legged means to an end. Through Carl, they were her entry into society and it was my job to prove that entry justified by competing in and winning the big society horse shows. I often wonder if she ever realized how much I had to learn at such a young age to be able to do that, and how willing I was to spend hours and hours in the saddle in order to do it well. It's not as if she ever returned the favor. When I was eventually working on movie sets, my mother never once came to see me nor did she ever acknowledge the craft of what I was doing there.

Still, riding was my being and my love was learning to ride the trained horses; I was the ultimate "catch rider." Carl was so proud of me and was my constant source of encouragement. I knew that whenever he took me out to breakfast, I would get to ride at the club that day. He loved good hotels, and our breakfasts were usually in the coffee shops of those hotels or in restaurants known for their quality breakfasts. Consequently, even though I was very young at the time, I can still remember the coffee shop at the Gunter Hotel in San Antonio and the Green Tree Inn in Old Westbury, New York. I still miss those private times with my father over breakfast. He knew everyone, and those he didn't know knew him. Breakfasts became a ritual that I loved and eagerly anticipated. Even when we moved to California, Carl still maintained the tradition by taking us to breakfast every Sunday morning at the Beverly Hills Hotel on Sunset Boulevard.

Everyone was upset that I did not start school in New York. This did not bother Carl and my mother, but others would remark how sad it was that little Martha would be seven years old before starting first grade. That was fine by me; I didn't have to waste time in kindergarten pasting cutouts when I could be out riding horses. Anyway, as it happened, at the time I would have started school in New York they were closed because of a polio outbreak. So, I started my first grade back in San Antonio, Texas, where they were way ahead of California schools. Consequently, when we did eventually arrive in California I was promoted from the second grade to the fourth grade.

Prior to moving to California, we returned to New York one more time for the polo season. Carl and my mother took me everywhere, and I must have got a head start on most children my age with all that travel and the major events I was fortunate enough to see and experience. There we were, standing on the observation deck of the Empire State Building on May 27, 1936, to see the Cunard Lines flag ship *Queen Mary* dock after its maiden voyage across the Atlantic. I held tight to my mother's hand as I looked down over the parapet, which you could do then, to see cars and people so far below they looked like ants! We were all so thrilled to see the legendary ship coming into New York Harbor, the little tugboats clustered around her like horses with their riders corralling a steer. I really have so much for which to thank Carl. If it hadn't been for him, my dreams would have remained in my sleep.

I arrived in Hollywood with my parents at the grand age of six, when the world seems so new it's still shining. I had thought no place in the world could be more exciting than San Antonio and New York, but Hollywood really opened my eyes. My parents were soon moving in heady social circles where polo, the "in" thing in Hollywood before World War II, was in its heyday. Matches drew stars, movie moguls and film wannabes who sipped champagne at elaborate tailgate lunches while they cheered their favorites on the field. Many of the stars and wealthy men of Hollywood, though, actually fielded teams and rode in them and it took big money to do that. To support eight to twelve horses cost around $40,000 a year, plus three or four grooms, a trainer, and memberships in the right clubs. Laddie Sanford of the Bigelow-Sanford Carpet Co., for example, actually had world-famous polo player Cecil Smith under contract to play for him.

Carl, who had played polo on the West Coast many years before, was initially under contract to Leslie Howard, which is how we came to California this time, but Howard returned to England when war broke out. Carl sold him a number of horses to take back to England, and I went with Carl down to the harbor to supervise loading Howard's five or six polo ponies on board ship. As it was a passenger liner, stalls had been built on the main deck. My father took me up to see them there in their white halters looking out over the gates. I was just in heaven surrounded by all this. My mother, on the other hand, was not thrilled at all because her favorite pony, Big Train, was among those sailing to England.

In this publicity photo, titled "After the Game," taken in 1939 at the Uplifters Polo Club in Pacific Palisades, California, are (left to right) Charles Farrell, star of *My Little Margie* and owner of the famed Palm Springs Racquet Club; Mrs. Frank Borzage; oil tycoon Russell Havenstrite; Martha's mother Sharon Crawford; Harry the bartender (behind bar); Walt Disney and Mrs. Disney; and Frank Borzage, award-winning film director.

After Howard had left, Walter Wanger and his wife Joan Bennett employed Carl to train all their polo ponies and to play on their team at the Riviera Country Club. Joan would just sit in her box and read a book during Walter's games; when he made a good play or goal, someone would nudge her and she would clap briefly. She was missing a lot. There was always a thrill a minute during a game, due to the amount of risk involved. It was never a good idea to forget that polo could be a dangerous sport, even between club members. In 1936, well-known Los Angeles Chevrolet dealer Winslow B. Felix, who was famous for his use of cartoon character Felix the Cat as his Chevrolet dealership mascot, died from head injuries at only 42 after colliding with "Snowy" Baker, whom I would later come to know well, during a friendly weekend game at the Club.

Nevertheless, the sport attracted the rich and famous of Hollywood there. Walt Disney and Mrs. Disney were familiar faces. Frank Borzage, who was the first person to ever win an Academy Award for directing, was a regular on the field and in the clubhouse, along with fellow directing legend Michael Curtiz who directed such classics as *Casablanca, White Christmas,* and *Yankee Doodle Dandy.* He supported polo, but I believe race horses were his first love. His Hungarian accent was unforgettable; I remember him with my father in a conversation about horses' legs, saying that his horse had "beautiful underpinnings." Screenwriter Sy Bartlett, who worked a lot with Gregory Peck, and polo star Aiden Roark were often to be seen at the Club. Married to international tennis star Helen Wills, Roark was a very special person and one of the finest polo players to ever grace the game. At one time, they were besieged so regularly with party

Spencer Tracy and Martha present trophies to a winning polo team at the Will Rogers Ranch, Pacific Palisades, in 1937. From left to right: director Frank Borzage, Dr. William E Branch of the William E. Branch Clinic in Hollywood, Mrs. Joy Branch, Tracy, Martha and professional polo players Cecil Christianson and Tom "Red" Guy.

crashers at their house that the Roarks posted a sign on their lawn that read: "If you have not been invited, you are not wanted."

I would see Spencer Tracy playing polo every week; he was a favorite among all the players and a good sport. It was a family occasion with him because his wife, Louise, was also an excellent polo player in an era when women polo players were almost unknown. I once heard it said that she was a better player than he was! Tracy's children Susie and Johnny were my riding companions almost daily. When Johnny was diagnosed with nerve deafness as a baby, Louise had refused to allow it to hinder him and had set out to teach him to lip-read and eventually to talk by constantly chattering and reading to him. Then, when he was six, Johnny contracted polio and learned to cope with that, too. In 1936, when Johnny was twelve and his sister Susie was four, the Tracy family moved to an eight-acre ranch at Encino. Louise embarked on a mission to raise support for parents with deaf children and in 1942, after a call for help from twelve other parents, Louise and Spencer founded the John Tracy Clinic to provide parent-centered services to young children with a hearing loss, to help the children learn to communicate. Louise worked with the Clinic for the rest of her life, receiving many awards, and her "mother's group" has now grown to be the largest single-service provider to parents of deaf children around the world. Though he wore a brace because of a weakened leg, John had begun riding horses at nine and could play remarkable games of polo and tennis when I knew him at the Riviera Club. He could understand everything said to him because of his extraordinary lip-reading skills. He would simply remind me, "Just talk as you normally do—don't talk slow."

I first met unforgettable comic genius Red Skelton when I was about twelve years old. We used to enjoy watching him do his famous Guzzler's Gin routine on the polo field at half-time on Sundays at the Uplifter's Polo Club in Pacific Palisades. This was not too long after his screen debut and his entry into the world of films after a successful radio career. Red was known to have a true photographic memory. A few years after World War II, my father and I walked into Armstrong Schroeder's, a Beverly Hills restaurant frequented by the Hollywood in-crowd, for breakfast and as we were shown to our booth we heard, "Hello, Carl! Hello, Martha!" It was Red, sitting a few booths away, whose memory once again had not let him down.

Socializing after the game, of course, could be just as big an event as the game itself. The cocktail parties at Bing Crosby's and Lin Howard's

Binglin Farms were always sheer fun. I will never forget Bing Crosby coming up to my father and introducing himself by name, commenting that he'd always wanted to meet him. Crosby could be quite self-deprecating, never assuming that people automatically knew who he was. Both Lin and Bing figured prominently in the thoroughbred racing picture; Lin's father, Charles Howard, owned Seabiscuit.

Dinner at the home of one of the wealthiest woman in the world, Ann Gavit Jackson, could also be quite an experience. She was related to Anthony Brady, one of the largest shareholders in American Tobacco, and married to Charles Hervey Jackson Jr., the grand-nephew of President Chester A. Arthur. The story was that when Pete, as Ann's husband was known, asked her father for permission to marry, that man had said, "Everyone will say you are just after her money, so I'll give you a million dollars in your own name and then no one can say that." The home they built in Montecito, near Santa Barbara, was like a film set and used to just take my breath away. The living room had chestnut wood panelling and a ceiling brought over from a castle in Europe. There was a full-sized tennis court in the basement, and the round horse barn was lined in solid mahogany trimmed with gleaming brass hardware. However, in spite of the formal atmosphere and overwhelming decor, Ann was remarkable at putting everyone at ease. When dinner was served, she would cheerfully announce, "Soup's on!" A very experienced horsewoman and a true horse lover, Ann (and Pete) had also purchased the Alisal Ranch in the Santa Ynez Valley in 1943. Now the Alisal Guest Ranch and Resort, it is still in the family and was where my friend Clark Gable married Lady Sylvia Ashley.

The most impressionable years of my life were spent riding my father's polo ponies. He would school them, and I would settle them down for him on the trails around the golf course at the Riviera or around the sprawling grounds of the Uplifters Club or the Will Rogers Memorial Polo Field. He taught me the finer points of riding that stayed with me all my life. He would dwell on "good hands," as he was known throughout the business for the good mouths he developed on his horses that he would sell. Though my mother would laughingly say that my father "couldn't sell a gold brick for a dollar," he would never sell a horse to someone that did not fit them or that they couldn't ride to play on the field. That upset more than one potential customer who often wanted to buy a horse on which they saw my father playing because he looked so good on it, without really considering whether it was the right horse for them or even whether they had an aptitude for polo. For example, Mark Stevens, who starred with

Olivia de Havilland in *The Snake Pit* for Twentieth Century–Fox, once thought he could learn to play polo and insisted on buying a certain horse in my father's string. Carl told him that he wasn't suitably proficient and that the horse could get him hurt, so Stevens went off and purchased one from someone else. The last I saw of him, that horse was running off with him through the stable area where he put Stevens head first into a huge manure pile. I have always thought that my morals and high ideals came from my father who not only believed in them, but lived them.

I was too young to realize at the time how fortunate I was to be part of all this. To me, Shirley Temple was just another likable playmate with whom I competed in the Egg and Spoon race on Easter Sunday at the Desert Inn Hotel in Palm Springs. We were required to run to a designated area with a spoon, retrieve the colored egg and run back to the finish line without dropping the egg. I was first and Shirley was second. She lived quite close to us in the Santa Monica area and was an absolutely delightful friend. As many of the celebrities did in those days, my parents took me everywhere with them and so I was always one of the children's group playing at those parties. I often rode out with Mickey Rooney at the Riviera Club where my father's ponies were stabled. An excellent rider, Mickey showed a pure white jumper named Moonlight. Although I enjoyed the time we spent together, my childhood crushes were on future film stars Robert Stack, Jackie Cooper and Tim Holt.

Robert Stack was the ultimate gentleman and such an excellent horseman that Carl would mount him on his own ponies when Bob wanted to play polo. Whenever I saw Jackie Cooper, another horse lover, he was always waving and smiling from ear to ear, and we all loved gentle, classy young Tim Holt whose father was himself a masterful horseman. Jack Holt had appeared in scores of western movies, yet few guessed that the impeccably dressed and well-spoken gentleman refereeing polo games was the same person. Having played polo in military academy, Tim was such an excellent player he had been a member of the team that won the first Will Rogers Memorial Tournament.

As experienced horsemen and gentlemen, Robert, Jackie and Tim were hard acts for the callow young men of my generation to follow, but Heaven knows they tried. Once, while attending Hollywood High, I dated a star football player who wanted me to teach him how to ride. Much against my better judgment, I agreed. We talked my father out of a gentle horse and after the football player was mounted, laboriously I might add, we headed to the riding ring. By the time we reached it, the horse

Martha's much-loved father, Carl Crawford, relaxing at the Uplifters Polo Club, Pacific Palisades, in 1941 just before the Japanese attack on Pearl Harbor.

had about sized that football player up and evidently even he thought this was a dumb idea, because the minute we stepped into the soft, sandy ring, that perceptive horse promptly sat down in it and refused to budge. So much for that lesson. I can recall at least one other horse disagreeing with my choice of men so intensely that my prospective date actually described quite a graceful arc through the air before biting the dust. Naturally, his wounded dignity prevented him asking me out again.

Despite my riding partners, I dated few show business personalities. In any case, with the lifestyle I was leading I had little time or occasion for interest in boys my own age. For a while, I was fascinated with show horse trainers but of course they were older and my mother put the brakes on that idea. The one actor I dated for any length of time was Jerome Courtland, who did a lot of work for Walt Disney as the lanky Southern kid in many of his films and sang the title song for *Old Yeller* just prior to becoming a Disney producer.

The famous Western film star Jack Holt, father of the equally famous Tim Holt, presenting a trophy to Martha at the Riviera Country Club Horse Show in 1937. Martha is riding film producer Walter Wanger's horse.

The Riviera Polo Club held monthly shows where I was constantly competing with the children of the rich and famous, such as Susie and Johnny Tracy; Sooky Landi, niece of actress and writer Elissa Landi; Frances, daughter of horror film star George Zucco; and Toni Vidor, whose father King Vidor would have a record 67-year career as a film director.

Our riding group was known as the "Geebungs," a name given us by the club's Australian riding master, Snowy Baker, who was also a director of the club and its major operating partner. A national sporting hero and horse-riding actor in his own country before coming to America in 1920, the dashingly handsome Baker was known to have competed in twenty-six different sports and to have excelled in all of them. Needless to say, we were just a little in awe of him. Baker took our group's name from "The Geebung Polo Club," a famous Australian poem by A. B. "Banjo" Patterson; perhaps his lines, "But their style of playing polo was irregular and rash/They had mighty little science but an awful lot of dash," said something about us. Still, we were all the same age and had a great deal of fun together. The older group of young riders in the Riviera Club, who included Jackie Paley, daughter of CBS president William Paley, would just put their noses in the air as we hurtled by, laughing hilariously.

    I soon became very good friends with Charlene Wrightsman, whose

Here, Martha is winning the Junior Jumping competition at the Riviera Country Club, Pacific Palisades, in 1940.

father was a well-known polo player and Standard Oil tycoon. We had met earlier in Houston, Texas, and now really hit it off. She lived at the Uplifters Polo Club, a residential enclave in Santa Monica where many stars had homes. The Uplifters had all of the amenities, including polo fields, stables, tennis courts, swimming pools, and a ballroom where many celebrity functions were held. Charlene and I spent hours riding the club's wooded trails. In a shady area behind the clubhouse was a playground with a child's paradise of monkey bars, swings, rings, and slides. Quite unknown to Carl, I often used this playground as my secret stunt-riding training field, eventually becoming quite adept at riding one of the polo ponies under the rings, catching hold of them and swinging off the pony. Charlene was my scout. She would let me know when the coast was clear to ride under the rings, and then she would catch the horse for me. Before long, I had developed my upper body strength so effectively that I could do one-armed cartwheels across the entire 300 feet of the polo field.

Another of my scouts was Jay Silverheels, a Native American who had played many roles in movies before he became famous as Tonto, the Lone Ranger's famous sidekick, who rode a horse named Scout. A frequent visitor to the Uplifters Club, Jay was in person much like his Tonto character: a man of high morals and a role model for youngsters. His career had received an early boost from comedian Joe E. Brown, who was also an Uplifters member and who often lunched there with my father and Jay while, unknown to them, I was swinging away on the rings.

Like most youngsters I knew, I spent my Saturdays in the friendly darkness of the Criterion Theater in Santa Monica at the all-day kids Western matinees, all day for a dime. We had so many cowboy heroes to choose from: Gene Autry, Roy Rogers, John Wayne, Gary Cooper, William Boyd, Buck Jones, Johnny Mack Brown, Tim Holt, Ken Maynard, Bob Steele (who later became a fine stuntman) and of course the Lone Ranger himself, Clayton Moore, and his faithful sidekick Tonto, my friend Jay Silverheels.

Suddenly, quite out of nowhere, Carl was offered a contract to be the playing manager of the major polo club in Manila, in the Philippines, at $1000 a month. All his horses would be supplied, and we would have a house with three servants, a cook, a housekeeper and a driver. Hardly able to believe it all, we were ready to go in no time at all with our passports in hand. Then, the night before we were to leave, he sat down at the dinner table with us and, looking around at each one of us, he said that he had a bad feeling about Manila and he'd decided not to take the position.

Well, we were completely surprised but we trusted Carl implicitly. Much later, we learned that the polo player and his wife that went in our place were held prisoners by the Japanese when war broke out, and all the polo ponies were confiscated by the Army. So, perhaps it was Carl from whom I developed my tendency for the occasional experiences of precognition that I have had. Many times I told my mother of a pending earthquake.

During the war years, polo almost came to a standstill as a source for pleasure and entertainment for the film colony. My father had a big six-horse van and was given extra gas coupons for it that enabled him to move the horses from the polo club to their retirement areas. The polo sport that had been at its zenith before the war was never the same again. After the war was over, the long-awaited comeback never came. It used to cost in the neighborhood of $40,000 a year to maintain a polo stable, at a time when the average blue collar worker was making $400 to $600 a year, and so when the government tightened the tax screws, the wealthy players did not want to reveal they had the resources to privately maintain indulgence in such an extravagant sport. Eventually, the film stars drifted back and it was still a delightful diversion for many of them, but it was in a very scaled-down fashion. Polo was never again played in Hollywood as it had been in the thirties. However, my exquisitely beautiful mother continued to be an official timer of the United States Polo Association, while Carl continued on in club management.

Meanwhile, my riding improved to where I was ranked as one of the top equestrians on the California horse show circuit and a candidate for the Olympic show-jumping team. Unfortunately, the U.S. Olympic Committee denied me the opportunity to compete in the Olympics because as the daughter of a professional, I was considered a professional. The rules have long since changed so that current members of our equestrian teams are no longer required to be amateurs; aspiring riders usually work at training horses or teaching. That amateur rule prevented the U.S. from fielding its best riders for many years.

However, I didn't languish for long. It so happened that Carl frequently played polo with studio head Darryl Zanuck, and one day my name happened to pop up in post-game conversation. It was probably not by chance. My mother had never liked the direction in which my love for horse-riding was taking me, and it would have been just like her to persuade Carl to try and get me the chance to become the film star that she had never become. The end result was that, probably after a few drinks, the two fathers managed to convince themselves that I could be the next great female Western movie star and they promptly organized a screen test for me. Despite their good intentions, though, it very nearly didn't work out.

For whatever reason, the test director decided to style my hair in tight curls and dress me in a short, strapless, black velvet evening gown. I was given a cigarette, although I didn't smoke, and told to walk across the room and put the cigarette out in an ashtray while saying a line or two of dialogue. The character felt so unlike me that I knew instinctively I couldn't carry off the role. Needless to say, I was less than convincing on screen. I later learned that the reviewers reported I had the figure of a woman of twenty-five but the voice of a girl of seven. As it happened, I tested on the same day as another young lady with a little-girl voice, Marilyn Monroe, but unlike me she actually did want to be a movie star and didn't want to ride horses and so was naturally much more successful. Strange as it may seem, I was not greatly disturbed when I heard the verdict.

"Miss Crawford, I'm terribly sorry, but I cannot offer you a contract based on that screen test," stammered a very nervous Ben Lyon, director of casting for Twentieth Century–Fox. "Now, if you feel like trying again, I can of course arrange for another test...."

Lyon had delivered this crushing news to many an aspiring starlet, but this situation was a tad different. He would have been well aware of Zanuck's friendship with Carl, and so he was naturally hesitant to upset this young lady with such an inside connection. Of course, what he didn't know was that I had not been consulted at all about this possible future of mine in the movies. Typically, well-bred young ladies weren't necessarily consulted by their fathers about their futures at that time, and I had been no exception. So the outcome of this exercise didn't really matter to me one way or the other. Anyway, there was poor Ben Lyon obviously trying desperately to think of how he was going to diplomatically break the news that I was a flop to Zanuck, who was accustomed to getting what he wanted, without endangering his own future career. I couldn't help it; I just burst out laughing which only added to the poor distressed man's confusion. Then, I had an idea.

"Oh, Mr. Lyon, I know that test was awful," I reassured him. "It's quite okay, you know; I never wanted to be an actress in the first place. On the other hand, there is something I do want to be."

Breathing a deep sigh of relief, he leaned back in his chair and, raising one inquisitive eyebrow, he gave me a long, somewhat cautious look over his reading glasses as he waited for the other shoe to fall.

"What I do really want," I declared, "is a chance to do the riding scenes for Anne Baxter in *Yellow Sky*. As you know, to be able to do that I need my Screen Actors Guild cards."

Lyon continued to study me silently for what seemed an eternity, then he tipped his chair forward so that his elbows thumped loudly on his desk. His eyes stayed fixed on me.

"Are you sure you can do those riding scenes?" he asked.

"Absolutely," I replied emphatically. "I grew up on horses. I can do whatever you call for."

A happy smile slowly dawned on his face as he saw the solution to his predicament. This could be a way for us both to end up looking good. We sat there grinning at each other like fools as we struck our deal, knowing that we had found a solution with which everyone would be pleased.

As I look back now, it seems inevitable that I eventually arrived at this juncture of involvement with horses and movies. I sometimes wonder what would have happened if that door to riding in the Olympics hadn't closed for me and the other door to the movies opened. I probably would have been content to show horses the rest of my life but, one way or the other, my parents certainly wanted more for me, even if their individual aims were somewhat different. It was their aspirations, after all, that prompted the conversation with Darryl Zanuck, the infamous screen test, my deal with Ben Lyon, and my ensuing debut as a stunt double.

2

Yellow Sky

It was a moment for being a woman — for only a woman's weapon could keep her alive!
> — advertising slogan for the film

Ben Lyon was true to his word; in no time at all I had my Screen Actors Guild and Screen Extras Guild cards. Usually, these were extremely hard to get because you had to be accepted for a role to be issued either of those cards, but you couldn't apply for that part unless you had one of the cards in the first place! Kurt Vonnegut would have been proud of that situation. I needed both of the cards because stunts were usually done on the Actors card and photographic doubling work was done on the Extras Card.

Once that was sorted out, Lyon saw to it that I got the job in the summer of 1947 on the set of *Yellow Sky* doubling the female lead, Anne Baxter. This would be the only time that I ever had to ask for a job in films. Ironically, I wanted to work on this movie because I admired Anne Baxter, who then proceeded to totally ignore me throughout the entire shoot. This was my first inkling that stars are not always as likable as the characters they play on the screen. Baxter, the granddaughter of Frank Lloyd Wright and the daughter of a Seagrams Distillery executive, had been raised in luxury with the best acting coaching money could buy, starting work with Twentieth Century–Fox when she was sixteen. By the time she wasn't talking to me on set, she was already a celebrity for her roles in Orson Welles' *The Magnificent Ambersons* and *The Razor's Edge* for which she had won an Academy Award for Best Supporting Actress. However, I did feel somewhat better when I found out that Baxter hadn't wanted to work with Peck and was barely speaking to him, too.

I joined the crew on location in the Alabama Hills just outside of

Lone Pine, California. A golden-brown granite wonderland of rounded hills and arched rock formations, the Alabamas were named by Southern-sympathizing gold miners in 1864 when they heard that the Confederate raider *Alabama* had sunk more than sixty Union ships within the last two years. They have become a popular site for moviemakers since 1920 when Fatty Arbuckle starred there in a silent film called *The Roundup*. More than 300 films have been made in this area since then, including modern ones such as *Gladiator, G.I. Jane* and *Maverick,* and television series such as *Have Gun—Will Travel, The Rockford Files* and *Wagon Train.* Looking around me, I could see why this location was so popular. The snow-capped High Sierras, dominated by Mount Whitney, and a clear blue sky formed a stunning backdrop to the brown, weather-worn rocks of the valley that in some places looked like a moonscape. Before the coming of white settlers, the Paiute Indians had wintered in these hills, taking shelter in the caves and outcroppings. The tribe was banished to a reservation in the 1860s but, ironically, cowboy and Indian skirmishes continued to take place here for the cameras. Now, this 30,000-acre site is preserved as the Alabama Hills National Recreation Area, and the town of Lone Pine even has a Film History Museum and holds annual film festivals honoring the movies shot here.

When I arrived on the set, I was introduced to director William Wellman who was working again with producer Darryl Zanuck and screenplay writer Lamar Trotti, the team that had made the successful The *Ox-Bow Incident* in 1943. When he heard my stepfather's name, Wellman commented, "Carl Crawford the polo player? I used to be married to his first wife! Tell him I feel sorry for the time he spent married to her."

We had a good laugh at that memory and formed an instant bond. Wellman was a colorful, rowdy man who was married five times and was known for getting the most out of actors, even if it took some bullying and a lot of profanity. He had earned the nickname "Wild Bill" as a fighter pilot with the French Foreign Legion's Lafayette Flying Corps in France during the First World War, as a result of which he had been awarded the Croix de Guerre, and the nickname fit him like a well-worn pair of leather gloves. This genius filmmaker, who had at one time actually been a wing-walking aerial stunt pilot, directed over seventy-five movies during his career, including the 1927 silent *Wings* that won the first-ever Academy Award for Best Motion Picture. He had a passion for history, perhaps because he was a great-great-great-grandson of Francis Lewis, a signer of the Declaration of Independence, and a reputation for getting things done on schedule. He once said that studios hired him to be fast and cheap, not slow and expensive.

Wellman had assembled a great crew for *Yellow* Sky. Working on that set spoiled me, because I then assumed all movie productions would be done with such professionalism. The cinematographer, Joe MacDonald, worked on as many films as Wellman, of which three were nominated for Academy Awards for cinematography, and may well have been involved with more Westerns than anyone else in his line of work. Ben Nye, the makeup artist, was one of the industry's best. In the cast were some of the hottest stars in Hollywood at that time: Gregory Peck, Richard Widmark, Harry Morgan and, of course, the aloof Anne Baxter.

The plot of the movie concerns the classic struggle between good and evil, as do so many of the Western genre, along with some warnings about greed. Bank robbers led by Stretch (Gregory Peck) ride into the desert to escape a posse who then abandon them there because it saves the trouble of hanging them. Lost and near death from lack of water, the outlaws stumble into the ghost town of Yellow Sky where they are shown at gunpoint to water by the granddaughter (Anne Baxter) of an old prospector (James Barton) who are the only residents. When the outlaws learn that

On location in 1947 at Lone Pine, California, while shooting *Yellow Sky*, Martha is ready to double for Anne Baxter.

the prospector has a cache of gold, they plot to rob him. Then Stretch falls for the granddaughter and tries to foil the plan.

My job was to double for Anne in scenes that called for riding, climbing around amongst those huge rocks, and shooting a rifle. I quickly discovered that I enjoyed living the life of the Old West so much I would have paid the studio to let me do it! It was the most thrilling thing I had ever done. I even loved the outfit. Before I went on location, I was told to report to the wardrobe department at the main studio in Hollywood. There I was fitted with jeans and a soft paisley shirt. When it was ready for me to try on, I felt a shiver of excitement at the label in the collar that read, "Double — Anne Baxter — *Yellow Sky*."

The location for *Yellow Sky* had a good feel to it, something that could not be said for every location to which I was assigned. I loved watching the cast and crew at work on this production, noticing the individual skills and teamwork. This was my introduction to some of the technicalities of stunts. Doubling for Gregory Peck was Jock Mahoney, considered by his peers to be one of the greatest stuntmen in the business and later to become a star in his own right on television's *The Range Rider* and *Yancy Derringer*. I always thought Jock was more like a cat than a human being; I once saw him leap over four horses! He claimed to have once been a circus acrobat, and I could believe it. In one scene, Greg's character was to ride down a very steep incline. To make it more spectacular, the crew greased the slide so that Jock and the horse absolutely flew down it. It was a breathtaking stunt that demonstrated that even though Jock was not a great horseman in the finer sense of the word, he was an extraordinary athlete who could do practically anything. When a stunt person jumps off a cliff or a stagecoach and pulls someone off the back of a running horse, it's called a "bulldog." Well, when you were bulldogged by Jock, you hardly felt yourself hit the ground. He would jump off a balcony onto a standing horse, and the horse would hardly flinch. At last I felt privy to how movies were made, welded into an entire magical quilt from a patchwork of pieces.

Cast and crew stayed in Lone Pine at the wonderful old Spanish-style Dow Hotel, built in the nineteen-twenties mainly to house moviemakers like us on location. Believe it or not, after long, hot days in the sun making one, in the evenings we often went to a movie: Greg, Jock, Harry Morgan, Dick Widmark, and me. Actually, it was the only movie in town. They showed a different one every night for us and I was always asked to come along by Greg or Dick. Anne Baxter would invariably decline to join us. Other times we just sat out on the long arcade of the hotel veranda, a popular gathering place where there was standing room only during the radio broadcast of the rematch between world heavyweight boxing champion Joe Louis and Jersey Joe Walcott.

My respect for Greg Peck deepened a great deal while we worked on this set. A good horseman, but an unlucky one, Greg had already broken a leg in three places when a horse fell under him in the San Fernando Valley back in 1946. A few weeks beforehand, knowing that Bill Wellman expected his actors to be as tough as he was and as prepared, Greg had gone over to Ralph McCutcheon's stables in the Valley to pick out a horse for the film shoot. Unfortunately, while he was working with one possible horse, it slipped on a turn and went down so fast that Peck couldn't get his foot out of the stirrup in time and his ankle broke under the horse. Usually an ankle takes months to heal, but Peck was only four weeks out from the shoot so finally his doctor set it in a special cast that would allow him to walk carefully. Wellman had to photograph him from the knees up or from the right to keep the cast out of shot. Although he must have been in a lot of pain, Greg never complained. However, he never quite regained full use of that ankle again.

Each weekend, while the rest of us stayed in Lone Pine, Greg would set out in his car to drive two hundred miles back home because he had just purchased a house in Mandeville Canyon, close to the Riviera Country Club, for himself and his wife Greta. Unfortunately, his property turned out to be overrun with rattlesnakes, so one Friday the ever-helpful stuntmen on the set caught a bull snake for him, a non-poisonous species known to do a great job of chasing off rattlers. With the crated snake in the back seat of his car, Greg made the four-hour drive home but when he got there and lifted the lid, the crate was empty. That snake was nowhere in sight! Unnerved by the prospect of the snake emerging unexpectedly one day from the bowels of the car, Greg quickly sold the vehicle. He never got any complaints from the buyer, so the snake's disappearance remained a mystery and a great story for cocktail parties.

After we had finished work on *Yellow Sky*, I often crossed paths in the following years with the stars and crew of my debut film. Hollywood can be a very small town. When working on a later film, Greg Peck asked my stepfather to help him brush up for a riding role and the two became good friends. Carl often rode out with him and was always happy to provide him with horses. Greg was a kind, considerate man and a good horseman. He had absolutely no ego about his fame. In fact, he seemed awed by all of the attention.

Dick Widmark and his wonderful wife Jean later asked me to teach their daughter Anne to ride, and we both had a lot of fun. As it turned out, I passed more on to Anne than horsemanship. Carl had not only instilled in me a strong sense of responsibility and fair play, but also the value of being a "lady." I could ride all day if I wanted to, but when I was done I was expected to go home, and not to hang around the stable. Without realizing it, I passed these same values on to Anne, and Dick and Jean were very grateful. As I visited the Widmark home over the years, I watched Anne develop into a lovely lady who eventually married Sandy Koufax, the Hall of Fame baseball pitcher.

The very thought of Harry Morgan always makes me smile. He was a delightful human being and a professional's professional when it came to acting. After *Yellow Sky*, whenever he saw me at a distance, he would wave wildly and yell, "Hello, Martha." I would later work opposite him as a double for his screen wife, Gladys, on the television hit, *December Bride*. True to her form, though, we never did see much of Anne Baxter on the set of *Yellow Sky*. Every day she disappeared into her room at the Dow as soon as the set wrapped. She was as cool then as an Eskimo's belt buckle and just as cool every time I ran into her after that. It puzzled me because by then I had proven myself as a competent stuntwoman and star double. In fact, I was often told I looked a lot like her. Other than in appearance, though, we could not have been more different.

Many years later, I would hold my *Yellow Sky* shirt in my hands again.

3

Flying High

The art of being wise is the art of knowing what to overlook.
— William James

No sooner had I begun my movie career, however, than it was put on hold for a while. Love is probably about the only thing strong enough to motivate a person to put a new career in cold storage, and love indeed this was. All through high school I had dated William P. Lear, Jr., son of the world-famous aviator and innovator who, amongst some 150 patents, had designed and built the Learjet, co-developed the automatic pilot, invented the eight-track tape player, and been the co-inventor of American car radios and thus co-founder of the Motorola company. Bill and I met while attending Hollywood Professional School, a private school fully accredited with UCLA that met the demands of many school-age stars when their showbiz careers made it impossible for them to attend school during regular hours. HPS hours were from eight to twelve in the morning, and the list of stars who graduated from there reads like a who's-who of Hollywood. I was attending so that I had as much time to devote to my riding as possible, while Bill needed to have time for flying.

He was my first love, my first romance, my first venture into marriage. In short, he was pretty much my first everything and he seemed to be as much in love with me as I was with him. Whenever I had a date with someone else, flowers would arrive a half-hour before my date picked me up with a note attached reading, "Please don't forget me." After almost three years of an increasingly hot and heavy courtship that included dancing once a week at the Cocoanut Grove to the music of Freddy Martin, Bill started talking about getting married. Neither of us was prepared for it but we were young and I truly loved Bill, with all of my eighteen-year-old heart. Even though I did think that getting married would be an excit-

31

About to take off for their honeymoon in 1947, newlyweds Martha and Bill Lear Jr., son of aviation legend Bill Lear, happily cram into Bill's Lockheed Lightning P-38 *Martha J* that he flew in the 1946 and 1947 Bendix Air Races.

ing way to escape parental supervision, the way I felt about Bill was far more real to me than "puppy love."

We were married in Santa Barbara, California. As we were kneeling at the church altar, the only thing I could think of was whether I had forgotten to take the price tag off the bottom of my new shoes. I heard nothing but my thoughts. After a lavish reception at the Santa Barbara Biltmore, we left the following night for San Francisco on the Southern Pacific's luxurious *Starlight*. We stayed overnight at the St. Francis, and then the next morning we crossed the Bay by ferry to Oakland for the final leg to Portland on board the Southern Pacific's all–Pullman train, the *Cascade*. From Portland we journeyed to Baker, Oregon, where we picked up Bill's P-38 fighter that he had flown in the famous Bendix Air Races in 1946 and '47.

I slipped into the piggyback seat behind Bill wearing my backpack parachute. Originally there had been armor-plating behind the pilot's seat and then behind that on the shelf where I sat, which was actually part of

the wing, had been a rather bulky and heavy four-channel VHF transmit-
ter-receiver that Bill had moved to the nose. When Bill had removed the
armor plate to reduce the aircraft's weight and to allow room for a passenger, the back of the seat was still too high, so Bill had simply sawed off
the top of it. *Et voilà!*

Prior to take-off, Bill went through the emergency procedures with
me. Now that I was firmly belted into my piggyback seat, he casually
informed me that I would not actually be able to get out once we were
airborne unless the plane was turned upside-down and the Perspex hood
was jettisoned. Oh, and he had to bail out first.

"What?" I exclaimed. "You could have told me that before I got in
here!"

He reassured me that with the help of gravity I'd just be able to fall
right out, or wriggle out, any way I could. It was a long time later when
Bill finally confessed to me that, really, there is no way to get out of that
seat in a P-38 while it's in the air. Ah, such trust we have in each other
when we are young. So we taxied onto the strip and, as we lifted off and
levelled out, Bill aimed us in the direction of Boise, Idaho, towards his
new career with All American Air Shows and our new life, and it all turned
out to be as exciting as he had made it sound. Bill was a wealthy playboy
of the first order and our brief life together was a whirlwind. I wanted for
nothing, and I flew thousands of miles with him to those air shows in that
piggyback seat of the P-38 accompanied by Rusty, a cocker spaniel that
we'd found in Idaho. I just knew this had to be love.

What I didn't know was that Bill's sudden desire to get married had
been largely inspired by a potential paternity suit. The wings started to
fall off our storybook marriage barely a week after we had checked into
our Boise hotel when I got a call one day and a female voice announced
over the telephone, "Mrs. Lear, I am going to have your husband's baby."
The woman said she had not been able to get in touch with Bill and so
felt she had no choice but to tell me. Suddenly, and by no means gently,
I was made aware that as I had been sitting at home waiting for Bill, he
had been waiting on somebody else and, as if that knowledge wasn't
enough, here she was on the phone delightfully telling me all the details
of their tryst.

Now, I'm not a vindictive person but right then and there I told that
woman to come right on up to our suite and I would make sure she and
Bill could talk. Gotcha! I could hardly contain myself when I asked her
to come right on in and Bill saw her standing there. "I almost fainted!" he

wrote later in *Fly Fast, Sin Boldly: Flying, Spying & Surviving*, his autobiography. Bill, a master at surviving tight situations in the air, was about to crack up on the ground.

Through it all, though, I somehow never doubted that Bill loved me. I never thought for a minute that he was in love with that woman. Bill fell into the age-old trap that catches so many men who are in the spotlight: being unable to say "no" to the kind of women who preys on and flatters their vanity and egos. He had been caught in the web of an opportunistic female who was in fact already pregnant and who had tagged along with the Air Show looking for some way to ensure her and her baby's survival. Though Bill was certainly guilty of being unfaithful, he was not, despite her claims, the father of that woman's child. While I had been terribly hurt, I could never really be too mad at Bill. Despite his failings, he was a living doll and a colorful celebrity just like the rest of the Air Show pilots. They were all naturals for those women and Bill was a prime target, not just because he was the heir to his father's fame, fortune and good looks, but also because of his own celebrity as the star of the show.

After World War II, the taxpayers were almost frantic to see the war birds for which they had paid so much. Air shows gave them a chance to inspect, close-hand, the vestiges of where their hard-earned dollars had been spent. The audience always went away sunburned from watching with their mouths agape as those daredevil pilots defied death with their low-altitude aerobatics. The public got their money's worth, but the poor pilots were always at the mercy of the air show promoters and were rarely paid anything substantial. Fuel, oil, maintenance, rat-trap hotels and bad meals were usually the order of the day and were, more often than not, paid for by the promoters with bad checks and "vouchers" just before we had to skip town.

But the awed public wasn't aware of those problems; to them, those daring young pilots were so darling to look at, and there could be no doubt that Bill was an extraordinary pilot. He was so skilled at such an early age that it made a person believe in reincarnation. One time we headed off after an air show and, before we knew it, we were in the middle of a very severe storm. The nearest airfield where we could set down and wait it out was at Garden City, Kansas, but there was no control tower and therefore no radio contact, so Bill had to buzz the field until people on the ground fired off a green flare to let him know it was safe to land. The rain was so heavy Bill couldn't see if the strip was dirt, asphalt or concrete and, in any case, the runway was covered with several inches of water.

It was a risky landing. If the strip was dirt, it was now mud; the wheels would dig in when we touched down, and we'd flip over. There was no way to tell. Some later declared it could not be done, but I was there and I can tell you that Bill's great skill had that P-38 still *flying,* that is responding to controls, at a mere 70 miles per hour prior to touchdown as a last-ditch effort to ease onto the runway in case it was mud. Fortunately, it proved to be hard-top.

The old man and his wife who owned the airfield invited us to stay all night at their home. They eyed our youth with skepticism, but nevertheless offered us dinner and a bed in their basement that was a thin mattress on top of old real springs and was the loudest squeaker you have ever heard. We started to laugh, and every time we laughed or drew a breath it squeaked more and more. The more we laughed, the more it squeaked. The next morning, the old couple were staring at us over the tops of their glasses during breakfast. We figured their imaginations had run away with them.

June Allyson (in dark coat) and Dick Powell (in suit with tie), with Bill and Martha, were honorary starters for the 1946 Bendix Air Race.

The Air Show team consisted of Bill and his Lockheed P-38 Lightning, a trio of North American AT-6 World War II advanced trainers that performed precision formation aerobatics, and a World War II PT-17 Stearman primary trainer with a huge engine in it. Paul Lee would do his "stolen airplane" drunk act in a locally rented Piper Cub while Tommy "Bat Man" Boyd would leap from 10,000 feet with his bat wings deployed, trailing smoke. Tommy always frightened us because on each jump he would open his parachute closer and closer to the ground. There were times when his 'chute opened only seconds before he landed!

Bill was always trying new things out in his P-38 to enhance his show. His airplane was like a glove to him. He didn't get into it; he put it on. He and that twin-engine P-38 were one. He perfected a roll on take-off and could perform aerobatics on just one engine. His *pièce de résistance* was presented at Scottsbluff, Nebraska, when he scared everyone half to death, including me, by appearing suddenly out of the sky to scream down the runway at 350 mph with *both* propellers stopped! He suddenly pulled straight up into the sky, did a roll and then frantically began to start at least one engine. Without power, that six-ton piece of iron had a very short glide time. We all held our breaths as Bill successfully started one and then the other engine just as he started to fall. He was as elated — and surprised — as we were that the stunt actually worked, but he never tried it again.

As a pilot, Bill's philosophy was always to put on a show for the public — not fellow pilots. Trying to impress them would eventually get you killed. Bill had seen that happen before and should have known better, but just once he'd let his ego trap him into a stunt to show off in front of pilots and even that one occasion, as Bill readily admitted later, was just dumb, dumb, dumb. Mind you, they were all duly impressed. They thought he was nuts. So did I. On the whole, though, air shows were fun. People would crowd around us wanting autographs and asking questions. Bill would look like he was a kid of about fifteen and become very shy. At one show an elderly lady spectator asked him, "Sonny, does your mother know what you're doing?" Bill could only stammer, "Yes, ma'am, she does."

But after the air show season "went south" for the winter and we were left with just each other, it became apparent that our experience with that pregnant woman had damaged our relationship irreparably. We'd never had a place of our own; Bill had no regular job apart from flying and so we'd been living with his mother. Though she was a lovely lady and so very nice to me, we could all see the handwriting on the wall. With great sadness, Bill and I agreed it would be best if we separated. We were too young for the adult problems that had been unexpectedly thrown at both of us. Maybe if it had been another time and another place we could have dealt with it, but I could only take so much of his girlfriends calling me up. I never have played by that set of rules, even if I did know that to a certain extent he was just trying to outdo his playboy father. At that time and in that place, we had to go our separate ways.

I will always have a place for Bill in a secret corner of my heart. He went on to a brilliant future in the Air Force and would later make his own name in the world of civil aviation. I moved on to train with one of the world's best horsemen. Bill and I remained friends for many years, though, and he would fly out from Texas for the funeral of my father, who adored him. Our marriage had made the front page of the *New York Times*; our divorce made the front page of the *Los Angeles Times*: **Stunt Pilot Afraid of Horses!**

4

Higher Learning

If you can't trust a cop, who can you trust?
— Martha Crawford.

Devastated by the failure of my marriage, I threw myself back into horses, depending on their gentle, honest hearts to heal the damage done to mine. I returned to my birthplace, Texas, to study and show on the Arabian horse circuit with Walter "Chappy" Chapman, one of the best horse trainers in the business, who taught me higher levels of horse training usually not seen outside of top circus acts. Chappy had trained Cass Ole, the "Black Stallion" of movie fame. Although at the time the credit had gone to Corky Randall, the stock contractor, insiders knew that Randall had acquired the horse fully trained from Chapman.

Chappy and his beautiful wife, Carol, were both extraordinary horsepeople; he was the trainer and she was the rider. Chappy was one of the first, if not the first to introduce the advanced principles of classical riding into the horse shows. He was a great student of James Fillis, who is still acclaimed as one of the greatest high-school riders and trainers of all time, even though he was born in 1834. Chappy had horses performing in the Arabian shows in ways that no one had ever seen before, and he zoomed quickly to international stardom and into the Hall of Fame. None of the horse shows prior to this had seen this type of advanced classical training.

Although I acquired a basic foundation in the type of training Chappy taught, I was like Carol; my thrill was in actually riding the highly trained horses. While polo ponies are beautifully trained horses, they're not trained in this particular way. I was fascinated by these horses that could canter backwards on three legs, dance with pirouettes all across the ring, and write their name in the sand backwards. The first time I rode one of them, I felt as if I had been doing it all my life and I realized where I fitted in.

At the time I started working with them, Chappy and Carol were training and showing for a major Arabian stable and immediately asked me to accompany them on the show circuit through such cities as San Antonio, Austin, Houston, Dallas, Denver, and Scottsdale. I showed a white Arab stallion named El Geya who was nearly unbeatable. Two events still stand out in my mind from this tour: one was the most dangerous and the other was the funniest. People often ask me if jumping a horse is dangerous for the rider but for a trained horse person it really isn't, as most of the time you are thrown clear of the horse if it falls. The one time I almost got seriously hurt was in a simple trail horse class at the old Denver Stock Yards Arabian Show.

It was one of those days that was trouble from the beginning. I had been in English classes earlier, but it was now time to change clothes for the Western classes. We had to change clothes in the horse van, and it was hot and humid. Much to my distress I discovered that, as hard as I struggled, I could not get my jodhpurs off. They were sticking to my legs and there I was, caught with them half on and half off. If I had a knife, I would have gladly cut them right off me. I was left with no choice but to seek help. I opened the door and looked out, but the only person in sight was a uniformed trooper watching the back gate. Oh well, if you couldn't trust a cop, who could you trust? I yelled and signalled to him frantically. Now, it's not every day that a cop on gate duty gets an invitation from a pretty girl standing half-dressed in the doorway of a van, so he rushed right on over. Then, as he listened to me explain that I needed his help to remove my pants, his eyes just got bigger. I really don't think he quite believed me until I demonstrated my predicament. To his credit, he then tried to keep his head turned away like a perfect gentleman as he valiantly pulled and pulled on the legs of my jodhpurs. We just barely got them off and my Western clothes on in time for the next class.

My horse was already saddled and tied to the horse van, so with one breathless leap I made it into the saddle and headed into the ring, flipping a heartfelt "thanks" over my shoulder as I did so. I probably should have taken the pants problem as a warning from fate. The metal gate into the ring was to be judged as one of the obstacles, and my right foot caught on it. As I asked the little gray filly to come closer to the gate, she leaned into it and the gate telescoped into itself. That was a big zero score for starters.

The next obstacle was a bridge consisting of a ramp of about five feet running up to a flat landing, also about five feet, from where another ramp led down on the other side. Chappy had said the filly would probably hesitate at the ramp and to use both spurs on her by the girth when she did. Well, no sooner did that filly feel those spurs than she completely jumped the ramp and landed with her rear feet on the flat area. As both feet slipped out from under her, she flew through the air and landed squarely on her back on the bridge. Fortunately, by some miracle I was thrown clear by then but if a foot had caught in a stirrup, or I'd not been thrown completely clear, then it would have been a very different story. Instead, my sterling silver saddle horn cap caught most of the force of the fall and that probably saved the filly from serious injury. When I looked at it later, the cap was absolutely flattened. Still, at least all was not in vain; the fall was the only part of the show featured on the evening TV news.

Carol had an extraordinary horse named Dusty, a golden palomino with a white mane and tail, that was eventually sold to the Mexican Olympic team as an exhibition horse for a huge sum of money. My future performing horse in Las Vegas, Frosty, was a full brother to this half Quarterhorse and half Tennessee Walking horse. When another palomino appeared in Chappy's training program, Carol thought it would be fun for the two of us to show them in a pair class at the Dallas Fair, so as soon as I arrived we met up to get dressed in our matching outfits at Carol's hotel. Then, we discovered that Carol had forgotten her boots. Now, Carol had a Master's degree in designing and made all of the lavish Arab costumes for most of the owners as well as our outfits for this class, but her talents didn't stretch to boot-making. By a huge coincidence we wore the same size — 7½ AAAA — so I rather jokingly suggested she could wear my left boot while I wore the right boot. When we stopped laughing, we realized it could work. Afraid our boot secret would become known, we kept those horses so together and so in stride that we won hands down. We looked like we were tied together. The classical training that these horses had received allowed us to do this. We almost could not contain our laughter till we left the arena.

One of the things that made Chappy such a fine trainer is that his horses, no matter how highly schooled, were happy. The movie trainers loved to buy horses from him as they were already schooled and made those trainers look a lot smarter than they were. If you watch Roy Rogers' horse doing a Spanish Walk or a Passage, for example, you will see that it is just lifting its legs as required. When a horse trained by Chappy lifted its legs, on the other hand, the lifting was lofty and elegant as though the horse loved doing it and wanted to be noticed. Many of the more famous movie trainers, such as Glen and Corky Randall, could not attain this attitude in their horses. On screen it is very obvious, and you can easily see who did the training. Chappy also liked to teach his horses a lot of tricks. He enjoyed playing with them; the horses responded accordingly and the owners loved it. When the Singing Sheriff from Seguine, Texas, left his parade horse to be trained, for example, he was amazed to find that within days, once the horse was left loose in the arena, Chappy could whistle and send him running over to the fence where the sheriff was sitting and go up against the fence for him to mount.

But while all this had been happening, I'd been thinking back to my time on the set of *Yellow Sky* and how much I'd enjoyed that work. So, while on a visit to California to see Carl, who was by now very ill, and my mother who was also recovering from major surgery, I stopped by to talk with the casting director at Metro-Goldwyn-Mayer studios, Jasper Russell. We discussed a potential job coming up that would require a fast bareback mount and jump from a standing position, something that Chappy had taught me to do with the ease of a ballet dancer. I assured Jasper I could do it, and so he guaranteed I could have the job of doubling Eleanor Parker in *Interrupted Melody*. I immediately made round-trip train reservations for a brief trip back to San Antonio to collect my beloved dog and to say a world full of thank-yous.

A very pale, fragile father took me to Union Station in Los Angeles where I boarded the Southern Pacific's deluxe *Sunset Limited* for a return to Texas. It was a long walk down the platform to my train car. I had just begun to seriously regret allowing darling Carl to do this with me when, with a sudden shock as if I'd been hit in the head right then by a stone, I realized I could no longer deny that this big, strong, athletic man I had always known and loved was going to die soon. Instilled in our family tradition, train travel was an integral part of my life. Somewhere deep inside me, though, as Carl and I waved frantically while the *Sunset Limited* rolled away down the platform, I felt that this would be the last time he would ever wave goodbye to my train. I wept, pressing my face to the cold glass of the window trying to see him for as long as possible.

5

Interrupted Melody

The trouble with you, Cyril, is that my success is going to your head.
— Marjorie Lawrence to her brother
in *Interrupted Melody*

No sooner had I arrived in San Antonio than I was immediately making plans to leave again for California, but while there I heard a story about a horse that would eventually change my life forever. By the time Chappy told me this story, the horse was six months old, but Chappy could remember the foal's birth as if it was yesterday. Later, I too would always remember my first meeting with him. It was like meeting someone I had known from another time.

The brilliant sun had just peeked over the horizon when the little foal arrived. He was the long-awaited son of a beautiful, white Tennessee Walking horse mare and a brilliantly colored, golden palomino Quarterhorse, and he was to carry on a great tradition. His full brother, Dusty, was already being acclaimed as a champion high school horse in Texas and Mexico, and so this new foal was expected to be a golden prince in Walter Chapman's royal family of horses. But as the morning sun gradually revealed him, the anticipation of those watching this important event turned to disappointment. Their cheers slowly died away. Standing on shaky little legs before them was a tiny, motley white foal, his curious small ears the only golden thing about him.

His mother didn't give any indication she cared, though. Seeming to sense the majesty within him and perhaps what was before him, she nuzzled and licked the wet, wobbly foal. Each nicker said how much she loved him, as these extraordinary mares do, and so he didn't know that he was too small. He never knew that he was supposed to be a disappointment. Mind you, he had plenty of opportunities to give up. Only a short time after he was born, his beloved mother was led away. The foal's heartbroken cries went unanswered. His lively, intelligent eyes found only the door of the stall where he had been isolated in a misguided attempt to protect him. He never saw her again.

The grooms gave the little foal a barn name, Sancho, which in Spanish means "orphan." For six months, he was kept in his stall. His owner wanted to keep him safe, but the little foal needed room to run and room to grow. Because he didn't have that, the stall stunted his growth. At six months, he was only the size of a normal two-month old. He couldn't see over the stall door, even when he stood on tiptoe.

As I listened to Chappy tell me the story, I knew that prospective buyers must have asked about him only for Chappy to hear disappointment in their voices when they saw how small he was. Meanwhile, the foal would have learned to identify the voices of the grooms who cared for him. Perhaps they laughed at him and teased him for his size. I like to think that, as he waited there, this little foal told himself he would grow up in the days to come to be big and beautiful just like his brother. One day he would have a pure white mane that would tumble over his neck and a long sweeping tail, and his mother would be so proud of him. He just knew that somewhere out there was someone who would see beyond his appearance to the magic within him.

However, right now I had other things to do that seemed more important. Once again I had to board the *Sunset Limited*, only this time with a mink stole over one arm and my cocker spaniel, Sancho, draped over the other. Tucking him comfortably into my Pullman compartment, I tacked a note on the door that read: "Please don't open — dog," and headed off to the Club Car. On the way, I ran smack into a cowboy in the vestibule who tipped his hat and said, "Read the note your dawg wrote, ma'am — real smart dawg!"

A little unsure of whether he'd been joking, but smiling anyway, I opened the door into the Club Car and proceeded to find myself a comfortable chair. I was lost in the pages of a horse magazine, naturally, when I suddenly felt someone plop down next to me. With a start I looked around, thinking for a second that it was the cowboy, but all I saw was a rather plain-looking gentleman with a bow tie that bounced up and down as he talked.

"Sorry to startle you, ma'am," he apologized, "but I see you like horses."

"Well, yes I do, as a matter of fact," I replied. Where, oh where was that cowboy when I needed him?

"I have a nice horse," he said, trying politely to make conversation.

Now I was beginning to feel guilty for thinking of ignoring him, so I smiled charmingly and asked, "Oh, you do? What's his name?"

"Swaps," he said with a grin.

Oh, dear. Right then and there, even with my limited attention span, I just knew he was no horseman. In those days, your ranking with me was determined by how much you knew about horses, and I had been raised with horses that had names like Vagabond King, Seabiscuit, and Man o' War. As far as I was concerned, nobody who knew anything about horses would seriously name their horse Swaps! Having judged the man and found him wanting, I said goodbye as quickly as I could without seeming rude and returned to my compartment.

Dropping into the chair by the window, I gazed out into the haze of the early morning hour and let my mind drift away to Chappy's foal. At this hour, he would be alone in his stall and I knew just how he felt. Hugging my spaniel, I thought about the other Sancho I was leaving behind. They had both been unwanted runts, and I felt their destinies were somehow tied to mine. I kept seeing the foal in the reflections of the double Pullman car windows as the train sped through deserts with their kaleidoscope colors. I had no idea if I would ever see him again.

Then I had to rein in my daydreams in order to give some serious consideration to my coming job as Eleanor Parker's double. My father, Carl, had often worked with Jasper Russell and MGM, supplying horses and players for polo sequences in various films, the most recent of which had been an Esther Williams film, *Neptune's Daughter*. Other than my work in *Yellow Sky* several years before, just being the daughter of a well-known polo player had been reference enough for Jasper when we had discussed what I would need to do for *Interrupted Melody* but, still, he had to be seen to go through the motions.

So, having arrived back in Los Angeles in the latter part of 1954, I was notified to attend what is still known in the industry as a cattle call. It's a standard audition routine required by the union even though most know ahead of time what the results will be. In my case, the call had gone out for "jumping horse" riders. By the time I got there, my competing prospective "doubles" were packed onto a long bench in the drab gray hall outside the MGM casting office waiting to be interviewed by the producer of the film. There were only ten or twelve women doing this type of work then, and they were all there in an attempt to claim the biggest prize of the year. They were not all necessarily jumping horse riders per se but their riding skills were such that they could, most often, do anything asked of them.

After a while, Jasper Russell came out of his office and carefully studied each girl individually, looking for those that would photograph well. While he knew each of us was qualified to do the work, of course he wanted someone who would look good doing it. So, he mentally screened the attributes of this unique group of rodeo trick riders with their skin-tight jeans, cowboy boots and big silver trophy buckles. Their tanned faces reflected confidence in their abilities as he acknowledged each of them by name. Now, because I happened to be the newest kid on the block here, no one had moved up to make room for me on the bench. I had made several attempts at conversation with the girls but they weren't having it, so I was still standing up leaning against the wall wearing my navy blue silk shantung dress and Delman pumps with my ranch mink stole casually slung over my right shoulder over which cascaded waves of reddish-blonde hair. Jasper's eyes landed squarely on me and held mine for just a fleeting moment.

I must have looked such an oddity amongst that group of women, perhaps even a somewhat mysterious threat as they had no idea of who I was. Even later, when people in the industry did know me, I never quite fitted the mold of a stereotypical stunt girl, and that day I looked as though I was being interviewed for a lead role. As he showed me into the producer's office, Jasper and I both knew that apart from my riding skills, my other major advantage would be the close resemblance I bore to Eleanor Parker; I was much the same age, build, height and hair color. As the producer, Jack Cummings, graciously came out from behind his highly polished mahogany desk to greet me, I could tell by the look in his eyes that we'd been right. He gestured for me to sit, and then they both asked me a few questions and seemed pleased with the answers. As I left the office that day, I was confident that unless something unforeseen happened, I had this job in the bag.

A few of us were then selected by Dick Webb, the ramrod wrangler on the film, to return the next day to the studio backlot for a riding test. This was most unusual even then, and I've certainly never had to perform one since. It consisted of a bareback mount to a standing horse within two seconds and then a short ride. The other trick riders all failed. While they were proficient at the mounts to running horses that they did every day of the working week, they all had problems negotiating the mount in the required time-frame to a standing horse. On the other hand, with the help of my acrobatic background and those fool-proof lessons from Chappy, I had no trouble at all with that mount. A few days later, I got the call to confirm I'd be the double for Eleanor Parker, one of Hollywood's biggest stars, in the biggest stunt job of the year. I was so excited I called everyone I knew to tell them the news.

While working on *Interrupted Melody* I was living with my parents at their apartment in Westwood, near UCLA, as neither of them was well. My father had had a number of heart attacks and was consequently confined to bed or the sofa. My mother was in intense pain because scar tissue from ulcer after healed ulcer had closed her stomach. It is one of the few medical conditions from which you can die of the pain. It soon meant an eight-hour surgical procedure during which two-thirds of her stomach was removed. What we wouldn't know was that during the operation, the nerve to the stomach that governs the supply of hydrochloric acid was severed, and so she could no longer absorb Vitamin A. She needed to take it as a supplement, but because no one knew she was deficient that never happened and this may have influenced her eventual death from breast cancer.

Fortunately, I was making friends as the days went by. Actor Jeffrey Hunter and his wife Barbara Rush lived in the same building, as did dancer Taina Elg who would later be nominated for Broadway's Tony Award for her work in the musical revival *Where's Charley*. Roger Moore, who was playing Marjorie Lawrence's brother in *Interrupted Melody*, lived just around the corner and rode with me every morning to the studio where I would drop him off at the main gate as I came in through the casting office entrance. Fortunately, one of Chappy's customers had been able to drive my much-loved, dark-green 1952 Buick Special to California for me on their way to a Santa Barbara horse show. The future James Bond was even then a very classy, handsome young man. Most of my friends were men in those days, probably because I spent most of my time working within a man's world.

Dick Webb was a pivotal figure in many of my jobs at MGM. Living nearby, and aware I was under a lot of strain at home, he would often leave a rose under my windshield wipers of a morning on his way to the studio. He visited with my father often, and that was a god-send as my father's medication was making him dangerously depressed and he came to look forward to Dick's visits. Though many say that "success is being there" and I was so there I could see that success on the horizon, I was still lonely and Dick understood. We talked a lot and, being a fellow horseman, he sensed my yearning to somehow rescue that little foal I had left behind in Texas. You know you never forget your first sunset over the ocean, and I would never forget my first meeting with this indomitable four-legged soul who would come to make my heart so much his own. Dick, being the friend he had become, listened as I shared my memories with him.

Looking for Chappy one day, I had peeked into what I thought was an empty stall to see if he might be in there cleaning it out. Instead, I could see a little foal that appeared to be about two months old, and I immediately figured that this must be the one that Chappy had told me about. As I leaned over the door, my blonde hair cascading over the edge, he quickly came over to me and buried his face in my hair. For several minutes, I listened to him breathe me in, savor my essence and make a decision. He looked up at me, and I was lost.

I had spent my whole life looking into the eyes of horses. I had seen fear, defiance, and even acceptance, but here was something else. Here was an old soul. I could see in his eyes the look of someone who had already seen too much and had refused to be beaten by it. I was face to face with a king, with a champion who wouldn't quit.

As I stood there, with one arm over the stall door, I looked around these Texas stables that had once belonged to my father. A nicker drew my attention back to the little Sancho. I had never heard a sound quite like it. It sounded like a toy. In fact, now that I could see him clearly, he looked like a toy with his dirty white face, small golden ears and angora fluff mane. I was astonished when the grooms told me that he was really over six months old. Joyfully, I could sense the Great Hoop of life encircling both of us as I realized that we had both been born in this same historic city of San Antonio where, in 1836, 189 defenders had held the Alamo against some 4,000 Mexican troops for thirteen days before it fell. That famous cry "Remember the Alamo!" had rung in my ears as a child, a rallying call for those who were down but not out. 'Perhaps that is a sign of things to come,' I thought as I continued to look around. I had been only six months old when I first came to this stable, and I had first learned to ride here when I was two, beginning my lifetime affair with horses. In my mind's eye, I saw my father in his sweaty polo clothes and my mother running to greet him in her chiffon dress, trailing behind her a faint scent of Shalimar. I could hear the sound of horses' hooves on the gravel road as they returned from the polo games.

Bringing myself back to the present, I looked down at the little foal

for a moment. Then, leaning down to him, I whispered a word that only
he could hear. It was a new word full of promise, and when he heard it
he looked up at me with his ears pricked as if he understood it immediately. Time seemed to stand still. I saw kindness and acute intelligence. I
stared into eyes that looked right through me, as Tom Smith once said of
his horse, Seabiscuit.

But I had to go and, tearing myself away, I backed up through the
door. "I'll see you again," I said to him as I closed it behind me. After I'd
walked a few steps, I hesitated and turned for one last look. I could just
see his little nose straining over the stall door. I knew that those old, wise
eyes would never forget the lady from California, as I would not forget
him, and that the golden ears would search for the sound of my steps and
keep listening. I knew he would never forget the smell of my hair. I knew
neither of us would forget the instant bonding we shared, I told Dick, and
I knew in my heart we would see each other again. He agreed.

While not my first film, *Interrupted Melody* would definitely be one
of my most memorable. It unfolds as the tragic and inspiring true story
of Australian-born opera star Marjorie Lawrence's long, hard road to the
top, her international success, and of her battle with polio that not only
abruptly ended her career but threatened her will to live. Despite such
adversity, she succeeded in overcoming her illness and in making a tri-
umphal comeback. Eleanor Parker had the title role of Lawrence, and
Glenn Ford co-starred as her doctor husband, Thomas King. Inspired by
the success of their 1951 film *The Great Caruso*, starring Mario Lanza,
MGM had purchased the screen rights to Lawrence's recently published
memoirs in mid–1952 for $27,000. After considering Lana Turner and
Kathryn Grayson for the lead role, the studio had then offered it to Greer
Garson, who was a personal friend of Lawrence. Like her, Garson had
been raised on a farm and had persisted with her dream of performing
despite family disapproval and illness, and so she dearly wanted to have
the chance to portray her friend on screen. It appeared that her lobbying
had been successful when MGM went as far as publicly announcing in
July 1952 that Greer had been cast for the role, and she then embarked on
intense preparation that involved learning an Australian accent and studying various operatic arias.

However, by February 1953 the budget for *Interrupted Melody* had
blown out to over $2 million and an unhappy studio boss, Dore Schary,
began to have second thoughts. With hardly any warning, he shut down
work on the picture and allocated Garson to other projects. Furious over

such treatment, Garson left the studio within twelve months and went to Warners. So, in early 1954, Eleanor Parker was offered the biggest chance of her career, and she knew it. There was only one tiny little problem: Parker couldn't sing any better that Turner or Garson. Grayson could sing better than all three of them, although whether she would have handled Wagner in the end will never be known.

Up until now, MGM hadn't really been concerned about the voice because they'd naturally assumed that Marjorie Lawrence could dub the singing, but when producer Jack Cummings listened to the tapes he realized that her voice was no longer able to handle the demands of Wagner. Needless to say, Lawrence wasn't at all happy when told they wouldn't use her voice. Bobby Tucker, who was working on the musical arrangements for the film, then suggested his friend Eileen Farrell, a well-known concert, radio and television performance artist (and future Metropolitan Opera soprano). Working on a huge soundstage with MGM orchestra conductor Walter DuCloux, she finished the dubbing work in two and a half weeks. Parker, who wanted her lip-synching to be absolutely convincing, would often drop by the control room to watch Farrell record and to hear where the engineers put in the beep on the recording to let Parker know when to imitate taking a breath. When Farrell was told she could earn more money if her name didn't appear in the credits, she took the money but it is clearly her voice, rather than an imitation of Lawrence, and everyone at the time recognized it. Because of the wide variety of vocal pieces used in the film, all the way from "Waltzing Matilda" and "Over the Rainbow" to Wagner, it is doubtful whether any other soprano at that time could have done it as well as Eileen Farrell.

My respect for the real Lawrence grew when I discovered that we had much in common when it came to riding. She had been only seven when her father threw her up on to the bare back of a farm horse and by the time she was ten there was not a horse in the entire district that she couldn't ride. Her greatest thrill as a teenager was to tear across the fields of Winchelsea, in Victoria, in the wind and rain without saddle or bridle, feeling the muscles of the horse beneath her as she sang the "Hallelujah Chorus" at the top of her voice. At night she would ride out in the moonlight and sing to the stars. Lawrence was certainly the first twentieth-century Brunnhilde, and may well have been the first ever, to actually follow Wagner's directions and literally ride her horse, Grane, into Siegfried's funeral pyre rather than lead it, as had been the tradition, during a performance of *Götterdämmerung* at New York's Metropolitan Opera House

in the mid–1930s. Despite opposition from the stage director, the conductor and a petrified chorus, Lawrence mounted her horse at just the
right moment with her brother holding the reins and, kicking the horse
in the ribs, she leaped through the flames, singing the high notes as she
did so. By the time she dismounted, the house was in pandemonium and
she took curtain call after call. Lawrence continued to ride her horse on
stage until 1941, the season before she contracted polio. She would recall
later that during what would be their final performance, Grane would
whinny every time she sang, the only time he ever made any noise on
stage.

My own big moment in this film would be that same leap through
the fire in *Interrupted Melody*'s $50,000 immolation scene at the end of
Wagner's famous opera, *Götterdämmerung*, at that time the most expensive indoor scene ever shot. Believe it or not, the first stage of my rehearsal

Martha mounted on Ski about to leap into the funeral pyre at the end of Wagner's *Götterdämmerung* during the shooting of MGM's *Interrupted Melody* in
1954. This photo was featured in the May 16, 1955, issue of *Life* magazine (Warner
Bros. Entertainment).

had to be lessons in German because I had to accurately mime the words that would eventually be sung by Eileen Farrell. After several days of that, we embarked on about three weeks of rehearsal for the elaborate shot that would take place on Soundstage 50, Metro's largest. A large hole (about twelve feet square) was cut in the studio floor and covered with a metal grate. On the floor level beneath, the special effects crew set up a circle of large pots filled with celluloid confetti and explosive charges. Within the circle stood a large motorized plastic wheel into which were inserted red and yellow plastic panels. Bright lights were then fitted underneath the wheel so that they would shine up through the panels and the hole in the floor. The crew brought in large tubs of dry ice onto which they would pour water to create steam and smoke effects. Once all of this was set in motion, you had what looked on film like a genuine funeral pyre conflagration.

Not only did this scene call for an enormous fire, it also required a very special horse and my special horse was Ski. During our three rigorous weeks of rehearsal while they built and configured the set, I discovered that this extremely intelligent horse actually listened to the music. Standing in front of him, per instructions to answer to the camera for the long shot, I would make the required operatic gesture and then, on cue, I would turn to face the back with my left hand on his mane, holding onto a chunk of it. My left elbow came to rest just above his shoulder, acting as a lever as I leaped, helping me sail up and onto the horse in a bareback mount. This whole maneuver had to be carried out in exactly two seconds to fit into the music. After a few days of this, I noticed that Ski would move his left foot forward, to brace himself, precisely one beat before I had to swing up onto him. If you watch him at that moment in the movie, you can see him do it and it was obvious to me that he was listening. Once I was mounted we turned, reared, and galloped towards the fire. Ski's cue to rear was when I touched him lightly on his neck. The celluloid wheel and lights were already rolling and the water had been poured on the dry ice to look like smoke. At the edge of the "fire," Ski reared again and then jumped on the grate. As soon as we jumped, the crew exploded the pots of confetti, making it look just like sparks flying up in a real fire. It truly was remarkable.

Even in the fifties, the humane treatment of horses was a first priority in films made in the United States and there was an SPCA representative on the set at all times. Many directors in this era had no qualms whatsoever about a horse being hurt or killed during a scene, but if a horse

Eleanor Parker and Martha looking remarkably alike, dressed for the big fire scene in *Interrupted Melody* (Warner Bros. Entertainment).

did happen to be hurt in a shot the director was not supposed to use the film footage. During the rehearsals for *Interrupted Melody*, the SPCA insisted that Ski had to be fitted with a sterilized bit, even though it was on his regular bridle, so every morning a sealed cellophane bag would duly be delivered to the lot containing a sparkling clean bit. According to SPCA regulations, Ski could only be used for rearing scenes and was limited to rearing eight times in one day. This may seem somewhat extreme, but such regulations prevented unknowledgeable and uncaring movie directors from abusing a trained animal and prevented physical or mental injury to a horse.

Handling a professional rearing horse is not easy. They tend to get routined quickly, and if they are mishandled it is soon almost impossible to get them from point A to point B on all four legs, because all they want to do is stand there and rear. One must never forget these are highly intelligent, skilled horses that can be masters at pre-empting you and your best-laid plans or thoughts. In a traditional rear, a horse has only one foot solidly on the ground and just the toe of the other foot for balance. This is where the fatigue factor will show first if the horse has been overused. The fire scene photo in *Interrupted Melody* that was featured in *Life* magazine, though, shows Ski's right rear foot about eight or nine inches into the air with his left foot solidly on the ground. He knew exactly what to do and so a bond was established, not only between he and I but also with Eleanor Parker. Possibly because of this and also because of our physical resemblance, we came to like each other a lot and I would work with both of them again.

However, despite all my hard work including learning German, that fast mount from the ground ended up on the cutting room floor. "It looks too professional," they said after studying the rushes, words I would hear more than once after this movie. In the end, Eleanor was given a fake rock to step up on for her mount and close-up on horseback gesturing and mouthing the German words, and then the camera cuts to a long shot of me galloping off across the stage and into the "fire." If you didn't notice that she's mounted on a different horse, the average person in the audience wouldn't be able to tell the difference between Martha and Eleanor. And that's how it's supposed to be, really. After all, who watches the horse?

While the stage scenes and interiors were shot on Stage 50, the exterior farm scenes of the young Marjorie riding and jumping fences were done at the Irvine Ranch in Orange County. One of the original timber ranch structures, probably a foreman's house, was used as the Lawrence farmhouse. For many years you could still see the green cottage as you drove the freeway to San Diego, behind acres of lima bean fields and the stands of eucalyptus trees that gave it just enough of an Australian appearance to be useful as a setting for the story.

Ironically, Ski's expensive leap into this fire may have marked the

Still looking as alike as peas in a pod, Martha is costumed here to double for Eleanor during their horseback dash to the railway station at the beginning of *Interrupted Melody*.

beginning of the end of major studio horse stunts, in much the same way that Rex Allen marked the end of the singing cowboys as he rode into the sunset in *Phantom Stallion* that same year. I adored Ski. He was a stocky, mixed-breed black gelding with a marvelously intelligent eye and a conformation best described in Laura Hillenbrand's words about Seabiscuit:

"An American legend, built like a cinder block." He was never less than a consummate professional.

So my days on this set, which had started with German lessons I had thought silly at the time, still ended up being an experience I always look back on with immense enjoyment. Months later, driving to MGM for a rehearsal one day, I heard over my radio: "The winner of the 1955 Kentucky Derby is ... Swaps!" "Swaps!?" I cried aloud. "Swaps from the *Sunset Limited*?" I had given the proverbial cold shoulder to one of the best known and most successful men in the history of horse racing — Rex Ellsworth!

My beloved stepfather Carl died when he was only 55 years old, before *Interrupted Melody* was released. He had worshipped the ground my mother walked on, and had not been able to bear seeing her in such agonizing pain for so long. His doctor, Bill Branch, said to me: "You can call it a heart attack if you want, Martha, but Carl Crawford died of a broken heart."

For the rest of her life, my mother steadfastly refused to ever watch any of my films.

6

Texas Lady

Blot, don't wipe!

— movie makeup person's mantra

In the summer of 1955 I found myself on location in the small Californian town of Murphys, way up in Sierras gold rush country, with the wonderful Nat Holt Productions film company to shoot the film *Texas Lady* for RKO, starring Claudette Colbert. She plays the part of Prudence Webb, who wins $50,000 from gambler Mooney. Webb takes control of the Fort Ralston newspaper and campaigns for a railroad spur into town, but she is opposed by cattle baron Ralston. Mooney arrives to help Prudence and defeats Ralston's gunslinger, Foley, but Ralston and his men blockade the town in a last-ditch attempt to regain control. Chris manages to contact the Texas Rangers, who ride to the rescue. Although we didn't know it then, *Texas Lady* would be something of a landmark in Western film history because this rare combination of people involved in making it could never be assembled again.

Texas Lady was the last movie of our director, Tim Whelan, who had begun his career as a writer, producer and director in 1923, developing stories and scripts for Harold Lloyd, worked in England for some years and then returned to Hollywood during World War II. It would also be the last produced screenplay of journalist, novelist and screenwriter Horace McCoy, released only a month before his death. Ironically, having earned nearly fifty screen credits during a long career working for most of the major studios, McCoy is probably best remembered for a story that was made into a film after his death: *They Shoot Horses, Don't They?* Having been on the staff of the *Dallas Journal* for nearly ten years and a member of the Texas National Guard, it's no surprise that references to the newspaper business and to the Texas Rangers were favorite screenplay touches of his.

Our director of photography was master cameraman Ray Rennahan, one of only six cinematographers to eventually be awarded a star on the Hollywood Walk of Fame and the man who had been the official photographer hired from Technicolor for *Gone with the Wind*. He had a natural feel for Westerns that was probably in his blood. He had, after all, been born in that little railroad town of Las Vegas, Nevada, a year before gold had been found at nearby Searchlight.

Dolph Zimmer was the assistant director and occasional second unit director. He was a delight to work for, always fair, and had a good knowledge of just how much a stunt was worth to the production. A second unit director takes the place of the film's director for the action shots so, because they were more often than not the shots I was in, he was most likely to be the person from whom I received my instructions. When we were hired to do stunts, we received a basic day rate for the duration, even if all we did some days was to sit and study the scenery. However, our individual stunts were then negotiated with the assistant director over and above that day rate as to how much they would pay per successful film. It might have been $100 or $500 or whatever figure we finally negotiated. If the first take turned out to be unusable for some reason and therefore not considered a print, then you and the crew kept doing it until you got it right and the director was satisfied enough to call, "Print it!" Hopefully, that was within another one or two takes; after each one, you and the crew would wait in anticipation for the director to call out those two magic words, knowing that then and only then would you be paid. Everyone was always pleased to see "Zimmy" on a set. Working with highly experienced crew members who knew their jobs, as this crew did, made for a pleasant working day.

When the call came for me to work on *Texas Lady*, I had been really excited. I was thrilled at the chance to do a stirrup mount, because I had yet to perform one of these on film. I had been through a lot in my life recently and whether or not I would accept this job had been a tough decision for me. So, I was pleased in a way that much of the shoot would be done on the studio lot before we travelled out to the location. It would give me a chance to get to know people and to work out how best to fit in with this group of men who had done it all before and often. This would be an education for me, as it was the first time I had worked with a group of regular stunt men. A former theatrical poster artist and stage manager, Nat Holt was aligned with several major studios such as RKO, Twentieth Century–Fox and Paramount during his Hollywood years but he maintained an independent, autonomous production unit throughout, specializing in westerns, and he would later be involved with television series work, in particular *Tales of Wells Fargo* and *Overland Trail*. Because he had his own production company, Holt developed over time a group of people with whom he could work easily and well. He consistently employed the same production crew including Rennahan, writer Frank Gruber, set designer Darrell Silvera and composer Paul Sawtell, a group of actors that included Randolph Scott, Forrest Tucker, "Gabby" Hayes, Paul Fix and Victor Jory, and the same stunt crew.

Back in San Antonio, Chappy was also facing another tough decision. The owners of the little foal had told Chappy to get rid of him. He was not salable and Chappy was going out on the show circuit again. He would have to decide what to do with him and the options were pretty frightening. It was right about then that I called him, a few days after my father's funeral. I could hear the phone ringing and knew that the outdoor telephone bell would be piercing the air at the Chapmans' and echoing through the barn area. Walter answered the phone from the tack room where he was cleaning a bridle. He was happy to hear from me, but he was so surprised when I asked about the foal that I heard the saddle soap thump on the floor as it slipped from his hand.

"Excuse me? Dusty's brother? Yes, I still have him but he stayed small, you know," he added.

I reassured him that didn't matter and asked if he would sell him to me.

"Of course," he replied, his happiness that his little orphan would have a home just about making the phone glow. "How about $100 delivered to Phoenix? I'm leaving tomorrow for the Arabian show there."

He told me later that after he had hung up he had to sit down on a tack trunk to savor the moment. The little runt had made his way into Chappy's heart, too. He said that the Mexican boys, grandchildren of those who worked with my father's polo horses thirty years before, had their hands full getting the horses ready for the big show in Phoenix. Some were division champions, and their tack and costumes had to shine, as did the horses themselves. The little foal had been in a caliche corral day in and day out, typically surfaced with a tan-colored mix of soil and calcium and very dusty. So, there was just no time to spiff up a little white runt, and he began his ride to Phoenix just as he was. He was never neglected, just unwanted. I had known from the beginning it would take a miracle to save him from some unkind, unknown fate. Now, that miracle was going to be me.

I was able to manage my time and take a few days to drive down to Phoenix and personally pick up Frosty, as I had already started calling him, short for Frosted Sundae. Well, it would be far too confusing to have two Sanchos in the household. I met Chappy at the Arizona Biltmore Hotel, site of the first and very lavish official Arabian Horse Show. Only a year after its opening, the Biltmore's ownership was taken over by William Wrigley, Jr., who along with his wife Helen became charter members of the first Arabian Horse Association. The Wrigleys, along with their daughter Deedie, were pioneers in breeding Arabian horses in the United States. The Wrigley family's pampered horses, kept on Santa Catalina Island, had been shipped by barge across the Channel to Long Beach harbor from where they had traveled by deluxe horse van to Arizona for the show. Well, my horse had travelled by van, too, or at least in a float, and then there he was coming down the ramp. He was still a little skinny and rather pathetic-looking, with eyes like deep pools of water reflecting the expression I remembered so well, but he was my Frosty. As we drove the endless highway home across that Martian landscape, I had as much time as I needed to dream about all the things we could accomplish together.

I joined the *Texas Lady* cast and crew as they were preparing to leave for the Sonora location where we would spend ten days. I had heard Nat Holt's stunt guys were full of vinegar, and so I really should not have been surprised that they would put me through some kind of initiation into their ranks. On our first day together, actors, stuntmen, and production crew all boarded a bus at RKO Studios for the long ride out to Sonora. Making myself comfortable in a seat by myself behind two of the stunt men, I began to read but eventually my mind drifted off to thinking about Frosty and how I was going to train him. As the miles went by, the rhythm of the tires on the road lulled me into a dream and my book fell open, unread, into my lap.

Suddenly my thoughts were interrupted as I realized there was a small stuntman inching his way forward along the carry-on luggage rack above our heads. It was the odd scraping sound that had alerted me. When he was over our seats, he reached down and slugged the guy in front of me on the head — twice — and then scrunched back into the luggage rack. Well, the fellow in front of me whipped around in his seat and was about to slug me in return when he saw I was a lady and calmed down. To this day, he probably still believes it was me that hit him on the head that morning.

Then, a few minutes later, the comic in the luggage rack began to make the undeniable and very loud sounds of someone who is going to throw up. Everyone became really nervous and began to check each other out. Then, to my horror, it happened! The stuntman in the luggage rack above us threw up all over the same guy in front of me. In no doubt this time that I was absolutely crazy, he leaped to his feet swearing a string of words I had never heard in my life. I thought he was going to kill me right there before the trip was over! I was desperately trying to convince him the guilty party had not been me when I became aware that an entire bus-load of people was roaring hysterically with laughter. Of course, it turned out that this had all been part of my initiation into their ranks. The fellow that "threw up" had not thrown up at all; he had just made the appropriate noises and had then thrown a cup of vegetable soup all over my travelling companion. After that, they all accepted me whole-heartedly, but for many days it would still feel to me like it had been a close call.

Sonora was a central jumping-off point for Columbia, Jamestown (Jimtown), and the quaint gold rush town of Murphys with the nearby golden grass hills still scattered with the famous China Walls which are quite visible in the film. Their origin is a mystery as they seem to have no purpose. The start-and-stop patterns of the rock walls render them useless as corrals or containment fences and they are too low to be fortifications. As early as 1904 they were deemed to be the work of Mongolians or even Aztecs, perhaps dating back as far as the 1700s. They were fascinating to a history buff and indeed monopolized a great deal of our conversation on the bus to and from these locations. It is still said that neither man of that early day nor men of the present could possibly put the large stones of these walls in place without appliances of some kind.

Murphys, known as the Queen of the Sierra, is a charming old town with a rich and colorful past. Founded in 1848, it is located in the central Sierra Nevada foothills between Lake Tahoe and Yosemite National Park, in Calaveras County, and is a treasure of gold rush history. It was one of California's richest gold fields; five million dollars worth was taken from a four-acre placer area in one winter alone. The town's red- and gold-colored tree-lined streets seemed to enjoy lending themselves to the atmosphere of the real west that we were creating. The studio dressed up the windows of the stores with gold-leaf lettering and dark-green, pull-down shades that quickly transported Murphys back to its glory days, and the set decorators even covered the main street with dirt to make it look more authentic. The 1856 Murphys Hotel hardly needed to have any attention;

Martha doubling Claudette Colbert somewhere outside of the California town of Murphys, in the Sierras, during shooting of *Texas Lady* in 1955.

it still had the original supposedly arrow-proof iron shutters they could close in case of Indian attacks.

I was on this set doubling for Claudette Colbert, who didn't like horses anyway, in order to do a difficult stirrup mount: a flying leap from my right foot to tuck my left foot in the stirrup, then grabbing the saddle horn to swing into the saddle and dash away. "All quiet" was called for on the set, and then I heard, "Action!" For a fleeting moment, I froze. You see, I still hadn't quite got over what had happened to me on the bus and the stunt crew's antics hadn't been confined to the bus since then, either. In the scene just prior to this one, the stuntmen were riding into town to rob a bank. While that group was seated on their horses waiting for the action signal, two other stuntmen who were not in the shot had walked up to them and, as they casually chatted away, had proceeded to tie the saddle strings to their spurs. When the "robbers" made their run into town, pulled up to the hitch rail and went to bail out of their saddles outside the bank, all of them were totally upended by being tied to their saddles! Horses snorted and ran backwards, some bucked and whirled around and reared. The saddle strings quickly broke, and riderless horses scattered everywhere. Wranglers had their hands full recapturing them all. "Cut! Cut! Cut!" pierced the air. It took a while for everyone to settle down, not in the least because most of us were laughing till we cried. Consequently, the makeup team had to re-do almost everybody. Their famous slogan, "Blot, don't wipe," was lost in the moment.

So with events like these fresh in my mind, I had a momentary flash of what they might have done to me when I wasn't looking to upend my flying mount, like tying my boots together. Time can be a strange thing. What can seem like an eternity can be really just a matter of a second or two during which I looked down, checked my boots were still separate from each other, and then off I ran and everything went the way it was supposed to. Once again, though, all my hard work was to no avail. In the end, the director thought my scenes showed too much action for a prim lady publisher of a newspaper and they, too, ended up on the cutting room floor. It was too bad. I did a lot of riding up hill and down across the country for Claudette, but my big moment was to perform that stirrup mount for her. I had always wanted to do this kind of mount and this had been my main reason for wanting to be involved in this film. I justified it all by telling myself that there would always be another day and another film, but I never did receive that call to do a stirrup mount again. Really, though, you seldom saw a lady of the west called upon to mount a horse like that.

I found Claudette Colbert polite in a shallow sort of way. Perhaps she was a little embarrassed about appearing in an ordinary Western. After all, this was the twilight of an acting career that had begun in 1927 and that encompassed over eighty movies, television appearances, an Emmy nomination, a Golden Globe award and an Oscar. This was to be her next-to-last starring role; she would make only one other silver screen appearance, coming out of retirement for *Parrish* in 1961, although she would continue to act for television and on stage right up until a series of strokes disabled her shortly before her death in 1996.

In 1955, the slim, 5' 4" Colbert was still every inch a star and she didn't have any qualms about letting you know her status. Although we were staying in the best hotel Sonora had to offer, she insisted on bringing her own satin sheets. At 52, famous as a legendary beauty, she was now requiring just a little help from the makeup department to preserve it, especially for this movie where she is supposed to be so attractive to a younger man that he helps her fight off the bad guys to win the day for the town and for the newspaper she has inherited. One of the simple techniques they often used for older actors was to apply a strip of tape, pulled snug, from one side of your neck to the other just under the chin to give you a more youthful neckline. Once in a while, the tape would come unstuck and the actors would usually be furious and thoroughly tear into the makeup man and then go pout the rest of the day. Well, sure enough, every now and then Claudette's tape broke and she would go right down that same road, and I would turn away with a little smile.

Secretly, you see, I had held an underlying resentment for her close to my heart for years. When my mother was given a screen test by Colbert's home studio, Paramount, she had photographed on screen very much like the star but looked far more beautiful. Colbert had happened to see that test and, feeling threatened, had duly blacklisted my mother. So it was that I, for one, cheered silently within myself whenever Claudette Colbert's tape snapped.

Our return bus trip to RKO was much more uneventful than the trip out. This time I could relive some memories of my Phoenix trip in peace. I had given Chappy an envelope with a signed blank check just in case he had changed his mind about the price. He held it while he gnawed on a piece of straw and shifted it from side to side in his mouth. Then, after poking the brim of his hat up with one finger, he folded the envelope with a quiet smile and put it in his shirt pocket without looking in it. Years later, when that $100 check was eventually returned, it was still in the same envelope. I put my

Taken circa 1940, this photograph of Sharon Crawford, Martha's mother, highlights her resemblance to Claudette Colbert.

arms around my friend and hugged him, and he held me for a moment as if to thank me.

I had taken Frosty for a long walk to let him relax and get his legs under him again. He was like a child in fairyland. Just as I had a short time ago, he watched the water fountains sending sparkling drops of water high into the clear blue desert sky. His eyes were like saucers at seeing the surroundings, as if he thought he didn't belong. I let him taste the green grass and drink the cool water. He held the water in his mouth as he watched the others looking at him. The show horses and exhibitors were out and about in all their finery, and they held their heads tilted up as we walked by. They looked down their noses at us in disbelief, this grubby little misfit and I.

As we walked, I held the lead rope in my left hand and walked with my right arm partway under his neck. I slipped my hand under the red halter and placed it carefully on his cheek. It made him feel secure, I could tell. I smiled and nodded to the "swells" as if I was leading the Champion of the Show. He could not have looked worse, nor could I have felt better. Right then and there, I could sense a presence within him that exceeded my wildest dreams.

And so a quest of the lonely heart, begun in the wide open spaces and dusty caliche corrals of Texas amidst abandonment, disappointment and isolation, ended that day in paradise. Little Sancho's journey had ended, but Frosty's journey had just begun. From the first day my eyes ever fell on him I knew he would, somehow, become a part of my life from that day forward.

It was dark by the time the bus pulled into RKO. I had fallen asleep with my dreams, my book still unread.

7

Coming Back

Less filling! More satisfying!
— Drewry's Extra Dry Beer slogan

With the impetus of my work in *Texas Lady*, my comeback to films in the latter part of 1954 and into 1955 took off like a rocket. My mother moved back to Santa Monica and I got my own place in the San Fernando Valley where I could have two horses. I even traded my '52 Buick Special in on a new Oldsmobile 88. The next day I was returning to MGM to discuss a commercial I was going to do. While driving down West Washington Blvd. with the windows down and my golden blonde pony-tail waving in the breeze, the traffic slowed and I was aware that someone in the car to my right was looking at me. With a start, I recognized Rex Harrison. I had heard that he was a big flirt, so I returned his smile. He promptly ran smack into the car in front of him! I thought it was probably a good thing that my new car could not talk or write and so could tell no tales.

I had a call service that most of us in the movie business used, called Teddy's. No sooner had I arrived home than the service was on the line to tell me that I had a call at Universal to double riding scenes for Martha Hyer, one of the stars in *Kiss of Fire*, being directed by Joseph Newman. Fascinated by movies since boyhood, Newman had started out as L.B. Mayer's office boy at MGM in 1925 and had begun his film work as an assistant director in silent movies such as *The Big Parade* and *Ben-Hur*. Thirty-one-year-old Hyer, who had made her first film when she was eleven, was almost halfway through her long career, three years away from her Academy Award nomination for her performance in *Some Came Running*, and eleven years from marrying famous movie producer Hal Wallis. I was thrilled, as I had received only one call from Universal prior to this, so I rushed over there to tell them I'd do it. As part of this job,

65

they told me, I would be riding side-saddle through some very difficult sections of the Universal backlot. Not a problem, I figured, full of youthful confidence.

Kiss of Fire told a romantic historical tale full of melodrama supposedly set in old Santa Fe, New Mexico, in the eighteenth century. Princess Lucia (Barbara Rush) receives the news that the king of Spain is dying and that she is the preferred heir. However, the viceroy of Mexico is backing the competition. The only man who can get her by the Indians and her rivals and off to Europe is the outlaw El Tigre (Jack Palance), whom she initially despises. Need I say she eventually changes her mind? Jay Morley Jr., whose father had been a western actor in the silent era, was finally able to showcase some of his more extravagant designs in this costume epic and they were absolutely exquisite. My wardrobe was a grand dress of gold velvet with a huge skirt trimmed with ruffles, crowned by a magnificent hat with feathers in it that was so typical of the Spanish influence.

I had arrived on the set prepared to ride side-saddle, so it had never crossed my mind that the stock contractor would not be able to supply one. After a few hard words and some deep thought, I figured I'd just have to ride using a regular western saddle with my right leg draped over its single horn. Side-saddles, as a rule, were fitted with a second "curved horn" that gave your leg support above the knee and enabled you to maintain control of the horse while in that position. A grand lady, as she was portrayed in this film, would be expected to ride correctly with her back completely straight, so that if her posture was correct it would look like she was astride when seen from the rear. It was extremely difficult to do this riding side-saddle in the wrong saddle over the harsh terrain of Universal's heavily wooded backlot that required us to duck under limbs, jump fallen trees, and dodge large rocks. One day in particular, my struggle with the difficulties of this set reminded me of a recent near catastrophe with Frosty.

I had been working out in the blazing hot sun, and so I decided to take Frosty for a ride through the heavily shaded walnut grove near my house at the end of my work day. Like where I was working on the Universal backlot, this landscape was also riddled with fallen trees, large rocks and the odd treacherously dangling limb just waiting to lift you out of your saddle if you weren't concentrating. We had headed north to ride as far as the training stable on Devonshire that belonged to Clyde Kennedy, one of the world's best horse trainers and judges who had prepared many stars for their work on horseback in upcoming films. Before long we had reached Clyde's property and turned to come back once again through the walnut grove. The coolness under the heavily leafed trees was a favorite place for both of us, and I would often fill my pockets with the wind-fall of walnuts on the ground. The sandy soil was deep and quiet with the only sounds being an occasional creak of my old Pariani saddle or the crunch of a nut underfoot hiding in the dry leaves.

Frosty put his head down momentarily and as he lifted it again, the rings on the running martingale caught and hung on the small catches that allow the rein to be threaded through the bit and secured in place. In an instant his head was caught with his chin almost touching his chest, and he was unable to get loose. Terrified, he immediately ran backwards so fast that eventually his rear went out from under him in the soft sandy soil. I stepped off and landed on *my* rear as he went over backwards, but I quickly rolled over onto all fours. I reached for the reins that had previously been in my hand but they had broken in the melee. By this time the rings had come loose, and he took off through the trees in a blind run before I could grab hold of them.

He seemed to have mistakenly assumed he had done something wrong. As the rings caught within a split second of his action, he was sure it was my instant correction for putting his head down. For a moment I could tell the strength of our wonderful bond was in question, as he did not understand what was happening. His only thought must have been that he did not know why he was being punished so severely. He panicked, as so often a young horse will.

He would not let me catch him and just kept moving away from me, so it was impossible for me to get hold of him. I was devastated and filled with remorse. We were both so distraught; I could not even utter our secret word. I had no idea how to explain this to him. After spending a long time attempting unsuccessfully to get hold of him, I was so exhausted I had to give up. I was so angry with myself that such a thing could have happened. I knew he thought I had hurt and frightened him on purpose. So, with a breaking heart I leaned against an old, gnarled walnut tree to catch my breath while I tried to reason with him, but it was to no avail. Finally I uttered a breathless, "Well, I'm goin' home." My knees were buckling from sheer emotion. I picked up my mashed hat from the ground and ambled off. Seldom have I ever felt worse; I was swallowed up in grief.

I walked off a little way, and then glanced over my shoulder. I could see he was still in the grove with his reins on the ground. I was covered with sand from head to toe, so I slapped at my jeans and shirt to dust off the sand, pausing long enough to brace myself with one hand on a tree so that I could shake the sand out of my elastic-sided jodhpur boots with the other. They had scooped up the sand like a shovel. Frosty watched me, but I pretended I didn't see him while I wiped the sand from eyes that were filled to overflowing with tears. I looked again. He had started to slowly follow me, and he continued to follow me all the way home with his body arced to avoid stepping on the dragging reins.

Back in his stall, Frosty plunged his nose all the way into his water bucket for a cool drink. He looked up as the water dribbled from his mouth. Eventually, I heard him sigh deeply, and I knew it was over. It was my turn to heave a deep sigh! I removed his saddle and bridle and gave him a nice long bath to relax him. When I had walked him dry, I turned him loose for a good roll and a bite of cool grass. I ended up spending most of the night in his stall talking to him and stroking him in hopes that he would forgive and forget but, most of all, that he would understand. I know that horses, like dogs, usually understand far more than for what we give them credit, and they are both capable of understanding an apology from us. I remembered that while hoping the only similarity with the ride through the walnut grove and this side-saddle ride at Universal would remain the ground we covered.

I quickly worked out that it is always wise when doing any galloping or running in side-saddle mode to keep your horse on his right lead. If he falls, he will then fall in the direction of his lead and your chances will be far better of being thrown away from him instead of directly under him. However, without the correct saddle I wasn't able to do that very well and had to ride using balance alone. I was very glad that I had spent so much time carrying out my acrobatics training on those bars and rings, refining my strength and my exceptional balance.

In the end, my only real problem was that beautiful, blonde Martha Hyer took one look at me in my gorgeous costume, heard the kind words amongst the crew about my performance, stuck her nose in the air and walked off, never to speak another word to me for the duration of the shoot. Not that it mattered to me. Those were my glamour days and, fortunately or unfortunately, I not only looked like a star that day but I felt like one!

Although I had a little black book full of boyfriends, many of whom were both handsome and great dancers, I had so many irons in the fire at this time that even romance took a back seat. I was on a roll. The calls kept coming in from RKO, Twentieth Century–Fox and MGM. As well as movie work, I also did three commercials that year. I was so busy from day to day that I never gave a thought to the future and that it might all come to an end someday.

I didn't realize it until later, but this was my year for meeting horses that became significant in my life. The next call I had from Fox was to double for Dana Wynter in *The View from Pompey's Head,* the script for which required her to do six or eight jumps in a riding ring. Not being a particularly good rider, Wynter wasn't confident she could carry it off and so the scene was handed off to me. The horse I was given, Jim, belonged to stuntman Clint Sharp. Jim and I rode around the ring a few times, carried out the jumps, and everyone was happy. Everyone, that is, except Dana Wynter.

Now, for all I know the willowy and dark-eyed Dana might have been a very pleasant person outside the studio, but within it she had an ego far greater than either her acting or her riding ability warranted. After all, this was really her first major co-starring role on the big screen. However, because she was dating hotshot Hollywood attorney Greg Bautzer, Dana could get her own way at the snap of her manicured little fingers and having such power on the set had completely gone to her head. Without realizing it, I eventually discovered, Jim and I had made those jumps look all too easy. Once she saw how smooth and safe he was to ride, Dana became convinced she could do the jumps herself, and she proceeded to pressure writer-director Philip Dunne to allow her to do it until she won out. Predictably, Jim looked much better doing the jumps than Dana did on his back, and so eventually the entire scene was quietly cut from the film.

Still, as one door closes another opens, and in this case it was two doors. I fell in love with Jim so much after working with him that, as soon as I could, I persuaded Clint to sell that horse to me. Jim was a thoroughbred chestnut of about sixteen hands that had originally been purchased at Caliente Race Track for $25 by Don Burt, the well-known AHSA judge and past president of the AQHA. He had been put through a crash course in jumping by Jimmy Williams, but for some reason he would not jump inside a show ring whereas out in the open he'd jump anything. On various movie sets he jumped moving cars, burning wagons, and lots of fences. Jim was the horse I was riding the day when I fell after jumping the wagon. I had him a long time and allowed selected people to use him in films on occasion. He doubled Flicka in the Twentieth Century–Fox television series

My Friend Flicka whenever Flicka was required to jump in or out of a corral, and his jump through a "plate glass" saloon window by Clint in *The True Story of Jesse James* with Robert Wagner and Jeffrey Hunter was famous. For *The Mating Game*, Jim jumped out of a pasture, over a fence and then over a moving car while ridden by legendary stunt girl Donna Hall doubling for Debbie Reynolds. It was through Jim that I would eventually meet Don Burt and my life would take yet another turn in what would be a totally new direction. He was not an easy horse for all to ride but was gentle as a kitten to work around on the ground. When he eventually developed a heart condition, I gave him to the Los Angeles Retarded Children's home where they brushed him and loved him like a dog. They even bought him an older gray mare for company. It was one of the world's best retirements for a beloved horse.

The second wonderful experience on this set was my first meeting with the delightful DeForest Kelley who, like me, was playing a minor role for which he'd get no credit. We had a few laughs together on that set, and I had the feeling we'd meet again later.

Although *The Man with the Golden Arm* was made by director Otto Preminger's own production company and released through United Artists, it was actually shot at the RKO studios. Many have said that while Frank Sinatra's fame and fortune predominantly came from singing, it was this particular film that demonstrated his extraordinary acting skills in his role as Frankie Machine, the card sharp battling with his heroin addiction after leaving prison who finally has to go "cold turkey" to beat it. Sinatra actually spent time in drug rehabilitation clinics gathering background, and he would be nominated for a Best Actor award not only by the Academy but by the BAFTAs and the New York Film Critics. Sinatra had wonderful support from Eleanor Parker playing his supposedly wheelchair-bound wife, Zosh, in a style that was quite out of character for her, along with Kim Novak and Darren McGavin. Preminger had specifically asked for Parker, by the way, because he had been so impressed by her performance as a wheelchair-bound invalid in *Interrupted Melody*. It was an unusual and brave film for that period when drug addiction was not approved film content. The Motion Picture Association of America consequently refused to confer its official Production Seal on it, which of course only served to convince moviegoers that it must be worth seeing. It was this audience reaction that put the final nail in the coffin of the MPAA code, the direct descendant of the old Hays censorship code, and its demise led to the development of the present-day ratings system.

I was on the set to double for Eleanor Parker in one of the final scenes where Zosh, found to be faking her paralysis and faced with losing Frankie, threatens to jump from the roof of a three-storey building. I would walk to the very edge of the roof on a real three-storey building on RKO's back-lot, and then I was to stand there while the plot unfolded as to whether she jumps to the concrete below or not. It was my first stunt, and I hoped my last, that would not be horse-related. Walking to the edge of a roof might sound easy, but it is not necessarily so. For one thing, my toes had to be even with the edge of the roof. Then I had to counter-balance for wind up-draft. Eleanor was down below me, standing on the ground peering up, looking about as anxious as I felt. It seemed as if the take lasted forever, and I was so very happy we got it right the first time.

I did the one scene for *Man with the Golden Arm* and that was it. For once, I wasn't sorry to go. It was a dark film and that's just how the set felt, even in just the short time that I took to look over the interiors and do my work. Sometimes, a job felt that way even before you got there. A few years later, I was offered the job of doubling Audrey Hepburn in the Amazon jungle for *Green Mansions*. Seldom do they give you an opportunity to turn down a job, but MGM said I could turn this one down if I wished with no hard feelings from them, and I did. The stifling jungles of Guyana and Venezuela were not somewhere that felt right for me at all.

The calls continued to come in, though. It was the fifties and people were happy. Evenings were spent glued to television sets watching the birth of a completely new future for stunt people like me in such successful, long-running series as *Gunsmoke*. This great western held onto its top rating for fifteen years and contributed to many a stuntman's pocket book.

I've always thought it interesting that when we get a chance to see and hear ourselves, we are usually not at all the person whom we think other people see and hear. Strange as it might seem, though I was a natural-born Texan I never thought I had an accent. Travelling as we did all over the U.S. and going to seventeen different schools, I thought any trace of a local accent long gone. Late in 1955, however, I appeared as myself in a Drewry's Extra Dry Beer commercial shot at MGM. Drewry's was a Canadian beer brewed in South Bend, Indiana, until 1972 that often had a picture of a Mountie or a sports scene on their cans. The script called for me to fall from a fire escape for about ten feet, pick myself up, lift a can of Drewry's into camera view, smile and say, "Hi! I'm Martha Crawford," and then comment about how refreshing that beer was after a hard days' work falling off fire escapes and such. I couldn't believe it when I heard my voice played back; my accent was so thick you could cut it with a knife. It was just as well I had a soft place to land because I really did quite a spectacular fall from that fire escape by accident when my heel caught on the metal railing and I flipped instead of "fell." Unfortunately, I never got to see the finished commercial on air because in those days you couldn't be seen drinking beer on TV in California outside of a Western! I rather appreciated the irony of performing in a beer commercial that I couldn't watch when I really did not drink. I didn't smoke, either. On one occasion, I actually lost a really good Chesterfield commercial opportunity riding a horse in a hunt scene with hounds because I had absolutely no idea how to smoke.

On the other hand, I could ride and shoot and I had ample television opportunities to do both. I did a commercial for Buick automobiles that was to be shown during the television broadcast of the 1956 Academy Awards. Dressed in a royal blue western suit with a white hat, I galloped across the desert as a new Buick drove alongside on the road. It looked outstanding on screen as the desert was a gold color at that time of year and it was filmed in Technicolor, but the commercial was shot especially for the Awards and was only shown the one time. There were no residual checks from that one. I did some skeet shooting for a Union 76 commercial and then some more shooting for Du Pont who had invented a type of bullet-proof material that looked like plastic. I shot three boxes of 30-30 shells into the Du Pont target and sure enough, it didn't faze the material. But, even though I was paid for my work, the sponsor decided that a "real" champion who was famous for having won contests would be more believable. So, a lady showed up with merit patches all over her jacket and they used her. When she was done, I'd hit exactly the same places.

8

The Rains of Ranchipur

Theirs was the great sin that even the great rains could not wash away.
— advertising slogan for the film

It was apparent right from the first day I arrived on the set that the 1955 *The Rains of Ranchipur* was a big-budget production and that Twentieth Century–Fox was going to spare no expense on special effects, even if this was a remake of their own earlier film *The Rains Came*. The opening sequence as Lana Turner, in her role as Lady Edwina Esketh, arrives by train in a bustling Indian city is the ultimate teaser of what is to come in terms of the illusions that Hollywood can create right at home. That bustling fictional Indian city of Ranchipur, or at least as much of it as is seen on-screen, was entirely built on the backlot of Twentieth Century–Fox Studios, only to be destroyed later in the film by torrential flood when a dam breaks as a result of a catastrophic earthquake.

Love stories that feature forbidden love, with glamourous stars tumbling in and out of bed set against a backdrop of natural disaster, provide such an instant combination of drama, tragedy and a chance for a good moral story that studios down through the ages have been unable to resist them. When it came to Louis Bromfield's 1937 novel *The Rains Came*, Twentieth Century–Fox had yielded so completely that they were making another version of it only sixteen years later! Their original 1939 version, starring Myrna Loy and Tyrone Power, had won an Academy Award for its special effects, so the studio was pulling out all the stops this time to try and do it again and here I was, right in the middle of it all. I have heard many people say since then that composer Hugo Friedhofer's choice not to score some of the extraordinary effects sequences actually added to the drama and the impending feeling of ominous doom, but I can assure you that we had that feeling long before those watching the movie.

73

At least a hundred men and women were involved in special effects scenes of dams breaking, earthquakes and monsoon rain created by Ray Kellogg with realism seldom seen on this scale in pre–CGI Hollywood. Not surprisingly, this movie turned out to be highly paid work for selected stunt people. Normally, a day rate at that time was $100 with further financial "adjustments" negotiated for each stunt you did that was a print. Our base pay on this shoot was $500 a day plus extra for the stunts! Overtime was calculated at a two-hour increment, then four hours. One minute over four hours and every minute thereafter was known as Golden Time because we went into double time. Of course, not all of the people you see in the flooding streets on screen were on "stunt checks"; many were extras that were strategically placed for us to work with, through and around. The Ranchipur set was designed with lavish temples standing in stark contrast to the sections of the city where the poor lived, shopped and took refuge. Most of our stunt work, though shot as usual out of sequence, involved the earthquake scenes followed by the dam-break and ensuing flood that washed out those humble sections of the town, all of which apparently took place amidst a killer monsoon with punishing winds.

On the appointed day, the storm clouds duly gathered. The dirt street had been soaked, with the help of fire hoses, until it had turned into mud and was soon teeming with extras and a goodly number of stunt men. Polly Burson, a motion picture legend, was the only other stuntwoman and horse-girl I knew to be there, but I do not recall ever actually seeing her. To be honest, I doubt I would have known her if I'd walked right by her because by the time makeup and wardrobe were done with us, we all looked alike! It was hard to tell who you were speaking to, our faces were so filthy (as well as our clothes). The call had gone out for stunt people who were swimmers, too, and it is not unusual for groups of stunt specialists working on different kinds of stunts to never cross paths on a set. Mind you, that requirement should have warned us what was coming.

My group was portraying the poorest of the poor. Helen Rose did the costumes for Lana Turner, and the rest were designed by Edith Head. Both women had done their research well and our outfits looked absolutely authentic. Actors who had royalty roles, for example, could be identified by their colored turbans but most stunt people were dressed as downtrodden Hindus in baggy, wet clothes, some wearing turbans that had originally been white but were now soiled for effect with Fuller's Earth. My own wardrobe could best be described as rags made of muslin with a skirt of tattered, very heavy material tied around my waist; it was repeatedly almost blown off me. I wore sandals and a scarf for a head covering that was immediately lost in the scuffle as we worked under the sprinklers and high wind generated by giant fans. In fact, we frequently found ourselves in the midst of chaos that was all too real as frightened people fled torrents of water in which you could actually drown and flying debris that could do you serious injury if you didn't see it coming.

I was one of those women trying to escape to a safer place with a few meager possessions, in this case the clothes on my back and an old cart pulled by a frightened horse. We were filming on one of Fox's extensive collection of set lots that included an entire western town, a New York street, whole trains, and a suburban residential street among others. On this day, we were working on the European Street that had been muddied and re-dressed to appear suitably Indian. As I waited for the director to start us all moving, I tried to prepare myself mentally to lead an unknowing horse into the elemental holocaust that I suspected was to come, despite having been told rather casually by a unit director that we would just be walking through some wind and rain. He was a small horse, but he had movie savvy written all over him. Most of these horses had seen it all and, consequently, nothing surprised or upset them. Today was just another working day for him, pulling a growling old cart with heavy, hand-made wheels that voiced their discontent with every rotation. However, despite all that we had been though during our collective careers so far, neither of us was really prepared for what was about to happen.

The assistant director called, "All quiet on the set." This was a precursor to, "Action!" and trained movie horses knew the sound of that word. This make-believe street in a make-believe city, though full of people, became curiously still. In those few, last, peaceful seconds I had a premonition that all hell was about to break loose, and I was not wrong. It did. I heard the sounds of water pressure through the pipes as the crew turned on the massive overhead sprinklers, and then the P-51 aircraft engines being used to create the 100 mph, storm-force winds whined as they accelerated to their full revolutions. I could see the stunt men on the street begin to move. They were to take the offensive, running up and down yelling and screaming, sometimes falling, in a last-ditch effort to warn the terrified people of the imminent breaking of the dam.

"Action!"

Suddenly, we were blasted with wind and stinging sprays of water as if from a fire hose. I was so stunned by the sudden severity of the blast and the freezing temperature of the water that my only clear thought was,

"I hope my clothes don't blow off in front of everyone!" I had never experienced anything like it in my life, on set or off. I managed a quick look at my horse when he first threw his head up at the sudden blow of the "storm" hitting him; his eyes were like saucers and his ears were turned away from the wind. The loose dirt, that had just moments before been mud covering the street, instantly became clay so slippery that it was almost impossible for the horse or me to stand up. I can remember very clearly worrying about getting stepped on in my sandaled feet. I could barely make out the other people there with me, let alone any details of the street. All we could do was just keep moving forward and keep out of each other's way! I was sure that my horse could not see any more than I, but we both put our heads down and leaned into the wind and the stinging rain. Director Jean Negulesco certainly got the results he was looking for that day, as the colored lens filters turned a beautiful California day into a dark, somber, seemingly chaotic Indian nightmare. As the horse and I pushed our way forward, it became more and more difficult to remember that this was not real life — just special effects. Right!

When the director finally called "Cut!" it was all over with the same abruptness as it had begun. The sprinklers and wind machines were turned off, and the silence was all but numbing. I had to admit that the effects had been so well engineered it was hard to separate illusion from reality even when it was over. My horse and I, both covered equally thoroughly from head to foot in mud, sighed deeply together. Yes, that's right, horses *sigh* just as we do. During my movie work, I learned that when a horse doesn't understand what is being asked of them at first, they will sigh when they eventually figure it out. Now I knew that I just had to somehow communicate my gratitude to this horse I had never met before, but that had shown so much trust in me. I smiled to myself, and with tears in my eyes I stroked his dirt-caked shoulder and attempted to wipe the mud from his eyes as I tried the best I could to tell him that I loved him for trusting me and allowing me to lead him into such a chaotic and dangerous situation. Then the wrangler came along and quickly led him away to be cleaned up, just in case we would be required to do it all again. Thank goodness, there was no call for a second take; the first one was a print.

The wardrobe men and women then had their hands full getting everybody out of their wet rags and into different costumes, because in our next scene we were to be innocent patrons packing a café-bar about to be inundated by flood water. Once again, apart from that simple script direction, most of us did not have a clue as to what was specifically going to happen, and I really think that was a deliberate directing choice. After all, if like the real population we had no idea of the kind of disaster about to befall us, then we would not just look terrified — we would *be* terrified! And we were.

We assumed from previous experience that the room would fill with water from around floor level and then rise fairly steadily. What we didn't know was that the special effects crew had built a tower outside the set on top of which was a tank filled with some fifty thousand gallons of water. On getting the action cue, they suddenly released the water and it roared down a chute and crashed through the swinging saloon doors and slammed into us. We were violently knocked into each other, into the furniture and into the walls. Even though those walls were padded, several of the stunt crew sustained broken arms and serious bruises. I made a dive for a stairway and so fortunately missed being amongst the injured. There was no

Martha dangling from the edge of a gulf while some other unidentified stunt people scramble to safety during the earthquake scene in the *Rains of Ranchipur* (1955, Twentieth Century–Fox).

Olympic swimmer that could do anything with that force. We were all just victims.

The next day a lot of stunt people were still angry about the way we'd been treated, and they complained. They could still remember that many years before, during the shooting of a spectacular film called *Noah's Ark*, several stunt men had died during the climactic flood sequence allegedly because the director, hoping to incur genuine panic in his performers, failed to inform them that they'd be deluged with tons of water. Our situation had been eerily similar. Complaining didn't make any difference, though; the studio just kept rolling along without caring about us at all.

Needless to say, *The Rains of Ranchipur* began to gain something of a reputation amongst us for being a *real* disaster. We began to feel an impending sense of doom as time wore on. I feel I can now say unequivocally that the day we worked on the temple set, designed to collapse on all of us while we were standing on the "marble" steps, was absolutely frightening. Even the old-timers had a queasy look on their faces. The collapse was deliberately engineered to achieve maximum effect from the supposedly terrified people that were fleeing the dam-break and who had sought shelter on the temple steps to escape the ensuing flood. Well, believe me, once again we were not acting our terror; it was real! The temple itself was made out of Styrofoam blocks but while the falling walls were not about to injure us, the howling gale-force wind, freezing water and flying debris certainly could. Not only that, but the combination of all those elements easily played tricks with your imagination if you were not careful, and real panic was often breathing over your shoulder.

The earthquake scene was extraordinary. On the screen it appears as if the earth is opening up and swallowing people into giant crevices. This was simulated on the set by using large platforms atop hydraulic lifts to form sections of the "ground" that could, at the push of a button, be either raised or lowered in much the same way as a car is hoisted for repairs in a garage. In the "up" position, the floor section would be covered with mud to simulate earth, and stunt people would be positioned on it as if they were standing on flat ground. Suddenly, on cue, the lift would be dropped and other stunt people, standing on the adjacent stationary floor, would attempt to grab for us to keep us from falling into the supposed bottomless abyss lest the ground close back up, as it often does in these severe earthquakes. It looked incredibly real in the completed film and certainly felt as close to reality as when we did it as I ever wanted to be. You could feel it in the pit of your stomach as the elevator dropped away beneath your feet, and if you hadn't prepared yourself for it your fear could be paralyzing!

It was hard and scary work, and even our $500 per day plus extra for the stunts and the double-time pay was not enough compensation on some days. When it was all over, I wouldn't have done it again for ten times that much. Stunts are usually so carefully thought-out and rehearsed that the mechanics of the actual performance can be really quite straight forward and, above all, safe. This was not the case on the sets of *The Rains of Ranchipur*. Every day it felt like you took your life in your hands just to walk out there. There was no doubling on this job, just utility stunts, and sometimes the real stunt was just to finish the day's work in one piece. However, even though no specific stunt skill or training was of value for me in this particular film, I knew by the time it was over that if I had to do anything like this again, I would be far better prepared next time for what was to come. This was my first experience with generalized crowd stunt work, and a pretty rough introduction it was. We were eventually well-compensated for our trouble, but the experience remained deeply etched into my memory. In the end, poorer casting and inappropriate plot revisions resulted in this remake being the weaker version of the story, and it never did quite equal the success of its predecessor. Like *The Rains Came*, it would be nominated for a Special Photographic Effects Academy Award, but unlike that movie it would not win it.

Needless to say, I was exhausted by the end of every day after this kind of work and I was eagerly awaiting those magic words, "That's a wrap, everyone." This film was both emotionally and physically draining and frankly I was glad when it was over. By the time we were done and there were some breaks in my schedule, I was yearning to be out there in the walnut and orange groves with Frosty. He was learning quickly as the regular exercise and attention added to his development and growth. He remembered everything he was taught and, though much is said about the memory of elephants, I will put a horse's memory in a test against that of an elephant any day.

Only those who might recall the San Fernando Valley of that era will remember the beauty of the early mornings in this semi-desert with its blue skies, dotted with white fluffy clouds that occasionally shaded you from the warm sun, and the unforgettable smell of orange blossoms permeating the air. Each new day was an inspiration to accomplish something, and these were the most wonderful of days for me.

North of where I lived was a vast expanse of undeveloped land scattered with eucalyptus trees that went for miles. I loved the sharp, astringent scent of these trees that erased the ugliness of my work on the *Rains of Ranchipur* set. That clinging odor of mud mixed with wet cloth and wet Styrofoam from the temple was something I wanted to quickly forget. In Australia, the thoroughbred mares foal on the leaves that have fallen under the big eucalyptus trees because they have natural antiseptic properties. By riding through this area, Frosty and I could also avoid the memories and associations that permeated our catastrophe in the walnut grove, as area associations are very strong with horses. Frosty had accomplished so many miracles in such short time, both physically and mentally. Oh, Chappy and I might have taught him a few tricks along the way but, as they say in the horse world, "He was born broke." As I watched him develop, hope was reborn in my heart and, I believe, in Frosty's heart too.

9

Love Me Tender

Now, what's-your-name-again, it's very important that you try and keep up with me.
— John Epper to Martha Crawford.

By the time I was working on movie sets, it was unusual for stunt people to be badly hurt or killed on a major movie shoot such as *The Rains of Ranchipur*. When I first became involved in the movie industry in the late 1940s, the days of trip-wires and reckless endangerment of people and animals were already over. Action stunts had become so well-planned and -choreographed that there were seldom major injuries of either people or animals. The ASPCA was always on hand to make sure the animals were well-treated. In any case, it has always been my golden rule that I would never be a part of any stunt that might hurt an animal or cause it distress.

At that time the premier stunt men, and they were almost all men, who worked at major studios could be counted on two hands. A tightly knit group, they were very aware of each other's capabilities and would not do serious stunts with people they didn't know. I quickly discovered that skills I acquired on one job helped me on the next, and I earned the respect of my fellow stunt people. As I've said before, professional stunt people usually specialize in a particular field and, though I did other stunts, my specialty was working with horses. Now, naturally enough in that testosterone-charged atmosphere, seeing a woman on horseback doing what they figured guys should do sometimes led to challenges from the male stunt riders. However, as the best-laid plans of mice and men and sometimes competitors do not always work, I did on occasion get the last laugh. One of the funniest incidents in which I was involved happened on the set of *Love Me Tender*, and I get a chuckle out of it to this day.

This was Elvis Presley's first movie, a Western love triangle. It takes place just after the end of the Civil War and involves two brothers and their love interest, Cathy, played by Debra Paget, who I was doubling. Interestingly, Presley and Paget were already connected in the minds of the viewing public because of their recent joint appearance on a gag in *The Milton Berle Show* where Paget had hurled herself at him like one of his teenage fans. Although only twenty-two, Paget was approaching the end of her big-screen movie career; within three years she had switched almost entirely to television. One of her best-known performances, immediately prior to *Love Me Tender,* is as Lilia in *The Ten Commandments* for which she was selected without audition by Cecil B DeMille because he considered the hand of God was on her. Now that's how to get into a movie.

Because this was early in Presley's career, *Love Me Tender* had not been originally written as a star vehicle for him. Robert Wagner had been considered for the role of Clint, the youngest brother, in a script (originally titled *The Reno Brothers*) penned by Robert Buckner, who had penned the memorable line, "Win one for the Gipper," for *Knute Rockne All American.* The screenplay had been sitting around on various Hollywood producers' shelves for some time before Elvis was signed to a part in which he doesn't even show up for the first twenty minutes. The title was changed to *Love Me Tender* during post-production when the song of the same name, released as a single two months ahead of the movie, replaced "Hound Dog" as #1 on the charts within a week, and remained there for five weeks, the first time a singer had knocked himself off the #1 Billboard chart spot. This was the first time advance sales for a single had ever reached a million dollars under any circumstances, and the producers wanted to capitalize on that as much as possible.

The songs for *Love Me Tender* were written by the film's music director, the noted conductor, arranger, singer and songwriter Ken Darby whose Ken Darby Singers can be heard with Bing Crosby on "White Christmas" and "Ghost Riders in the Sky." As vocal and music score arranger, Darby was associated with such films as *How the West Was Won, River of No Return, Song of the South, South Pacific,* and *The Robe,* and he had just finished work on *The King and I* for which he'd share an Academy Award with Alfred Newman.

Of the four songs Darby wrote for *Love Me Tender* the theme song is the only real period piece, for which he wrote lyrics set to the tune of the earlier 1861 American folk tune "Aura Lea." Rather than being recorded in a studio with Elvis' regular band, this song was recorded on the huge Fox Stage 1 with a group of session musicians. Because of a standard clause in all Presley contracts stipulating he be given fifty percent of the rights for any original song Presley used, Darby assigned the credit for the other fifty percent to his wife Vera Watson, saying that she hadn't written it either.

However, the title wasn't the only part of the movie to be changed; so was the ending! Fans were unhappy when they learned via the media that Elvis would die at the end in a gunfight with his brother, so an alternative ending was shot in which he was spared. That didn't work either, so a compromise ending was finally worked out in which, as his family walks away from his grave, a ghostly image of him appears crooning the theme song, "Love Me Tender." Nevertheless, Elvis' mother was reportedly so upset that his character died that Elvis refused to ever again be killed off in a movie.

Presley plays one of the Reno brothers, Clint, who marries Cathy (Paget), girlfriend of his brother Vance (Richard Egan), after word comes back towards the end of the Civil War that Vance is dead. Actually, he's very much alive and has stolen a Union payroll that is then split between him and his fellow Confederate soldiers. Vance returns home and at first graciously concedes his brother deserves his girl, but the Union is hot on his trail and his buddies set out to prey on his jealousy, hoping the two brothers will kill each other off so they can take Vance's share. The film plays off the characters' moral ambiguities with a touch of *noir*: Vance has yielded to greed, Cathy to lust; Clint has betrayed his brother and eventually yields to anger.

Everyone on the crew was prepared to dislike this hip-swivelling singer who had decided he could be a movie star, and so when Elvis bounded into the makeup department looking very handsome in a sailor suit, he received a rather cool reception. To be honest, though, it wasn't all a reaction to him; he'd distracted everybody from watching Sheree North, a famous stripper in her pre–Hollywood days, who was being made up for a movie test right then. An hour later when Elvis left the building, or at least the makeup department, wearing that big kid smile of his, it was a very different story. He had thoroughly charmed the entire crew, and everyone wanted to trail along with him as if he was the Pied Piper. He was one of the most charismatic men I ever met, and a consummate gentleman.

In the major chase scene, John Epper, doubling Richard Egan, and I were to run our horses down a country road and jump a bordering snake fence, a type of rambling post-and-rail, with twelve members of the Union

Army in hot pursuit. Epper was a well-known stuntman who had been very good at his work for many years. This was the first time I had ever worked with him personally, although I knew of him as we had both worked on the *Flicka* series at different times and he had daughters who he promoted in the business, including one he was trying to get under me for many of my jobs.

So there were Epper and I, lining up for this chase scene and waiting for the "action" cue, when to my disbelief he launched into this little lecture about how the horse he was riding just happened to be his very own ex-racehorse. He was in full vocal flight, so I just sat back and let him run with it. There was obviously no point in telling him that I, too, was on my own horse that had just happened to run not too long ago at Caliente Race Track and had gone through the Jimmy Williams "too-much-too-soon" jumping program.

Eventually he wound up his monologue with the words: "Now, what's-your-name-again, it's very important that you try and keep up with me. I know you won't be able to — but just try so it will look good!"

I sighed within myself. His voice had that inflection in it that I'd hear so often with men. He was being a gallant tough guy and letting me off the hook because I was a woman. Now, I have never been one to expect special treatment when working in a man's world, but neither do I enjoy someone assuming I cannot do what a man can do in the same situation under the same circumstances. I couldn't help myself. I looked over, batted my eyelashes back at him and replied rather too innocently in my best Southern drawl, "Okay, Mr. Epper. I will try so hard. I sure will."

"Action!" the director shouted, and my horse Jim went straight for the edge of the road, took off early at the fence about ten feet from it, sailed clean over and kept going flat out across the field. You can clearly see in the film that indeed I'm not keeping up with John Epper; I'm a good fifty feet in front of him, kicking clouds of dust back into his face!

At one point, I looked back over my shoulder and could see that all twelve of the Union's finest had fallen out of their saddles trying to make the same jump. Of course, that meant the jump footage was going to be worthless and would all be left on the cutting room floor, which must have been disappointing for Stanley Hough, who as second unit director was in charge of the major stunts. He would have known they didn't have the budget or the time for a retake of that jump. On the bright side, the chase footage was good to stay in.

I've always thought that Elvis Presley was something of a paradox between who he really was and who people wanted him to be. On the *Love Me Tender* set, as happens on most film sets and locations, we spent a lot of time waiting — waiting to be called for a stunt, waiting for the weather, waiting for actors, waiting while people discuss things — all kinds of waiting. My favorite thing to do while I was waiting was to find the tallest ladder not being used, climb up it and sit on the top rung. There were two good reasons for my choice of activity: For one thing, I could enjoy a bird's-eye view of what was going on; for another, I could avoid any of the 365 types of rattlesnake that inhabited the area. So there I was at the Fox Ranch perched on my ladder, when a small jet of water smacked me in the back of the head! I started and nearly fell off my perch, realizing as I grabbed for a hold that I was being targeted with someone's water pistol. After a few days of this, I finally caught the varmint in the act — Elvis!

In the interests of staying dry, I suggested he pull up another ladder and chat. He did, and from then on he would often pull up a ladder and talk with me as the days dragged on. As strange as it may seem, we never discussed his singing career. I discovered instead that, like me, he enjoyed studying the set from up on high with great curiosity and fascination, and he rarely missed anything that went on there. He liked to hear about my movie stunt work and I found out that he loved horses and being around them. I often think that had he followed his dream of spending more time outdoors, then he would have been less isolated indoors. Maybe his life would have taken a different path. I delighted in telling Elvis about my horse's various antics. By now, Frosty could say "yes" and "no," smile, untie knots, take off his saddle blanket, and remove things from my hand. I figured he had never had much fun, and I wanted him to know we could play. Although this was fun for me, they were confidence maneuvers for him. I thought it was so cute that I could tie his knees or ankles with a soft rope and he could untie the knot, but then we moved on to smaller and smaller rope and he became very adept at not only untying himself but at opening most any fastener you could imagine. He could open the smallest, slipperiest chrome snap in the blink of an eye.

In fact, he became so good at it that one night he let himself out of my barn and invited five other horses to go for a cruise through the neighborhood at two in the morning. Now, this was quite a new neighborhood and many expensive virgin landscaped lawns had been laid down not that long ago. One by one, the six horses paraded in single file across those new lawns and finally came to rest outside the sliding-glass doors of a neighbor's bedroom. The lady heard a noise and opened the glass slider to be greeted by Frosty and his friends. She screamed so loud, she woke everybody in the stree; the next minute all the lights in the neighborhood lit up. Well, then there was much wailing over the lawns and they were all threatening to sue me, and it took a while to get them calmed down, but we did it. Elvis and I laughed a lot over that story of "Frosty and the Midnight Marauders."

Elvis was fascinated to hear that I turned Frosty out in the dark of night when he went to pasture for a year. I explained that night release was a long-time custom in Texas, where vast expanses of fields and pastures were still bound by barbed wire as were these in the high desert of California. Turning a horse loose at night in a fenced area allows the animal to walk the fence-line and learn the boundaries. I told him that I had, I supposed, become not only Frosty's mother but his lead mare, a relationship that can mean life or death in the wild. He needed time to become "just a horse." I did admit, though, that thinking of all that barbed wire out there held my thoughts in a vise-like grip. Still, as chaotic as life might become for me, I could at least relax knowing Frosty was safe and that I was contributing to his well being. I was working steadily, but they were long hours. Often I had to report to the studio makeup departments by 4:00 a.m. Working all day and driving home late did not leave much time for anything, so having this chance to run and play with the other horses would develop his body as well as his mind. He would have tests to pass and decisions to make. He would have time to learn the things that only horses can teach each other. Still, I had to reassure myself over and over that I was doing the right thing by turning him out in the pasture. In the long run, I knew it was the right thing to do but, like a mother watching her child learning to ride a bicycle, I knew Frosty would have to take some lumps. I know it sounds a little melodramatic, but like most mothers I wished I could take them for him.

Elvis and I also talked about Jim, the horse that I had been using to double the cast horse for the chase scenes, and about the horse Debra Paget was riding — a sweet, kind, gentle creature owned by Jimmy Loucks, the ramrod wrangler. We even discovered that at one time Elvis had dated my best friend's sister at the same time as my best friend was dating a certain Robert Wagner.

Elvis was a lot of fun when he could be by himself and thus be himself, but in many ways he was still just a country boy from down South and already there was a lot of pressure on him to change. I could see even then that he was never going to survive Rexford Drive in Beverly

Martha and her horse jumped into this lake at the Twentieth Century–Fox Studios Ranch for *Love Me Tender*. When she tried to swim across it the next day with another horse, he became tired and tried to climb on her (Courtesy Jerry Schneider).

Hills where my best friend's sister lived. He confided to me his sadness that already he couldn't go any place on a date or just enjoy an evening out somewhere without being mobbed by fans. It just poured out of him. Perhaps he felt secure with me up there on our ladders as my association with horses seemed to reassure him that I was a ranch girl from a country background similar to his own. He told me how he longed to just enjoy a quiet evening out with a girl, but that his "dates" were now limited mostly to drive-in movies so he wouldn't be seen and so could be away from screaming girls who tried to tear off pieces of his clothing or snip locks of his hair. I have always thought there was an unfilled longing or ache in his heart that one could hear in his voice when he sang ballads.

The musical scenes from the school-raising section of *Love Me Tender* turned out to be a lot of fun. All the stand-ins, doubles, and extras persuaded the assistant director to let us mingle around the dancers and be part of the group to whom Elvis would sing in the shot. His renditions of "Let Me" and "Poor Boy," as he sang them that day, will always be my favorites. With his singing and Lionel Newman's magic touch with the music, it was a delightful day's work — and we got paid for it! Elvis seemed to be having as much fun as we were, and I must admit that I did a little double-take and my stomach turned over when he winked at me from the stage. Did Elvis just wink at *me*?

Much of *Love Me Tender* was shot at the Twentieth Century–Fox Ranch, as was *Butch Cassidy and the Sundance Kid*, *Planet of the Apes*, *Viva Zapata*, many of the Tarzan films, and the original *My Friend Flicka* movie and the follow-up TV series, just to name a few. The seven-acre lake there has probably been photographed from every possible angle, and I added to the list. I had several stunts to do in and around this lake. In the chase scene, after Epper and I had raced on horseback through trees and jumped fallen logs at a dead run, the script called for us to suddenly make a right turn off the road, jump the horses off a small dock into the lake (about a four-foot drop originally) and swim across the water to the other side to escape the soldiers chasing us. My horse was to lose his footing in the water and I was to fall off, and then we would swim together to the other side with the horses.

That was when my problems really began. By the time we came to shoot the water scenes, the lake had lost about two feet of water because it was summer and it had become dangerously shallow. Instead of a jump of only four feet, I was now facing a leap from the dock that was closer to six feet — a different proposition entirely. If my horse jumped and did a belly flop all would be well, but if he went in front feet first they could get stuck in the mud on a lake bottom that was now only about six or, at the most, seven feet down. Unable to keep his balance, my horse would probably roll over with me underneath.

With so much uncertainly surrounding this stunt, I refused to use Jim for it and so we outfitted another horse with kapok blankets under his saddle. Movie horses all had a number of stunts they did well in their repertoire so that they could be interchangeable. They just needed a little color change here and a blaze on the face there or some white stockings added or painted over, and off they went to either ride up the hill with the cowboys or down the hill with the Indians. It was customary for the horses that leaped into water to have these kapok saddle pads to keep them upright. Kapok trees are found in Indonesia and produce seedpods with a fiber in them that looks like cotton. This fiber is often found inside life jackets and buoyancy tanks because it is lightweight and waterproof. Water not really being my thing, I asked for a kapok vest too. Fortunately, the stunt went by the book. My horse did a perfect belly flop, and the kapok pads kept him upright just as they were meant to.*

Then the crew started to set up for the swim across the lake. They placed sand bags on the bottom of the lake in a random pattern, so that as I attempted to ride across the lake my horse would inevitably have to go up on a sand bag and then drop off of it and fall over. That was where I was to pitch off and start swimming with him. Now, I never forgot that is always dangerous to swim with a horse because, for one thing, if the horse becomes fatigued he is likely to try and climb up on you as he would a rock. Sure enough, by the time we were near the other side he began to tire and I had my first experience with a horse trying to climb on me. He was coming at me with his front feet because at that point I looked just like a rock to him. It was a frightening situation, and by now I had shed my kapok vest as it had been too heavy for me. Just in time, we found shallow water where we could both stand up.

I really loved working on these exterior day locations. It was so difference from working on the main Fox backlot in West Los Angeles where Century City now stands. We would report to the studio first thing in the morning and then, after wardrobe and makeup, would be taken by limousine on the forty-five minute trip to the Twentieth Century–Fox Ranch in Malibu for the rest of the day. The *Love Me Tender* set was such a happy film set to work on, too; Robert Webb's direction was smooth and he could make difficult tasks seem easy. After it was released on November 16, 1956, *Love Me Tender* would recoup its production costs of over $1,500,000 plus its publicity costs within three days, and it would become the second-highest grossing film for the year. Elvis would make another thirty movies after this one, but I would never meet him again.

---

*Just to make sure he had something to work with, the director shot the jump again the next day with another stunt person doubling for me. However, I can recognize myself in the final cut; my right arm jerks up as we jump and I remember being afraid that I had ruined the scene. I had been given a whip to use and I was probably tossing it, as I don't recall ever seeing it again. Epper's horse practically steps off the bridge instead of jumping.

10

The King and Flicka

When one particular scene bothered me, he took me aside and sat down with me, discussed the scene and rehearsed the lines with me.
— Barbara Nichols discussing Clark Gable

Frosty was home! Half-running to the barn, I found myself eager to lean on the door to his stall just as I did when I first saw him in San Antonio. A hundred thoughts filled my head as I opened the latch of the weathered, wooden stall door and looked in. No longer did I see a small, stunted little foal. Now I could see an innocent beauty, like a weakened butterfly that needs help to emerge from its cocoon. If the butterfly is handled correctly, though, it will soon fly and I wanted so desperately to see Frosty soar on his own wings. We had achieved so much in such a short time that my imagination ran wild. In my dreams I saw him a highly trained high school horse like his brother Dusty, but those old hinges continued to squeak as I opened and closed the door as if to wake me from my reveries. Standing there I took a few deep breaths, as I did most mornings before starting the new day, gathering my thoughts and savoring the smell of the orange blossoms that filled the early morning air. Then I buried my face in Frosty's warm neck and whispered our secret word out of a sheer need to share my enthusiasm with him. I loved that he still nuzzled my hair.

Earlier in the week, I had signed to do a Buick commercial for the 1956 Academy Awards. Dressed in a royal blue western suit with a white hat and riding a golden Palomino, I was to gallop across the desert in Apple Valley, California, with a new luxury Buick racing alongside me on the road. Although the awards were not yet broadcast in color, this Buick commercial being filmed in 1955 could well have been the first color commercial to be used on a televised Academy Awards show.

I had originally been scheduled to double Eleanor Parker in *The King and Four Queens* right after completing the commercial, but then for a while I was enjoying what seemed to be an unscheduled break. Although I knew the company was already on location in St. George, Utah, I hadn't received the call to join them yet and frankly I was somewhat puzzled by the delay, but I continued to work with Frosty and make the most of my idle time.

Sometimes a script rewrite can be more predictable than the politics involved in getting a film job. It was common knowledge that Eleanor now expected me to double her regardless of what studio had employed her. This knowledge was common to everyone except, apparently, one of the assistant directors on this film who gave the job to another very "persuasive" young woman. Now, this was the first of Eleanor's films that would list her name over the title up there with Clark Gable's, so she was carrying more than her usual amount of political weight. When the other girl arrived on the set and was introduced to Eleanor as her double, I heard later, the usually soft-voiced actor erupted in an uncharacteristic tirade, and consequently both the assistant director and his protégé were not seen again on that set.

The first thing I knew about all this was when the phone finally rang one morning while I was watching Frosty drag his favorite toy, a 2 × 4 board, around the arena. I had to pry myself away from the fun and, with Sancho on my heels, I proceeded to my house, plopped in one of the captain's chairs at my kitchen table and picked up the call. The voice on the other end of the line abruptly asked me how soon I could fly out to St. George and so, before I could catch my breath, I was in a limo whisking me to Burbank Airport where a chartered DC-4 was waiting with engines idling to fly me to Utah. I was the only passenger, and I could imagine the pilots were wondering who on earth I was to be awarded this status.

We arrived after an uneventful flight with a stunning landing on a runway that was only just the right length. Waiting for me was second unit director Tom Connors, Jr., who escorted me directly to Eleanor's dressing room. I suppose they wanted to assure her I was really there! He was grinning from ear to ear with a very self-satisfied expression as if he had corrected the mistake, but really we both knew it had been Eleanor who had done the correcting. She was her old delightful self, the ultimate star, being readied for a shot and wearing her favorite perfume, Marcel Rochas' *Femme*. I could smell it on the dry desert air before I entered her dressing room, something that would no doubt have made the famed designer happy. After all, he always used to say, "You should breathe a woman in before you've even seen her." This woman gave me a look that said it all, so we didn't have to say much in those first few moments except, "Hi!" We had been working together long enough to be able to exchange a meaningful roll of the eyes that said far more than words. The situation was fixed, and Eleanor had fixed it.

Eleanor was a woman who always inspired me; she was not only beautiful but effortlessly projected a quiet charisma and was the essence of class. Signed by Warner Brothers in 1941 at the age of nineteen, Eleanor had already appeared in some thirty movies and had received three Academy nominations. Having been involved with an amazing variety of roles, she was the epitome of experience and versatility in her profession.

As it happened, we were booked into the same motel, and before going to dinner she stopped by my room to thank me again for coming at such short notice. We discussed with a chuckle that while she had her script, I was going to need a good book. St. George in those days was a *very* quiet town indeed, quite a contrast to being the second fastest-growing metropolitan area in the United States, as it was declared in 2005. Deciding to eat together, we crossed the main street on our way to Dick's Café to see the night life and bright lights. Apparently, they consisted entirely of a display of Snow White and the Seven Dwarfs, each carved delicately out of wood and standing together in a glass display case on the rich, green grass outside the carver's home. It was a rare meeting of past and future movie stars and we stood there appreciating the irony of it happening here in St. George. Every night after that we would walk by Snow White and her companions imprisoned in their illuminated case, and each night this beautifully carved group seemed to take on more significance. They were not just the main street's predominant night time attraction, they were the only attraction! We began to understand how they might feel. We began to think we'd been in St. George far too long.

Eleanor and I talked often, as the bright days grew hotter, of how colors seemed more intense around St. George because of the contrast between the red cliffs in and around the city, the bright blue sky and the pure white of the many churches. I've always thought it was unfortunate that those contrasts aren't evident in the film that instead seems to use a more subdued palette, but we did agree that Lucien Ballard was a great cinematographer. Perhaps the color choice was a comment on the drab ethics of the characters, because the film certainly highlighted one of life's true paradoxes. Both Eleanor and Clark successfully played parts totally alien to their real personalities, demonstrating their professionalism and experience.

In *The King and Four Queens*, smooth-talking Gable arrives at the small ghost town of Wagon Mound where he hears the story of the Widow McDade, her four outlaw sons and their wives. Three of the sons are dead, but the fourth is expected to return at any minute and reveal to his family where the loot from a robbery has been hidden. The problem is that no one knows which of the four sons has survived. So, Gable sets out to seduce the wives one by one in an attempt to persuade them to betray the cache. In the process, he discovers that one of the wives is an imposter. Eleanor Parker's character is the only wife who won't play along, and of course she becomes the one he wants.

Clark was one-of-a-kind himself and everybody, cast and crew, just adored him. He had absolutely no ego, even though he was not only starring in this film but the company that he had formed with Jane Russell, Gabco-Russfield, was also producing it. By now he had left MGM, and this was one of his rare, independent filmmaking attempts. He and Kathleen had been married barely a year, and she impressed everyone by coming along with him on this film shoot in the desert country around St. George in mid–May of 1956. While the other eighty members of the cast and crew booked out every hotel room to be found anywhere in the vicinity, the Gables rented a house and proceeded to become part of the neighborhood. She would be up early every morning to cook him breakfast and to prepare a cut lunch and thermos of coffee for him to take to work, and while he was gone she'd do the shopping or join a town quilting bee. By the time he came home, dinner would be on the table and a drink freshly prepared. On the weekends, they could be seen out in the desert while he improved her shooting technique and taught her how to roll her own cigarettes. Their love for each other was already becoming as legendary as Clark's film career

Although Clark's status as an actor was almost mythical in the eyes of many, when he spoke to you he shed all of his own importance as if he had taken off a costume after a scene. For those few moments, it became as if you and he were the only people in the room. But sometimes when we talked together, I felt a sadness within this great man, a feeling that in spite of all he had become, he still did not think he had attained the dream that everyone thought he had. Then again, on many occasions I saw his sense of humor in action when he would delight in playing some practical joke, and on other occasions I saw a man of quiet refinement and good taste. What I remember best about him was his great love of life.

While I sat around on my horse waiting to work, when I wasn't sit-

Clark Gable and Martha, along with international polo player Peter Perkins, meet in 1949 at a Beverly Hills Country Club function to publicize forthcoming matches between the United States and Argentina. Clark and Martha worked together a few years later in *The King and Four Queens*.

ting on a ladder, I would often catch him watching me out of the corner of my eye when he thought I wasn't looking. I couldn't help but wonder what was up, until one day I overheard him commenting how much I reminded him of "Ginny," the actress Virginia Grey who was one of the long-term loves of his life but whom he never married. His eyes seemed to speak of a heart filled with very private wonderful memories as though trying to place me into them.

So, at the very first opportunity I went over to introduce myself and to remind him that we had actually met many years ago at the polo club in Los Angeles. A floodgate of polo talk opened between us. He asked about my father and some of the players of the day that he remembered well. Clark was not just a ladies' man, but a man's man too. When shaking hands with him, you knew you were shaking hands with a real man. Clark was an excellent rider in his own right, yet he was always considerate enough to defer to the wranglers on the set before taking anything for granted with the horses. He rode a horse called Steel in this film, and he had ridden the big chestnut enough to be comfortable with him, so most of our ensuing conversation took place while we were both on horseback. He loved polo, and when we spoke of my early polo days I could tell he would have liked to have played on the field himself. We talked about the big players of former days with fondness and familiarity, as if Clark was part of that era himself instead of being only an observer, and we spoke about horses in general and our mutual love for them. I told him of my rescue of the unwanted foal, bragging about his progress to date, and of my love of driving horses as well as riding them. This would be next on Frosty's agenda. I mentioned I had recently signed to do the driving for Shirley Jones in a movie called *April Love* about harness racing. Clark replied that he had a breaking cart (jogging cart) that he did not use and he could give it to me if I needed it and could pick it up. Eventually, I did. It was finished in a maroon lacquer with gold striping and the initials CG on the side in gold. It had to be the most beautiful cart I had ever seen, complete with an exquisite hand-made full harness for one horse.

Many have tried to fill Clark's shoes, but none have succeeded. He was a real, diamond-studded star who did not wear the tarnished tin crown that so many did; he had worn the real crown of the King of Hollywood. He was who the fans thought a star should be but few actually are. However, I became terribly concerned with his health while we were working together. I couldn't help noticing when we were talking together face to face that he had developed quite a tremor in his head. Mostly, Ballard would try to shoot around it, but you can see it in some shots if you look closely.

Eleanor was usually a very reserved person, but she did have a great sense of humor that you could see in her twinkling eyes when she talked to you. Working as I did with her on a number of occasions, I had plenty of time to study her and came to believe that whereas at first I had thought her distant, she was really quite unassuming and shy with people she didn't know. Being the great actress she is, she could project a rather smart-alecky, feisty character, especially in this film, which was not like her real personality at all. Eleanor took her work very seriously and would make sure she retired early to her room so that she had plenty of time to go over the next day's shooting. She was always totally prepared for her work.

That went for both of us, which is probably one of the reasons we got along so well. The main reason I had been flown out here was to double for Eleanor in a scene where she would jump onto a buckboard and chase Clark down the road at full gallop. I was fortunate to be given the best team of local horses that could be found, and this scene would require me to run this team, hitched to the buckboard, as fast as it would go. Typically, I preferred to do this kind of work using horses with which I was familiar. There had been more than one moment fraught with apprehension on occasions when I had to do something like this with totally strange horses. This time, though, I was assigned a great wrangler for a pick-up man to help me get stopped if I needed him, and we would be running a perfectly straight road. These were both comforting thoughts that helped to reduce my anxiety to a workable level.

St. George was a very difficult desert location at the best of times, and at this time of year it was well over 110 degrees every day with the sun radiating off the stark, red cliffs in and around the town and the harsh desert floor. In fact, St. George would be where the then-hottest Utah temperature of 117° would be recorded in July of 1985, a record that would stand for many years. For this chase scene, I had to wear over my dress a pure wool cape that was absolutely suffocating. Clark's gambler-type outfits were also all wool, but I figured if no one heard him complaining, then they were not going to hear me, so I focused on the job in hand. Fortunately, my team proved to be truly exceptional. They looked and worked like thoroughbreds and perhaps they were, but they also had wonderful mouths that most horses that are driven for chases and handled by a lot of different drivers do not have. Being local horses new to a film shoot, rather than studio horses, the horses were not thinking of just running and running, as so often happens when they are just used over and over for one special thing. They had that innocent, "Now, what would you like me to do?" attitude, and they slowed down as soon as I asked them. I could not have been more pleased as I viewed the "rushes" that night.

However, my pleasure was short-lived. Although Eleanor plays a lady in this film who is a little rough around the edges, the real Eleanor was the epitome of the word "lady." No one seems to have foreseen any issues with that, but right about this time one particular issue arose in a big way. Now, I always thought that if ever it was right for a lady to chase a man, it should have been right in this film. I mean, who would not want to chase Clark Gable? Nevertheless, Eleanor apparently had principles about that sort of thing and she could not be persuaded to deviate one iota from them for anyone. She flatly refused to be seen on film chasing a man, even Mr. Gable. Why no one thought of checking that out with her before the company flew me out to where we all ended up standing on the scorching sands of Utah, I don't know. But I do know that those principles cost someone, somewhere, a lot of money. The entire ending had to be rewritten and so, of course, the buckboard scene for which I had been primarily brought out to the set ended up, like so much of my work, on the cutting room floor.

As on most location shoots, the best restaurant in town is chosen to cater the lunches and then prepares for the whole film company to arrive at the end of the day for dinner. In this case, as I mentioned earlier, it was to Dick's Café that Eleanor and I would stroll every night, after our regular inspirational meeting with Snow White and her seven friends, to join the rest of the cast and crew. That restaurant would, without fail, produce food to die for every evening. Enormous serving trays would arrive at the table heaped full with freshly caught trout fried in corn meal. Then thick, char-broiled steaks with baked potatoes and sour cream and fresh vegetables were served. After all that, carts would be rolled around to the table with dessert selections out of *Gourmet* magazine. No expense was spared for those meals. It was a wonder we could still get into our saddles the next day.

As well as tables, there was a fascinating store in Dick's Café that became a gathering place for the actors after dinner. From this store, Dick sold his personal collection of real Indian jewelry, and I selected some lovely Navajo pieces from there as did most everyone else. There were great restaurants and fine accommodation in small towns such as St. George in Utah and Lone Pine, Murphys and Bishop in California, and studios would contribute a lot of money to the local economy while using towns such as these for locations.

Working on location for a TV show, on the other hand, was in stark contrast to movie shoots and the box lunches that would be handed us on those occasions, containing a sandwich and an apple, rather aptly summed up the differences. The set of *My Friend Flicka* was my introduction to just how far apart these two working environments could be from each other. Still, some aspects never changed and I continued to be amazed at just how much money could be wasted, even though the budgets were smaller. That old cliché, 'Throw away the dollars and save the pennies,' originated with television studios. On many days I was picked up by a studio limo early in the morning only to be left waiting around on the set enjoying my sandwich and apple. Nothing would happen. Then I would climb into the limo again at the end of the day and be driven back to my door.

However, there were advantages. Some days I collected my check for seeing what I love most — a good trainer working his horses — as I sat and watched one of the best horse trainers in the business, Les Hilton, train Flicka as well as Mr. Ed. Flicka was a very sweet Arabian that was doubled by my own horse, Jim, in any of the scenes that required Flicka to jump, such as in or out of a corral. Jim was a natural for the film business. I'd just show him the jump, take him back a ways, tap him on the rump and he'd find and jump what I had shown him. Although I never quite understood his very own way of doing things sometimes, I didn't tire of working with him or suggesting how to work with him to the trainer that happened to be on that particular set. He was a horse well known for his range of abilities and willingness to work, and so he was often the horse of choice.

The television series of *Flicka* was a spin-off from the 1943 movie of the same name about a boy and his horse. I was there to double for Anita Louise, who played the mother, while driving a buggy. During my first simulation of a runaway buggy, I was driving in a mad dash and the buggy was supposed to nearly turn over. To create this effect, a large rock was placed in my path so that when the left wheel hit it, the buggy would be tossed out of control. Fortunately, I was able to aim for the rock with the left front wheel of the buggy and hit it square on. Even so, the stunt worked almost too well. The buggy tipped precariously to the right and barely stayed upright as we continued at the full gallop, though tipped onto the two right side wheels, for about twenty feet before righting itself. It could not have worked better. Nor, probably, could I have done it again.

But what I really looked forward to now was going home each evening to a nice drive with Frosty in Clark Gable's jogging cart. The cushion in the seat of the CG cart was upholstered in corduroy in a golden color that perfectly matched the new hairs in Frosty's coat and was the exact color of his ears. We made quite a sight complete with the black driving harness!

On the whole, I got along with almost all the stuntmen on the *Flicka* set famously, although there always has to be one exception. A certain stuntman, who shall remain nameless, already had his young daughter employed on set as double for the actor Johnny Washbrook, the son with the horse, but he dearly wanted my job for his older daughter as well, and so he kept trying to get her in under me as double for Anita Louise. However, Fox Studios were always good to me, and I was never seriously threatened. Besides, I had evened the score on the set of *Love Me Tender* when I outran that certain stuntman on his best horse!

Anita was another on my list of fine ladies. She was very charming and loyal, even if she did tend to come across with that kind of distant politeness that made you feel you'd just been introduced to royalty. Acting for Anita had been a lifelong career, so perhaps she felt as if she qualified for some deference. Making her acting debut on Broadway at the age of six, she was appearing regularly in Hollywood films by the time she was ten. By her late teens, she was being cast in leading and supporting roles in major productions where she was highly regarded for her delicate features and blonde hair. Among her film successes had been *Madame Du Barry*, *A Midsummer Night's Dream*, *Marie Antoinette*, and *The Little Princess*. In the 1950s she had moved to television and was now playing one of her most widely seen roles as the mother, Nell McLaughlin, on *My Friend Flicka*. She was frequently described as one of cinema's most fashionable and stylish women; her reputation was further enhanced by her role as a society hostess and her parties were attended by Hollywood's elite.

The series was a joy to work on. Gene Evans, who played Rob McLaughlin, was a fine and professional actor and a really nice guy who never could resist an opportunity to kid around on the set. He was interested in discussing horses as were many other guest stars such as "Big Boy" Williams, the famous cowboy star whom I had known since childhood. Williams was a fine polo player who had often ridden on the field with my father. A sweet man, he was as strong as an ox. I once saw him dismount and bulldog to the ground a polo pony that had upset him in the middle of a game. Then he mounted up again and everything went fine. Sheb Wooley was a scream. Better known as scout Pete Nolan in the *Rawhide* series, Sheb also wrote the song "Purple People Eater" that went #1 for six weeks in 1958. Wooley really had been a cowboy and rodeo rider, and turned to character acting and country and western singing when his injuries took him out of competition. He was such a character, always ready for a laugh and to sing and always teasing me about falling off the fence on which I was napping. He, too, expressed a few thoughts about his apple and sandwich lunch and for all I know he probably wrote a song about it. Claude Akins, who appeared in a few *Flicka* episodes, played a tough character many times but was really as charming a person as you could ever meet. He was always quick to recognize me and would hold the limo door open. Naturally enough, they all associated me with horses which is why, no doubt, they were the main topic of many of our conversations.

I also had a chance to work with the delightful Harry Morgan, playing Spring Byington's neighbor Pete Potter, in the role of his wife Gladys on the hit TV series, *December Bride*. Not that you will ever recognize me because, although she is heard and often talked about, Gladys is never seen except when dressed in a gorilla suit. Although the only skills involved in this gorilla call were being able to fit into the suit and breathing, they were two really important skills! I actually got the job because I was the only stunt person who could fit into the small suit, but once they fitted the head on I'd start laughing, imagining how I must look. Once I was in the suit, though, there wasn't a whole lot of air with which to be laughing, and I'd quickly run out of it and start gasping. They had to keep taking my head off so I could breathe. Now there's a new concept. Then, the wardrobe girl set a tiny feminine hat on my big gorilla head, complete with a veil, and we were falling about the place laughing again. We were just in tears because we were all laughing so hard, and we couldn't get the lines said for a long time. There I was, as Gladys, sitting at an afternoon tea with my legs crossed, holding a tiny china cup with my enormous gorilla hand, being sure to curl my little finger, and sipping the tea. It was truly an unforgettable job. It was so wonderful seeing the one and only Harry Morgan again, too. We had always been such good friends since I had worked with him in *Yellow Sky*. Harry was truly one of the most talented performers in film history and one of the nicest you could ever meet.

Cheyenne, the 1956 Warner Brothers production that launched Clint Walker's career, was the first one-hour Western series on television. In Episode 8, during which they run the standard gambit of killings, lynch mobs, and guilt or innocence, an angry neighbor (Barton MacLane) tears out of the ranch on his horse and runs over Sheila, played by Beverly Michaels, killing her. Naturally, I was the person who was really in the horse's path.

It sounds simple enough — aim horse at stunt person and ride over them — but it took several shots to get it done. Now, before I got to the set that day, I had heard what would need to be done through the grapevine. Consequently, unbeknownst to but a few, I had practiced this at home with Frosty despite being aware that it was against all basic rules of survival in the stunt business at that time to practice anything. You see, if you got hurt on the set you were covered with their insurance, but off the set you were on your own. My friend Donna Hall, perhaps the most versatile riding stunt girl in the business, was furious with me for being so careless as to actually take risks at home. But, practice I did. I conned Donna into riding Frosty by me where I stood beside a pile of wood shavings about four feet deep. When he came by me, I stepped into him and put the flat part of my arm (elbow to hand) against his shoulder which would knock me safely back into the soft wood chips. Of course at that point Frosty would come to a full stop, regardless of what Donna said, and look back at me like I was nuts. When I went for the interview, they asked me what made me think I could do the stunt and I told them I had been practicing many times over at home! They were so impressed, I landed the job!

All that practice was nearly to no avail. The director had no idea that unless a horse is stampeding from fear he will not willingly run over you, for which many a person has had cause to be grateful, I'm sure. Now, Sheila is supposed to be deranged and to wander into the street in the path of the running horse. Time and time again that director tried to have the horse ridden into me, and time after time he veered off until finally I couldn't contain myself any longer. Taking the director aside, I told him that the only way this was going to work would be if they shot from the other side of the horse while I stepped into the horse's shoulder, just like I had practiced with Frosty. By this time, the frustrated director had no choice but to go along with me on this. Just as I knew he would, once they set up the shot, the horse ran by me as I stepped into his shoulder with my arm in front of my chest, bent stiff at the elbow. The "blow" sent me backwards and down, and it looked like he had run over me and killed me, just as they wanted. Of course there was no soft pile of wood chips out here, so I was strapped into the hip and elbow pads that all stunt people wore, similar to those of football players, and it was no problem. The hip pads were like a girdle with pad inserts over the hip and tail bones and fully elastic. We always carried our "stunt bags" to each job, filled with pads for every occasion.

As an example that some stunt techniques never change, a similar issue occurred during the shooting of *Silverado* in 1985. In the scene where Scott Glenn is hogtied on the ground and apparently trampled by a horse, it's not really happening for the same reason. A horse wouldn't naturally do that. Once again, the camera is shooting from the other side while the horse is being ridden along a line past Glenn while he rolls around as if being trampled. In fact, when it came to shooting the climactic cattle stampede in that movie, they couldn't even get the cattle to run towards people. When the first person showed up in front of them, they all veered off. The scene had to be shot in short takes and edited later to make it look like one continuous, uncontrolled stampede with bad guys getting run down.

After days at the studios that were as physically challenging as that one, I would stagger in my front door completely worn out. Frosty and I were using some different muscles, both in my work and his training program. Still, I did discover that taking him away from his work area and me from mine gave us a mental break, as well as a physical one. There were few hills for us to ride over as this was, after all, a valley but there was one fairly good incline to the north by the Veterans' Hospital in Sylmar, so we would ride off through some of the olive groves, with Frosty picking his way between the trees like a cutting horse. Sylmar was not too far to ride and was once the site of the world's largest olive groves — hence its name, which means "Sea of Trees."

Not a day would go by that Frosty didn't remind me of "the little foal who didn't know when to quit," and he did so on this day as he carefully picked his way through the trees. He was always interested in doing anything new, and forever let me know how he felt with his eagerness to please. I shifted my position in the saddle often as he created a zigzag path around these beautiful trees. We stopped once on top of the slight elevation. It was enough of a rise to allow me to look down on the changing colors of my beloved San Fernando Valley. I swung my legs over the saddle and dropped to the ground. Frosty stood three-legged, totally relaxed, while I leaned against his warm shoulder. The olive, walnut, orange, and eucalyptus trees and acres of grass surrounding them were all different shades of green. The perfume was unequalled by anything.

When I slipped the rein over his head, Frosty quickly began to investigate the various weeds under his feet on the little hill and found something, as he usually did, that was a delicacy. There was no martingale on these reward rides, allowing him to easily stretch his neck or put his head down to look for something great to nibble on. Occasionally he paused, raising his head with his golden ears pricked to listen to something beyond my range of hearing. I would try to guess what was in his mind as I saw once again the look of kindness and acute intelligence in his expressive eyes. I held him and cradled his head in my arms in what was our own private ritual. I cooed his secret word and reached out my hand to rearrange his foretop and pluck out a whisper of a weed. I so enjoyed spending this time with my horse, being constantly amazed by his rapid development in so many ways.

After we had both surveyed the valley below, I put the rein over his head, swung back atop the saddle and we headed off down the slope. It was a long ride home, and I lazily leaned with my hand on Frosty's back behind the saddle. We were refreshed, and I was looking forward to another day while he looked forward to his end-of-the-ride belly button scratch. Whenever we rode out like this, after I removed his tack and before his roll, I would rub his belly button and he would raise one back leg, stretch out his neck and curl up his nose with his head high in the air. He had already given me so much pleasure, how could I not return as much of that to him as I could?

11

Dakota Incident

That shot's no good! He lost his hat!
— director Lewis R. Foster.

Some film work stands out in my memory, not necessarily for quality and popularity, but for the circumstances and for what took place during the shoot. *Dakota Incident* is one of those.

If ever there was a film star who seemed to fit into the western genre so seamlessly that he could have been part of the real-life environment, it was Dale Robertson. Not only did the handsome six-footer look the epitome of a cowboy but he was born in Harrah, Oklahoma, where he worked with horses from a young age. By the time he was a teenager, he had such an excellent local reputation that on at least one occasion he was training seventeen polo ponies at the same time! A natural athlete from his college days, he used to box in professional prize fights to earn money; he retained that charming Oklahoma accent and just seemed to fit the image of everything Western. He always used to say that he had heeded the words of Will Rogers Jr., who once advised him never to take acting lessons. "They will try to put your voice in a dinner jacket," Rogers had said, "and people like their hominy and grits in everyday clothes." It proved to be very good advice for Dale.

I was thrilled to have been selected to double Linda Darnell in this film, as she and I had not seen each other for some time. We had first met back in 1948 on the set of the Twentieth Century–Fox production *Unfaithfully Yours* in which she co-starred with Rex Harrison. It so happened that a cousin of mine who badly wanted to be a film starlet at the time was appearing in this movie and she had managed to wangle a job for me as her stand-in so I could have some extra cash. This was my first time on a film set and I was trying hard to look as though I did it every day. For some reason I took Rusty, my cocker spaniel that had flown behind me in the P-38 piggy-back seat with Bill Lear, Jr., to work with me one day and Linda fell in love with him. We got talking and I told her about my marriage problems and she commented that if it looked like I'd not be able to keep Rusty, that she'd be glad to have him. Well, in the end, it turned out that I couldn't keep him as I had to go back to living with my parents and they couldn't have dogs in their apartment. Linda seemed so lonely, so I took Rusty over to her place near the Riviera Country Club and it turned out to be a match made in Heaven.

I had already heard that Republic had put together a great cast, including Ward Bond and John Lund, in a wonderfully authentic setting. *Dakota Incident* was to be made almost entirely on location in the Red Rock Canyon area (now Red Rock Canyon State Park) on the northwest edge of the great Mojave Desert, which has been a famous location for many westerns since the thirties. Because of its moonscape qualities, it's also been the setting for a number of science fiction films such as *Capricorn One* and *The Andromeda Strain* and television series such as *Lost in Space* and the original *Battlestar Galactica*. The studio would be using a stunt crew who knew their stuff, too, and so I was really looking forward to this shoot.

Our director Lewis R Foster had started out as a journalist in San Francisco and then worked as a screenwriter before becoming a director in the late 1920s. His best-known story was probably that of *Mr Smith Goes to Washington*, directed by Frank Capra in 1939, and Foster maintained parallel careers through most of his time in Hollywood, occasionally adding that of songwriter as well. However, *Dakota Incident* would be one of his last big-screen movies; he had already become involved in television work, directing a number of episodes of *The Adventures of Jim Bowie*. Later he would write and direct episodes of *Wonderful World of Disney* and *Tales of Wells Fargo*.

When the limo picked me up, I was surprised that Dale and I were the only passengers in the back seat for the drive. Naturally, with our common background our idle conversation soon turned to horses. Dale is an enthralling storyteller, in true camp-fire style, and so as we rode along to Red Rock Canyon I listened to the tale of a little stallion named Figure. He was purchased by a fellow named Justin Morgan and was so gentle that a child could ride him, but he was also so hardworking and fast that none could out-pull him or out-run him. Figure became so famous that he was seldom called by his name; he was simply referred to as "Justin Morgan's horse." Eventually, the Morgan became the oldest of all American horse breeds and strong enough to contribute significantly to almost every other American breed, while retaining its own identity for over two hundred years. It was three hours by car to Mojave, and I sat spellbound for every minute of that drive listening to Dale's story. It was an experience I will never forget.

As he spoke, I realized just how much of this tale touched upon things that my horse, Frosty, was learning at home. In years to come I would look back on what I had taught Frosty and understand that the two horses shared a special quality. The simple exercises that Frosty mastered to overcome being stunted at an early age, combined with the discipline they required, became basics for almost anything he was asked to do or learn, and they became part and parcel of how Frosty accomplished his difficult routines in his eventual career. Both Frosty and Figure demonstrated an intense passion to excel at what they were doing. This was the quality they shared.

On my first day on the *Dakota Incident* set, they shot the scene after the stagecoach wreck. The costume department dressed me in a chiffon blouse and satin skirt on a day when the wind was blowing hard and cold, and we just froze out there! It was so typical of what usually happens. I would find myself working in summer clothes during winter and in winter clothes in the summer. The costumes for Linda and me were beautifully made of cherry red satin, topped with a hat full of feather plumes, but underneath it all we wore tightly cinched "merry widow" corsets and, consequently, we found it impossible to sit down. Instead, we had to lean against tall, angled back-boards and pass the time catching up on news; we often talked about that little dog I'd given her. While that corset might have been bearable standing up, though, I had no choice but to take it off to work on horseback and in the stagecoach. My normally 25-inch waist did not take kindly to being squeezed into 20 inches. Linda and I both laughed our heads off at our predicament, but our ribs were squeezed so tight even that was not easy to do.

One of the funny stories she told me was about the first script reading for the movie. The evening before the first day's shooting, the cast had gathered in Linda's motel room to read through the script together. This was the first time they had all been able to get together in one place to do this, so it should have been a pretty intense work session. But, for some reason, one by one they started chuckling over their lines and the more they read, the more it got out of hand. By the time they were all out of the coach and pinned down by hostile Indians in a creek bed, Linda was rolling on the floor crying with laughter. It was a good omen for the rest of the shoot.

Even people like me who have worked with so many different stars are occasionally star-struck. There were some who were exceptional people, not just exceptional performers, and Linda was one of them. Kind, gentle and considerate, she was reputed to be Hollywood's youngest leading lady (just sixteen) at the time she was given the lead in her first movie. She even had the rare distinction of starring in a film, *Star Dust,* based on her own life. Her premature death came in 1965 at only 42, as a result of injuries she received in an early morning fire at the home of her former secretary in Glenview, Illinois, not long after they had been sitting up watching a television rerun of *Star Dust.* No one really knows why she went back downstairs into the fire, although one theory was that she might have been trying to save her friend's young daughter. If so, that would be apt for this gentle being. The most beautiful woman I ever saw in all my years in films, Linda was sensitive but she was also lonely, and cameras can be cruel with their favors. Hers was a beauty that no camera could entirely do full justice, perhaps because so much of it radiated from within.

Red Rock Canyon was a small desert community with little or no entertainment. Not that we needed any; everyone was tired after working in the cold and wind and retired early, willingly, after yet another great restaurant had supplied us with choice food. The most action off and on the set was to join the hunt for turquoise nuggets after a member of the crew found one the size of a fist. With its unique geology, formations and coloring, the canyon is an extraordinary place of natural wonder, and it always felt strange to see the big generator trucks parked in the middle of it all supplying electricity to the set's lights and sound systems. I could not help but wonder what the local Native American Kawaiisu people or the pioneer survivors of the 1850 Death Valley trek would have thought of the place now.

Then the shooting schedule took us backwards in time to the runaway stagecoach wreck itself. This was to be the big scene for us stunt people and crew, but it unintentionally became a classic example of how quickly a stunt with horses can become a life-threatening incident. Driving one horse at full gallop can be complicated enough under certain circumstances, but driving a team of four leaves little room for error and can easily get you seriously injured or even killed. Things can get out of hand as fast and with as little warning as a lightning strike.

The script called for our coach to be attacked by Indians. In the process of trying to escape, the driver would "lose control" of the horse team so that they bolted downhill with the coach until it wrecked, whereupon the survivors would escape and seek refuge in a dry gully while the coach was burned. In the words of that famous writer of the west, Louis L'Amour, travel in those pioneer days "was often more travail than travel," and that certainly applied to stagecoaches. They were not designed for passenger comfort, but to enable a horse team to pull them over difficult terrain with a minimum of effort. So they were often far smaller than you would think, customarily sitting six people facing each other, sometimes with room in the bigger coaches for three more on a kind of jump seat in the middle with a leather strap as a back. Luggage either went up on top or into a "boot" on the back, above which there was room for another two passengers to sit on top. The driver at the front would mostly be alone, unless there was reason to have someone riding "shotgun" either as a backup driver or as a guard. The studios and those who supplied the livestock to them had extraordinary collections of authentic stagecoaches, buckboards, wagons and carriages of all kinds. For some reason, this particular coach we were using was even smaller than usual and, as it happened, that turned out to be a very good thing.

As I was to be the only passenger, I was loaded in first — not an easy task in my fine red satin dress with huge, full-length skirt, complete with half a dozen petticoats. It was a stunt in itself just getting me into that stagecoach. I sat back and relaxed while I waited for the shot to be organized. This was going to be a complicated scene, so I knew it would take a while. Sitting in that old coach, I filled in the time by brushing the dust off my red satin dress, making sure my plumed hat was not being crushed, and trying to envision what it was really like in the days all this represented. Then, for a while I let my mind drift effortlessly to the same place it always did these days: Frosty. His was a life so extraordinary that I felt one day it would read like a book. He would become big and beautiful and he would have the white mane and tail of his dreams. I just knew that one day I would help him become a celebrity like his brother, as I promised him the first day I ever saw him. I knew then he needed a miracle and that miracle was going to be me. He was the one with the magic within him, and his desire to achieve was written in his eyes. If I could come up with the right training and development, I knew he could discover his challenge. I had absolutely no doubts he could do it. And still we waited....

Our particular stagecoach was for all intents and purposes being

This is only a two-horse hitch on this Concord coach, so imagine how much faster Martha's coach was going downhill behind a four when their coach ran away during *Dakota Incident* (Courtesy Hansen Wheel and Wagon).

driven on this occasion by the star, Dale, who was seated up front holding token driving lines to four horses along with a stuntman sitting next to him riding shotgun. As driving a team of four horses is a highly skilled feat usually performed by a professional, there was actually one of that rare group sitting inside the coach holding the real driving lines to the horses. He was referred to as the "blind driver" because you couldn't see him and he was pretty much, well, driving blind. Slipped through a small opening in the front of the coach, the real driving lines can often be seen in a Western if you know where to look.

Once the action got underway Dale, following his script as the apparent stage driver, encouraged the horses to run and so run they did — and then they ran faster. Unfortunately, when he shouted, "Go!" they misunderstood the command as meaning, "Run as fast as you can!" Almost as soon as they were moving at speed, they were out of control on a narrow road with a steep drop-off on one side, towing a heavy vehicle sitting on which was the star of the movie! There was a sharp turn coming up, and there was no way we were going to make it around that curve at the speed we were traveling.

Dale, who didn't even have any means of contact with the real driver, had absolutely no idea the team was now out of control for real. Kneeling on the floor, peeking out the slit cut for the lines, squeezed in between me and another passenger, the driver had no room to lean back and so put any drag weight on the lines. When I saw him take a double hand wrap on them, I knew he'd realized he could not stop the team and that we were in some serious trouble. I looked out the window and could see that we were rapidly coming up on the turn. Meanwhile, Dale was still up there on the seat obliviously encouraging the horses to outrun the Indians to our doom. As fine a horseman as he was, Dale wasn't used to driving teams and did not have the experience to feel the danger we were in.

Now, Lewis Foster was a fine director with a many great films to his credit, including many Westerns, but things were happening so fast he really didn't know what he was seeing when one of the most miraculous feats I have ever witnessed on a movie set took place. The stuntman riding shotgun alongside Dale had evidently also realized what was happening and had been thinking out his move. Suddenly, I saw a pair of boots coming through the small window beside me as that stuntman lowered himself over the side of the madly rocking vehicle and squeezed in through the window beside the door. Climbing over my lap, with the team at a dead run, he seized one set of lines while the blind driver hung onto the other and, between them, legendary stunt men Joe Yrigoyen and Davy Sharpe pulled those runaways to a halt. As the cloud of dust slowly settled and I climbed out on very shaky legs, I heard the director declare: "That shot's no good! He lost his hat!" Foster had not been inside that coach to see the heroic and skilful act that had saved all our lives.

In these days of lower budget, made-for-television and made-for-DVD Westerns, it is rare to see a full team pulling a stagecoach, and so most people have no idea of the power and speed that a full team can produce when hauling a heavy coach. Let me tell you, it can be impressive enough when the driver has full control of that team, let alone how scary it can feel when you know it's the horses who have taken over. The original script had called for a six-up and thank goodness it had been changed to four. There would have been no way to stop a runaway six-up in the time allotted, considering the length of the road and the sharp turns as chosen by the location manager.

There was no story of Justin Morgan on the limo ride home. Left to my own thoughts, I couldn't help but consider how special our two horses were. I wasn't to know then, of course, just how much Frosty would show me of his special qualities in time to come. A few years later, during his career in Las Vegas, an unusual event occurred that still brings tears to my eyes when I remember it. On this occasion, I was riding him in the famous Helldorado Days Parade in which, because he was under contract at the time as the "spokeshorse" for Arden Dairy, he was dressed as the Arden Dairy Milk Man. As always, it was the unrehearsed things Frosty did that stole the show. In this long parade, he usually never offered to do anything but walk and dance (Spanish Walk or Passage) unless asked. However, this time he seemed to become distracted at one particular spot on the route and wanted to go to the side of the road, which I allowed him to do. The road was lined with hundreds of people, mostly children, calling to Frosty from either side. Suddenly, of his own free will, he stopped in front of a little girl in the front row who was sitting in a wheelchair and lowered his head, decorated with his Milk Man's cap, almost into her lap. It was the most glorious thing that could ever happen to that child! How Frosty knew this little one needed special tenderness, I'll never know for sure, but I *am* sure she will never forget it. What I do think is that the lonely orphan foal, inside the glorious horse he became, recognized another aching heart. Then, he was content to return to business as usual, following the band in the parade. That year in Vegas he had requests for 30,000 pictures from the children who had seen him perform.

However, there would be many more stagecoaches to ride in, buckboards to drive and stunts to do before we rode in that parade.

12

My Tin Star Year

Don't I know you? You look really familiar to me.
— Martha Crawford to Henry Fonda.

Every time I think of Janice Rule and *Gun for a Coward*, I think of water and mud. Janice, for whom this was her first Western, was a very talented and versatile actress who played the whole spectrum of human life roles in comedy and drama during her career after her first screen appearance in 1951. Eventually, though, she would move on from acting to focus on her New York private practice as a psychoanalyst after earning her doctorate in 1983. Just about the entire time we were on that set at Universal, it seemed to me, they were constantly flooding it with "rain" from overhead sprinklers. My wardrobe was really simple: a rain slicker. I was not doing any horse stunts on this film, just photographic doubling, but it was not hard to understand why Janice had requested a double. We were all soaked all of the time. Whether on a horse or just walking from one canasta game to the other, we were in mud.

A few months later, she and I would find ourselves in more water and mud together when I doubled her again in the first episode of the television series *Have Gun—Will Travel*, "Three Bells to Perdido." Her character, Nancy, was scripted to fall into a mud puddle while running and to emerge with her rifle still in one hand and a duck in the other. Then, still holding these, I was supposed to leap on my horse bareback, wet and muddy, and ride off. For a short while there, I was afraid I would have to do all this holding a live, flapping, quacking duck but as it turned out, the duck was stuffed. It was just as well; I would probably have broken its neck. The rifle was real enough, though, and that actually made the mount easier. The weight of it as I threw my right hand over the horse while I held the duck, the reins and the mane in my left helped me propel myself up and over in my vault from the ground to the back of the horse. What I learned that day I later put to good use when I performed a similar mount while doubling Jean Simmons on *The Big Country,* a highlight of my career. Demonstrating to everybody that I could deal with situations like this formed the basis of my reputation and became a pivotal point in my success with Frosty.

I was working steadily, but the days could be long. Often I had to report to the studio makeup department by 4:00 in the morning, working all day and sometimes into the night until the director had the shots that he wanted. I wouldn't reach home until late, and that kind of schedule didn't leave much space for anything else, including worrying over Frosty. Late in the evenings, though, I would sit down with pencil and paper and try to outline the pattern I wanted to follow for Frosty's development. I knew so well that he had all the muscles; it was just that some had never had a chance to develop due to his early confinement. I gave great thought to designing the exercises that would develop his chest, his rump and the loin muscle, and fill out his neck. While this type of rehabilitation was becoming standard for human accident victims and polio sufferers, to my knowledge this was the first time that exercise kinesiology, as it would become known, was applied to a horse! But I had no one with whom I could share these thoughts, no one to reinforce my ideas, nor anyone who knew Frosty like I did.

When I first sat down at my kitchen table to create a daily schedule for these exercises that I could see in my mind, I stared at the blank piece of paper in front of me. It stared right back at me. Hours later, I was still sitting there with my blank piece of paper, gazing at the patterns made by the knotty pine on the wood that lined the kitchen walls in my one-storey wood frame house. All that was filling my head was a bunch of questions. What if I could not do this? Did I really know what I was doing? Was I just chasing a dream? I knew it was not going to be easy, and I was terrified I might not be able to do all the things I had convinced myself so easily that I could do. I had no formal education in rehabilitation, just a lifelong love of horses. I was more worried that I might let Frosty down than concerned over any failure of my own.

In the end I grew angry at my own fear and said a few strong words to myself. I remembered the look in my little orphan's eyes, the desire and faith he had in me even in the darkness of his lonely stall. I saw again little Frosty, bedraggled and unkempt, walking through the laughter of the snobs in Phoenix, and I took heart in what he had already accomplished.

I knew I could not give up on that great heart and mind inside that scrawny little body. But how to accomplish all that needed to be done? The task was daunting, to say the least. I needed to take it one step at a time, and it was that night after I'd returned from shooting the mud puddle scene with the duck that I slowly began to write those steps down on paper. It dawned on me that I had been faced on that set with what seemed an impossible task, much like how I was feeling about working with Frosty, and yet I had found a solution from within my own experience. If I had done it then, I could do it with Frosty. It would just take time.

There were hours upon hours, even days, of doing nothing much on *Gun for a Coward* while the crew adjusted and readjusted the rain-making system. It was just as well that the cast members were all card players and canasta was the game of the moment, for as those damp hours of waiting dripped by, the canasta games kept rolling on. It wasn't just about playing cards, of course; the games were social events and gave us a valuable chance to catch up on studio news and friendships.

I was reminded again that Hollywood could be such a typical small town. On the one hand it could be one great big family, yet on the other it could be clannish and riddled with politics. I worked primarily for Metro-Goldwyn-Mayer and Twentieth Century–Fox, and very occasionally for Universal, so I knew a lot of people who worked for those studios. However, I knew virtually no one who was in my line of work over at RKO, for example, or Paramount or Republic or even Warner Bros. Those studios even used different horse contractors and wranglers.

Gun for a Coward tells the story of the three Keough brothers, played by Fred MacMurray, Jeffrey Hunter and Dean Stockwell, who take over the family ranch after the death of their father. While the eldest and youngest seek justice with their guns, the middle brother is more interested in peace and reason. Jeffrey told me that his opportunity for this role had come about because of sad circumstance. James Dean had originally been scheduled to play the middle brother, but he had died the previous year in a car crash and production had been suspended until now. I knew Jeffrey from when he and his former wife, Barbara Rush, had been living in the apartment next to my parents in Westwood Village. My father adored him and the feeling was mutual. An experienced stage actor by the time he made his first movie appearance in 1951, Hunter had just finished *The Searchers* with John Wayne. He would later move about as far away from Westerns as you could get, to appear as Jesus in *King of Kings* and as the first captain of the USS *Enterprise*, Christopher Pike, in the original

Star Trek pilot. Unfortunately, he would die when only 42 from injuries sustained in a fall, after suffering from a second stroke.

Actress Betty Lynn and I knew each other from working at Twentieth Century–Fox, and we always had fun catching up on our lives whenever we met. She once said that she wanted to be an actress so people would like her, but I always thought it was impossible not to like her. After this role, her career was almost entirely involved with television, and she is now best remembered for her role as Thelma Lou on *The Andy Griffith Show*. As strange as it may seem, she now lives in the North Carolina town where Andy Griffith was born and which was the inspiration for the town of Mayberry in that television show. Fred MacMurray, in the role of the eldest brother, was making one of his rare excursions into Westerns in a long and varied career before he moved to working for Disney in 1959 and also becoming one of America's favorite fathers in the television series *My Three Sons*. As the youngest Keough, Dean Stockwell was making is first appearance in an adult role having started acting in films at age nine. Bud Westmore was doing my makeup which always gave me a thrill, too, as the whole Westmore family were legends in the field of motion picture makeup. Before long I would be working again with hair stylist Joan St. Oegger on the set of *The Big Country*.

Before then, I was called for a few days' work to the set of the low-budget western *The Tin Star,* in which veteran bounty hunter Morg Hickman (Henry Fonda) rides into a town to find that the sheriff has been killed and inexperienced young Ben Owens (Anthony Perkins) has been temporarily deputized in his place. Ben dearly wants to have the knowledge and experience to become the permanent sheriff and when he finds out that Hickman was once a lawman, Ben asks for his help. Rather than teach him how to handle guns, Hickman teaches him how to handle people. In the process, Hickman not only teaches Ben but is able to recreate the family he has lost and so rediscovers himself. It's a tale with a moral about what's more important in life, about community, and perhaps because of that added depth *The Tin Star* received an Academy Award nomination for Best Story and Screenplay.

Nineteen fifty-seven was already looking like it would be one of my biggest years. I was in solid with the studios, and the phone was literally ringing off the hook with work offers. I'd told Teddy, my call service, to accept them all. Teddy spoiled us as she was so much more than a call service. She knew the business and her stunt men and women and what they could and couldn't do. She could filter the calls when needed, so it was like having a private secretary. This was a year for three-cent stamps and for Iron Liege to win the Kentucky Derby. He won as the result of an embarrassing moment when the rider of the favorite Gallant Man, legendary jockey Bill Shoemaker, misjudged the finish line and stood up too early which caused his horse to slow just enough for Iron Liege, ridden by Hall of Fame rider Bill Hartac, to win by a nose. I knew how Shoemaker felt. If I had won an award for *The Tin Star*, it would have been for Stunt Girl's Most Embarrassing Moment.

I arrived on the *Tin Star* set, the Western street on the backlot at Paramount, for my first day of work to double Betsy Palmer, who plays Nona Mayfield, in a buggy-driving scene. This was going to be a piece of cake, I thought. I had driven many a horse and buggy in my time, and I'd not long ago performed a wicked near-wreck for the *My Friend Flicka* television series. From that little stunt, I'd evidently acquired a reputation as a dependable driver of buckboards, buggies, carriages, and wagons who could handle any situation. The wranglers always brought the equipment with the horses all hitched up to the set and I just stepped into it. They would stand off-camera to take the horses when you were finished or, in the case of a chase, they were already mounted on horses ready to run up beside you and "pick you up" (take hold of the horses' bridle) to stop you if you could not get the team or horse stopped on your own.

However, on this particular day the buggy became a buckboard on which I was to tear into town, make a sharp right-hand turn onto the main street and stop in front of the hitch rail at the hotel. It could not have sounded simpler. The four-wheeled buckboard, with its origins way back in the eighteenth century, played a large part in the settling of the West with its versatility for rough terrain. Steered by the front wheels, it has a pivoting front axle which enabled me this time to apply my new-found skill of performing a "brodie" in the turn, an inside term for sliding a buckboard through a turn. I hit the brake for the rear wheels just as I turned the horses, slowing the rear wheels just enough to cause the back end to slide out slightly in the opposite direction. In the movie, you can see the dust hanging in the air where we turned. However, if you hit the brakes too hard, the rear of the buckboard could fishtail and flip you over. You needed a deft touch, and I got it just right.

So, as I neared the hotel, I was filled with more than a touch of smug self-satisfaction at demonstrating my prowess so successfully. This stuntwoman had just made a perfect dash and turn under the watchful eyes of some of the very best stuntmen in the business. Even Terry Wilson and

Driving a buckboard flat out down the main street of the Paramount Studios Western backlot, Martha is doubling Betsy Palmer in *The Tin Star* (Paramount Pictures).

Frank McGrath, who would later work on the *Wagon Train* television series, were there that day. I had left a cloud of dust on the dirt street bigger than my wildest dreams. But as I neared the hitching rail, my dreams vanished in a puff of wind. The next thing I was supposed to do was pull to a halt outside the hotel, jump out of the buckboard, tie up at the rail and run through the door. Unlike when leaving your horse at the rail after riding into town, if that horse is harnessed to a buckboard you never tie up with the reins. Instead, it's customary to wrap the reins around the brake handle so that they don't fall out or become tangled. You actually tie up to the rail with a piece of rope that you carry on the floor down near your feet. However, as I frantically scanned my equipment, the team, the rail and the path I was to follow, I could see nothing in my line of sight with which to tie up the horses! They duly pulled up just as we planned (I sometimes think they read the scripts), but I couldn't just jump out and turn them loose. So, I did the next best wrong thing; I took the lines with me and did a wrap around the hitch rail. "Cut! Cut! Cut!" wailed the director, Anthony Mann, and his assistants all together. It was a far cry from the "Print that!" which I was used to hearing.

I just thought I would die right there on the spot. All my confidence and newly found arrogance blew away like the dust on the breeze. To make matters worse, much to my chagrin, when I looked in the buckboard again there was the rope in a tight little coil right alongside where my left foot had been resting. How could I have missed it? I felt like crawling under the buckboard, not getting back into it. However, after making sure that rope was still there, I did climb back in for the second take, scooted around the corner, pulled up, took a wrap with the lines around the brake handle before jumping out, and then I tied the horses to the rail with that rope just as should have happened in the first place. I remember hearing that Eugene O'Neill's play *A Long Day's Journey Into Night* was produced posthumously and won both the Tony Award and Pulitzer Prize that year. Well, it certainly felt like a long day's journey into night for me before I was at last in the security of my own kitchen. I plopped into a chair and stared at the patterns of the knotty pine, reliving a day of work that would gather me neither awards nor prizes. On the contrary, I felt it was a day that would go down in infamy like Pearl Harbor. I can't remember ever being called by Paramount again.

Still, my time on the set was not a total loss as I renewed friendships with three wonderful people. I had previously worked with Neville Brand on *Love Me Tender* and, though he always tended to play a tough guy as he did in *The Tin Star*, he was really nothing like that. He had actually been highly decorated during World War II, was a gentleman and a fine, fine actor and it was always a pleasure to work with him. Then there was Tab Hunter, who was a frequent visitor to the set as a friend of Anthony Perkins. We got to talking between takes about horses and our mutual friend and Hall of Fame horseman Clyde Kennedy, at whose training stable I had met him. Tab was a nice guy and such a fine horseman that I think he could have had more fun and fame had he followed a career in the professional horse world. He and Fox star Dan Dailey were top jumping horse riders. I also had a chance to talk again with Henry Fonda, who

Opposite: **This 1956 poster for *The Killer Is Loose* includes Martha up close with Wendell Corey in the illustration at the top. Joseph Cotten and Rhonda Fleming are below (MGM Clip+Still).**

remembered me from when I was fifteen or sixteen and had just won a Working Hunter division on my horse Yellow Sleeves at a cross-country horse trial. I was still on my horse getting my breath back, anticipating another class, and I had just removed my black velvet hunt cap when this friendly gentleman came up to me, put his hand on my knee, and congratulated me. In my naiveté all I could say was, "Thanks, but don't I know you? You look really familiar to me." He never said who he was; he just laughed and walked away. A while later, it suddenly hit me: "Oh no! I've just told Henry Fonda that he looked really familiar!"

I always found director Oscar "Budd" Boetticher a real-life human interest study. I often met him in passing at the San Fernando Valley Saddlery, owned (along with the surrounding property) by one of the very top custom saddle makers in California. The favorite of most show horse riders and film people, this man was known for his distinctive oak leaf leather carving and lightweight saddles, and he also boarded horses. The Saddlery was a favorite watering hole for stunt men, celebrities, rodeo stock contractors such as Andy Jauregui and top rodeo performers. When he wasn't working, you could count on seeing Budd there absorbing all the western ambience he could. He just loved it, and that affection carried over into his movies. Among the thirty-six films that Budd directed, as well as a number of episodes for television shows like *Maverick* and *Zane Grey Theater*, were some of the most memorable Westerns of the fifties, such as *Seven Men from Now* and *Ride Lonesome*. Most of them were shot using the area around Lone Pine that I knew well from my own work there, and they often featured Randolph Scott. Given my background, you would think that the studio might have called me to do stunt work in one of those. Not a chance. I never even had the chance to corner him and impress him with stories of my Frosty with which I know he would have been impressed! When I finally got to work on a Budd Boetticher set, it was for one of his few noir thrillers, *The Killer Is Loose*, shot in fifteen days at Warners during 1956 with cinematographer Lucien Ballard.

In this cops-and-robbers scenario, a desperate savings and loan employee named Poole (Wendell Corey) successfully plans the robbery of his workplace while making it look as though he's a victim. At first, he is considered a hero for his actions during the robbery but the police quickly figure out he's involved in the crime. They catch up with him and his young wife, Doris (myself), at their apartment. During the arrest, detective Sam Wagner (Joseph Cotten) accidentally kills Poole's wife and Poole swears vengeance at the trial as he is sentenced to prison. Three years later, Poole kills a guard and escapes and it becomes clear during the manhunt that Poole is obsessed with a particular goal, but it turns out not to be the goal that everyone presumes.

Wendell Cory and Martha discuss their script on the set of *The Killer Is Loose* (MGM Clip+Still).

A wonderful group of experienced actors was put together for this film including Corey, Cotten, Rhonda Fleming, Alan Hale Jr., and the Australian actor Michael Pate who must have had the longest career of any white actor playing indigenous Native American roles. Despite the somber context of the movie, these actors were great fun to work with, light-hearted and sometimes hysterically funny. I expected Joseph Cotten to be very sober in person because he had played so many serious roles, but he revealed a fabulous sense of humor. Rhonda Fleming, breathtakingly beautiful in person, had such a cute personality she was just delightful fun to work with. Wendell Corey also surprised me. In contrast to the deadpan characters he often played he, too, could be very funny in person

Though my screen time as Doris was going to be very short indeed, the studio wanted to interview me and asked me to bring pictures. I arranged for a photographer to shoot them at my best friend's house on Rexford Drive in Beverly Hills, and United Artists liked three of them so much they promptly used them for publicity. Between those and the studio shots, I think I received more press for this short flash on the screen than for any of my other work.

Usually you are brought into the studio for a wardrobe fitting, but my time on the screen was going to be so brief that the studio told me just to wear a dark suit and report to hairdressing. So, I wore the navy-blue silk gabardine suit that I had worn when I briefly worked for Eastern Airlines and my favorite Delman pumps. Well, after I'm shot, Wendell Corey was supposed to pick me up in his arms, but between his Italian silk suit and my silk gabardine we were both so slippery that I kept sliding out of his grasp. After a few takes had come to nothing, we were laughing so hard it was difficult to get the shot. Finally, even though I was supposed to be a body at that point, I put my hand behind his neck and held on to keep from sliding away again.

In those days, theaters had box offices which sat alone in a forecourt area. Glass cases lined these areas displaying large poster previews of coming attractions, used to entice the passerby. The front cases that faced the sidewalk, however, had actual stills of scenes from the film now showing. Which still do you think was the main one they used for *The Killer Is Loose*? That's right; the one where the "dead" wife is hanging onto Corey's neck and trying not to laugh.

A year later I found myself working with Rhonda Fleming again. This time I was doubling for her in a fight scene on the set of *Gun Glory*,

One of the photos that Martha brought along to the MGM studio interview for her appearance in *The Killer Is Loose* was this swimsuit shot, taken alongside her best friend's pool on Rexford Drive in Beverly Hills (MGM Clip & Still).

starring Stewart Granger. MGM enlisted its top costume designer, Walter Plunkett, and makeup artists Sydney Guilaroff and William Tuttle to enhance this story of a gunslinger, Tom Early (Granger), who returns to his home town to retire and live a quiet life only to find that his wife has died in his absence and his son is understandably resentful. That son, by the way, is played by Steve Rowland, son of the film's director Roy Rowland. Then there's the cattle baron (James Gregory) who wants to drive his cattle through the valley where the town and their ranch is situated. Early hires a housekeeper, Jo (Rhonda Fleming), of whom he grows fond, only to find his son has taken a liking to her as well. One way or the other, it is not going to be a peaceful path to settling down.

Some of the movie was shot on the MGM backlot, so you might recognize the same Western street and store from *Seven Brides for Seven Brothers* and *The Fastest Gun Alive*. However, the panoramic outdoor locations

Martha trying not to slip out of Wendell Corey's arms while playing dead in *The Killer Is Loose* (MGM Clip & Still).

were shot in Northern California in CinemaScope and look absolutely stunning on the wide screen. Rhonda Fleming, with her impish personality, was a strange pairing with Granger, who was almost as serious in person as the character he portrays. Granger himself thought he didn't have the right build to be a gunslinger, but by then he owned the T4J ranch in New Mexico so he rode a horse very well. In fact, in *Gun Glory* he's riding his own highly intelligent horse, Sundown, that he had trained to cut out steers. Although the horse balked the first time on set and jumped sideways because it thought the whirring camera was a rattlesnake, after that Granger could ride it up to a mark and it would stop on the spot.

In his last year of a seven-year contract with MGM, Granger was trying to make the payments on his T4J ranch and that was a primary incentive for him to take on the gunslinger role in this film. Although familiar with guns as a hunter, Granger wasn't familiar with drawing a revolver fast from a holster and firing, so he trained with a Native American named

Lightfoot. After some intensive work with an empty gun over a few days, Granger was doing very well indeed and so the gunfight scene was set up for a shoot with his opponent opposite, and a crowd of us stunt people, extras and crew gathered off-camera to watch. Once the six-gun was loaded with blanks, though, Granger became overly conscious of the spectators and grew nervous. On the first take, he pulled the trigger while the gun was still in the holster and burned both his clothes and his leg from the flash. On the second take, he got the gun out of the holster but forgot to fire before he went to fan the hammer with his left hand; when he pulled the trigger, the sharp striker on the hammer promptly went right through the palm of his hand. Finally, on the third take he got it right; it was a blindingly fast draw and fan and the bad guy bit the dust. Silence. "Sorry," called the cameraman, "the camera jammed." The fourth take finally worked out, but it wasn't quite as fast. It was always somehow comforting to see that actors had bad days, too.

Martha getting slugged while doubling Rhonda Fleming in *Gun Glory* at MGM in 1957 (Warner Bros. Entertainment).

The climax of the film involved a stampede of five hundred cattle supplied by Frank Wingfield's ranch at Nogales, on the Arizona border. He and Granger got to talking about ranches one day, and he invited Granger down to stay with him and view some properties for sale. Consequently, Granger eventually purchased a 10,000-acre ranch, Yerba Bueno on the Santa Cruz River, along with a herd of Santa Gertrudis cattle that he promptly replaced with a more expensive Charolais herd. He and Jean Simmons had to sell both the T4J ranch and their Hollywood house to pay for it all, plus keep up a solid work schedule to make the annual $50,000 payments for the next five years. Evidently, the strain of it all became too much for their relationship; a little over two years later, Jean filed for divorce. At times like that, I knew why I had stuck to stunt work and felt lucky I had Frosty to come home to.

13

The Seventh Sin

Dr Walter Carwin: "The dog it was that died."
—from Oliver Goldsmith's poem "Elegy of a Mad Dog"

I was trying unsuccessfully to smile at Bob, the camera operator and my traveling companion, while we stood at the foot of a loading ramp at Los Angeles Airport. It led to the first step on the initial leg of our location trip to faraway Hong Kong to film the background shots for a new MGM film, *The Seventh Sin,* a remake of the old Greta Garbo film *The Painted Veil* based on the Somerset Maugham novel of the same name. The close-ups would be done later in the studio in Culver City. We were embarking on our 8,800-mile trip to meet the other six members of the MGM production company that had gone on ahead. Little could we guess that the action in this film would not be limited to the script nor the sins to seven.

Right after we had hurriedly introduced ourselves, Bob had asked me, "Didn't they teach you how to smile?" I was somewhat confused by his question. I was the only female cast member on this plane, having been asked to once again double for Eleanor Parker. Indeed, I was the *only* cast member on the plane; no other actors were making this trip. However, I was anticipating flying out of Los Angeles much too eagerly to allow anything or anyone to cast a shadow over it all. So, balancing precariously on the high heels of my Delman pumps, carrying a white Borgana coat in one hand and fiercely clutching my red leather Elizabeth Arden makeup case that contained the $5,000 "fall" for my hair in the other, I quickly climbed the stairs and stepped through the door into the aircraft. As Bob grabbed the window seat, I finally found the breath to answer his blunt question as I plopped down into my own seat. "You know, I guess they forgot that," I replied, and then in my lowest voice I added, "By the way, did they teach you how to ride?"

This job offer had been unusual. When a major studio called a stunt person about work, the offer usually didn't come with an option. It was a fatal mistake to turn the job down if you were available; if you did, it was highly unlikely the studio would ever call you again. I can only recall ever being presented with the full details of a job and then actually being asked if I wanted to do it on one other occasion: doubling Audrey Hepburn in *Green Mansions*. "Feel free to turn down the work for *The Seventh Sin* if you want to," Jasper Russell, MGM's casting director, had said. "They're going to shoot in Kowloon and there's been quite a bit of unrest there because of Communist activity." I was, in fact, aware of that and had only recently heard of a European diplomat's wife having her arms pulled off as professional agitators dragged her through the streets. The studio was obviously taking the situation there very seriously, so accepting the work had certainly been a calculated risk on my part. I knew the money they were offering was very good, and I felt secure in working within a major film company on that location. I would not have even considered the job if it had been with one of the small independent companies.

On the other hand, Eleanor Parker had not been offered a similar choice. She had to appear in a certain number of films as stipulated in her contract, but she made sure her feelings about the matter were understood by refusing to go on location to Hong Kong for reasons of ill health. So, that was how I came to be employed to go to Hong Kong and be a photographic double for all of Eleanor's long shots, while she remained in the U.S. for the close-ups at the studio. I knew that Eleanor would have specifically asked for me, because of our long association together, and that also influenced my agreement to go.

Much to my amazement, I was fitted in wardrobe by the living legend designer Helen Rose. She could not get over the similarities between Eleanor and me. Not only did we have the same measurements but the same physical peculiarities: a high right hip and low left shoulder. Helen often remarked she could do fittings for both of us while using just one of us. That lovely wardrobe was very tempting to own, but at a price of $10,000 I had to pass. I was mesmerized watching the wardrobe department pack those clothes for shipment to Hong Kong. Each item was packed with tissue paper so that when unpacked, they would be absolutely wrinkle-free. Once I arrived in Hong Kong, I would have my own wardrobe lady, makeup man, hairdresser, interpreter and driver.

We flew via San Francisco to Honolulu. When we were about an hour or so out from the Hawaiian Islands, I was chatting with the stewardess and the conversation led to my recent marriage to, and divorce from, Bill Lear, Jr., during which flying had become a part of my life. Soon after, the captain came to my seat and invited me to the cockpit for the remainder of the trip. It was a delightful surprise. He and the co-pilot had donned full uniform for my benefit, complete with shiny silver wings and flight caps, and they were looking the image of traditional airline pilots. Inviting me to sit in the jump seat between them, they were eager to talk with me (as we cruised on auto-pilot) about my time in the P-38 and Bill's Bendix Air Race. After awhile, though, our conversation trailed off as the most extraordinary sunset I had ever seen appeared in front of us. It seemed to appear out of the blue sky where just a moment before it had been out of our line of vision. We all paused for a breathtaking moment as we sat looking ahead through the main cockpit window of the DC-6. Then, before too long, the lights of the islands started to appear, and as they twinkled in the fading sky I felt as if I had just "touched the face of God." I came out of my trance, thanked the two men, and returned to my seat with a blissful smile. Now somewhat more impressed with my presence, Bob couldn't help asking me what that had all been about, but I just kept smiling mysteriously. Perhaps I had earned some new respect.

After a brief lay-over in Honolulu with just enough time to stretch our legs up and down a few crowded streets, we boarded the Japanese Air Lines DC-6 *City of Osaka* and prepared for the 7,000–mile trip to Tokyo's Haneda Airport. Considered the best of its class in those days, these aircraft carried only forty-eight to fifty passengers in a configuration of two seats each side and were crewed with pilot, co-pilot and two stewardesses. Bob promptly took the window seat again! We crossed the International Date Line somewhere short of halfway from Honolulu to Tokyo, before our re-fueling stop in Guam, and we celebrated with the serving of an elaborate buffet meal. After that, however, the situation on board the plane became very curious indeed. Up until now, the stewardesses had been dressed in what was then the usual American-style fashion for female air personnel, but after the meal they both reappeared in traditional Japanese kimonos and their manner changed along with their outfits. As we traveled across the date line into the future, their attitudes traveled back into the past. Neither stewardess ever spoke to us again. Their animosity towards Americans was a silent presence that filled the aircraft.

After landing at Tokyo's Haneda Airport, we caught a cab to the Nikatsu Hotel as the legendary Imperial, designed by Frank Lloyd Wright, was being renovated and our reservations had been reprocessed. The

Nikatsu was very nice and my room for our overnight plane connection was on the tenth floor with a private balcony overlooking the city, although my expectations of being able to take in a view of this city of lights were somewhat dampened by the enormous Coca-Cola sign directly opposite. That evening, Bob and I enjoyed dinner in the hotel dining room where a balcony of violinists entertained us at our formally set table. I revitalized my taste buds over a plate of Sashimi. As I dunked my first piece of thinly sliced raw fish into the soy and ginger sauce, I finally asked Bob about his "smile" question. Always the cameraman, Bob replied that he was alluding to the standardized set of expressions used by stars in publicity photos.

"Oh!" said this naïve stunt-girl, who should have known better by now. "I thought those expressions were, well, just the way they looked."

Bob sighed dramatically and proceeded to enlighten me about how celebrities were actually taught such expressions, including smiling, by their studio.

"So, is that all?" I replied. "And here I thought you were implying I was being difficult."

Bob just shook his head silently and applied himself to his steak. We still had another eighteen hundred miles to go.

As we made our approach to Kowloon and the Kai Tak Airport, we could see the entire area as the old airport was just a mile from the city center. The landing approach felt as if we were landing in the city itself. The pilots actually used a checkerboard painted on a hillside to guide them down to the runway, and conditions were generally regarded as so dangerous that no night landings were allowed. Old Hong Kong with its touch of colonialism was not remotely like the Hong Kong of today. I had been anticipating our stay at the famous and luxurious Peninsula Hotel on Kowloon's waterfront, but by the time we arrived political unrest was becoming worse and so we were sent to the Gloucester Hotel in Victoria instead. At this time, Hong Kong was still a British colony consisting of Hong Kong Island, and then Kowloon and the New Territories on the Kowloon Peninsula connected to the Chinese mainland. One boarded the Star Ferry in Kowloon to journey to Hong Kong across the historically important deep water port of Victoria Harbor, bustling with Pearl River junks, British destroyers, and U.S. aircraft carriers often sharing the harbor with the occasional luxury liner, freighters and old-fashioned sampans. Victoria was the heart of the business center, while across to the southern shore of the island was the fishing village of Aberdeen and the famous floating restaurants. We would be working mainly in Kowloon and Aberdeen, Bob said, and then perhaps taking a few shots in the crowded streets of Victoria.

I was given a very large suite at the Gloucester, consisting of a sitting room and bedroom with large closets that would be ideal for my wardrobe. The furniture in the room was made from a strange wood and I had trouble with the smell, but then there were many strange smells in Hong Kong to which I had to become accustomed. Eventually they must have been absorbed into my body, because when I returned home my beloved cocker spaniel would not come near me for several days. In fact, it took a good week for me to unwind from the stress of the trip.

Directly across the street was a construction site for a new building. They worked twenty-four hours a day and so did their pile driver. Whoooooosssssshhhh — BANG — thumped over and over again about every thirty seconds around the clock. It was awful. Then, there was the water rationing. Public faucets had water for only two hours every other day for two million people on an island of only 32 square miles. Hundreds would be lined up for water and it was not unusual for there to be several killings in lines over water allocations. Nevertheless, every day when I came back to the room, the bath tub had been filled about half full, and there were pitchers of fresh water on the tables. I had quickly figured out that you were much more likely to be able to complete washing yourself by using the tub. It was not that unusual to meet someone running down the corridor, wrapped in a towel, asking if you had any water as their shower had turned off while they were still soaped up!

We shot street scenes in Victoria and in close proximity to the hotel, but they were rather mundane as I merely walked down the very crowded street and entered and exited an office building. However, while we were working on these street scenes, director Ronald Neame decided he would have cinematographer Ray June photograph me as close as five feet from the camera if I walked straight to it and then veered off to one side. That was very unusual practice with a double, but he estimated it would work because of the close physical resemblance I bore to Eleanor. Neame was a fascinating man with a history in films that went back to his parents: His father was a silent movie director and his mother a film star. He had worked his way up the studio ladder from errand boy to cinematographer to screenwriter to director and producer. In one capacity or another he worked on such classics as *Great Expectations, One of Our Aircraft Is Missing, Blithe Spirit* and *In Which We Serve,* and later films such as *Tunes of Glory, The*

Prime of Miss Jean Brodie, *The Odessa File* and *The Poseidon Adventure*. His son and grandson would both carry on the family tradition of filmmaking. I had heard that Neame had only taken this job because he would get a tax break out of it, as it meant he would be out of his home country over a certain number of days during the year, and that could go a long way towards explaining the tedium of the final product and why he was eventually replaced by Vincente Minnelli.

We worked long hours to make use of available light and to get as much on film as possible, given the short time we had to be there. Usually we had to be ready to leave the hotel by six in the morning, and we would return around six in the evening. We filmed on Victoria Peak (referred to simply as "the Peak" by local people) probably Hong Kong's most enduring tourist attraction from where many breathtaking views had been shot in 1955 for *Love Is a Many-Splendored Thing*. The seventy-year-old cable-hauled railway took us 1300 feet almost straight up in just seven minutes to where the view of Victoria, the harbor and Kowloon left us speechless.

When we were done there, we moved locations to Aberdeen, a fishing village where people lived either on the large junks that were about 40 to 150 feet long with large masts and black sails, or on the smaller sampans. These boats served as both their livelihood and their homes, and typically you would find the entire family on board, old and young, along with dogs and chickens and whatever tools and supplies they might need for their work. Some of them had reached ninety years of age and had never lived on land. It was full-time living on water. The worst part for me was that the only rest rooms for most people, including us, were out-houses extended over the water. I tried once, and after that I chose to "hold it" till we got to the hotel at night. There were times when that was a really difficult challenge, but it shows what you can do when you consider there is no alternative.

Most of the population seemed never to have seen anyone with red hair! For a few days, we were shooting aboard a floating restaurant that looked like an enormous, long pagoda covered at night in neon lights. You arrived there by motor launch, so there was much filming of me entering and leaving and embarking and disembarking. The first day we were there, I attracted a great mob of people who gathered around me giggling and pointing to my hair, which was reddish blonde to match Eleanor. When I wasn't working, I was usually sitting in a chair under an umbrella surrounded by the Chinese hairdresser, makeup girl, and interpreter.

However, these crowds were downright intimate and friendly compared to the frightening size of the crowds that could gather in Kowloon. Hong Kong might have been only about the size of California's Catalina Island but something like two million people lived here, and some days it would seem that most of them had nothing to do but gather to watch us work. And gather they did on the day that we shot a high-speed car scene along a steep, narrow and winding road in Kowloon. I was doubling once again as the car passenger for the long shots while Bill Travers was ostensibly driving us to a formal party. Consequently, I was dressed in an exquisite Helen Rose red satin evening gown teamed with jeweled dangle earrings to accentuate my strawberry-blonde hair and to add to the dazzle. The script called for us to be in the midst of a terrible argument while we were hurtling around bends and dodging people. Neame's philosophy was similar to the one I had encountered on the set of *The Rains of Ranchipur* which was that people's reactions would be more realistic if they didn't know what was about to happen. So, the locals along the road weren't informed that a movie was being filmed. Neame wanted their spontaneous reaction to almost being run over while they attempted frantically to get out of the way.

However, by our third take down that same road, the community had caught on, and when we stopped this time, our little black English car was instantly drowned in a sea of people before we could even get out. There were so many packed into that space, their faces were pressed flat against the windows. Unfortunately for us, the locks had been removed from the doors in case we needed to exit the car quickly if it ran off the road, and it didn't take the crowd long to discover that. Soon they were jerking the doors open and slamming them shut, laughing at the noise. The car began to rock back and forth under the impact of the doors and the pressure of the crowd, and it was quickly escalating into quite a frightening situation that might easily get out of hand considering the political climate. At the time, professional Communist agitators were known to infiltrate similar crowds in this neighborhood, often with violent results. Finally, Neame and his crew broke through the mob to rescue us. I was so relieved. It seemed to be growing in numbers by the minute, and I could sense the feeling of good-will beginning to fade. The director ordered me taken straight back to my hotel; I don't think I could have stood up to another take under those conditions. When I look back on it all now, they were probably just a highly inquisitive group of Chinese citizens who had never seen anything quite like a film being shot before or quite like me, for that matter. Once again, my red-blond hair had seemed to be the strangest thing they had ever seen. They were staring at it and pointing it out to others in the road, accompanied by loud exclamations. At the time, though, it felt like a potentially volatile situation that I was very glad to leave behind me.

Stressful as it was because of the crowds, we chose to eat each night at Jimmy's Kitchen, a restaurant that resembled an American steak house with an American menu and booth seating. Their steaks were extraordinary and their shrimp cocktails made your mouth water just to look at them. Now, the American Chinese cuisine of the 1950s didn't really have a lot in common with authentic Chinese food, and so for many of us, this was our first exposure to the real thing. We realized we had a lot to learn. I recall one Hong Kong restaurant in particular because it was a French restaurant that served Chinese food. The place was elaborately decorated in thick red carpets and gold trim on the walls with white linen table cloths, quality china and real crystal. The waiter for your table came by and spread the napkin in your lap. I was all prepared for a dining experience like I had at the Forbidden City in San Francisco, owned by polo player Charlie Lowe. But when they brought me a bowl of shark fin soup and it kept slipping off the spoon, I suddenly lost my appetite. Bob said that if I liked the food, I should just eat it and not ask too many questions about what was in it, but before long we were back in Jimmy's Kitchen and their comfortable booths.

When I was leaving Hong Kong, my hairdresser gave me a very fine china tea set. I carried it personally all the way home on one airplane after the other and it arrived with nary a chip. A few years later, I moved to another area and had a professional moving company pack and ship my things. When I opened the box, that precious tea set was in a hundred pieces and not one cup or saucer could I save.

My journey home was just as exciting as the trip out. This time, we flew a different route in a TWA Constellation over the Aleutian Islands off the coast of Alaska, advertised as the shortest route with the slogan: "Never more than a hundred miles from land." I was quite sure I could not swim a hundred feet, let alone a hundred miles should the need arise, so that line did not impress me in the least. What did impress me, however, was that the Constellation had berths like a Pullman car on a train; they made up into the most comfortable beds.

Of course, these planes had nothing like the fuel capacity and flight endurance of modern planes. Long-distance flying in the fifties was still a series of hops between one re-fueling point and the next, even in large aircraft such as the Constellation. So, we landed at Shemya Island for re-fueling. Shemya is considered the Black Pearl of the Aleutian Islands, located near the western end of the chain approximately 1,500 miles from Anchorage, Alaska. It was literally just a long landing strip in the middle of the ocean that had been used extensively by the military in World War II. All passengers had to vacate the plane during the re-fueling process, but I got to stay in my berth because I had an awful cold.

After our tanks were topped off, everyone was re-boarded and we lined up on the runway for the last leg of our journey to Seattle. But as we were tearing down the runway towards our lift-off point, the pilot suddenly began to apply the brakes, threw the engines into reverse thrust and endeavored to stop the aircraft before we ran out of runway. We howled to a stop at the end of the tarmac with me folded up against the head board of my berth. As the dust settled, an apologetic pilot's voice over the speaker said the cockpit fire warning light had come on as we were almost at the lift-off point and so the take-off had to be aborted. With our full wing tanks, we would have had to circle and dump the fuel before landing again, an extremely hazardous procedure if there really was a fire somewhere. Needless to say, it was a terrifying experience for us all. Finally, after about an hour of checking every possible thing, the crew concluded that a change in atmospheric pressure, not a change in temperature, had caused the warning light to go on, and so we took off hoping they had come to the right conclusion.

Maybe it had all been just as traumatic for the pilot as for us passengers. About noon the next day, the captain came wandering into the main cabin as drunk as the proverbial skunk. The co-pilot quickly appeared right behind him to assure us that there was someone else who could fly the plane and that *he* would bring us into Seattle. I think that somehow we all understood exactly how that captain felt. He sat down in the main passenger cabin and remained with us for the rest of our several hours' flying time. When our wheels eventually touched ground again in Seattle, we all breathed a deep sigh of relief, then shook that captain's hand and thanked him for saving our lives. Sitting in my seat on the short flight back to Los Angeles, I reflected that while it was usually the action in our movie work that was the highlight of a location trip, this time there had been more action off-camera than on.

Unfortunately, while we certainly worked hard making *The Seventh Sin*, the movie apparently didn't work for the audience. Perhaps that's no surprise, considering it's full of hospitals, cholera, brooding husbands, selfish wives and melodramatics topped off with some wooden acting by Bill Travers. Nine years later, he would be wonderful in the role of George Adamson in *Born Free* but Travers' heart just didn't seem to be in the role of an obsessed doctor married to a selfish wife (Parker) who eventually embarks on an affair with a French businessman (Jean-Pierre Aumont). When her husband finds out, he gives her the choice of joining him in Hong Kong fighting cholera or being pilloried in a public divorce. She chooses Hong Kong where she is initially bored, angry, and potentially distracted by George Sanders. She finally comes to see the light and appreciate her husband's devotion to the good of mankind.

However, this version brought no new insight to Somerset Maugham's original story. While his exotically scented brand of soap may well have had his readers in a lather, you can't keep washing in yesterday's suds. Worse still, given the lack of spark in Travers' personality, it was a tad difficult for many women in the audience to accept that Parker would choose to be with him in cholera-ridden Hong Kong rather than escape into the arms of the incredibly romantic Aumont or suave Sanders. It was also regrettable that, considering the beauty of the Hong Kong scenery, the producers chose to shoot in black and white. Perhaps Warner thought time would change perceptions. In 2007 they cranked up the soap machine again and released yet another version of *The Painted Veil*, starring Naomi Watts and Edward Norton. This time around it was possible to shoot most of the movie on location in China and, of course, to do it in color, but just like our version this one also received mixed reviews.

I had hated leaving my Sancho and the horses, but this was scheduled to be only a week-long trip. To my surprise, they all treated me as a stranger upon my return. I must no longer have smelled like myself, but like some stranger from the East. Since then, whenever I have walked into a store and inhaled that same scent, I'm taken back to Kowloon and those lights on the water and that endless sea of faces.

14

April Love

Everything wonderful happens in *April Love*. Springtime! County fair Time! First-kiss Time!
— advertising for the film in which Pat Boone actually refused to kiss Shirley Jones because of his principles

Sometimes the location or the circumstances surrounding the filming of a picture far surpass the memories and charm of whatever work you were required to do on it. *April Love,* a musical remake of Henry Hathaway's 1944 film *Home in Indiana* starring Walter Brennan, Lon McAllister and Jeanne Crain, was one of those films. Most people seem to remember the theme song rather than the film, which is quite understandable. While Pat Boone's version of the song "April Love" became a #1 hit in the U.S. in December, 1957, and was nominated the following year for an Academy Award for Best Music and Lyrics, the film is one of those bland, happy-ending moral fables the fifties era was so good at producing. Young Nick Conover (Boone) is forced to leave Chicago for the Kentucky farm of Uncle Jed (Arthur O'Connell) and Aunt Henrietta (Jeanette Nolan) after being put on probation for car theft. Uncle Jed is still getting over the death of his boy and so Nick isn't exactly welcome. Fortunately, he has sweet Aunt Henrietta and two pretty young neighbors, including the delightful Shirley Jones, to help rehabilitate him, along with the inevitable wild horse that needs to be tamed. Well, after all, this is Kentucky! Probably the liveliest thing about this film at the time was Boone's flat refusal, for religious and family reasons, to kiss Shirley Jones on-screen.

Though Lexington, Kentucky, is usually recorded as the primary location for the film, much of it was actually shot at the Devonshire Downs Race Track and Fair Grounds in Northridge, California, which is some twenty miles northwest of Los Angeles and was then a gem of a rural area in the legendary San Fernando Valley. Northridge was a mecca for those Hollywood stars who liked horses or just enjoyed being out of town. In 1935 Barbara Stanwyck moved to Northridge and with her neighbor, agent Zeppo Marx, jointly formed the 140-acre Marwyck Ranch where they raised thoroughbreds. She commissioned an English Manor–style house from Paul R. Williams, one of Hollywood's favorite architects, but after marrying Robert Taylor she sold her share of the business to Marx and the home and land to comic actor Jack Oakie in about 1941; Oakie renamed it Oakridge. The Oakies would hold Sunday afternoon pool parties that became legendary amongst neighbors such as Lucille Ball and Desi Arnaz, Gordon MacRae, Lionel Barrymore and William Holden.

Not far away was Northridge Farms, another large breeding ranch for thoroughbreds, that sprawled along Reseda Boulevard. Betty Grable and Harry James owned the fifteen-acre Baby J Ranch at 18102 Devonshire, where they had nine mares and their stallions Big Noise and Laughin Louie. Fred Astaire's twenty-acre Blue Valley Ranch was at 10901 Melvin Avenue, Chatsworth, Lou Costello owned the Bold Bazooka ranch, and George Brent had the fifty-acre Royal Oaks Farm. Cowboy star Montie Montana was actually honorary mayor of Northridge for many years, always appearing at the head of the annual equestrian parade, the Northridge Stampede. Among other ranch-dwelling residents were Walter Brennan, James Cagney, Jim Davis, Al Jolson, Slim Pickens, Roy Rogers and that famous cowboy Ronald Reagan. The smell of orange blossoms seemed to permeate the air among the walnut groves, pepper tree–lined driveways and acres of green grass criss-crossed with white fences. And of course the ubiquitous eucalyptus trees will seldom be forgotten by those of us fortunate enough to have lived there. My bedroom window had a huge orange tree just outside. Early every morning, a little breeze would drift in the windows filled with the smell of orange blossoms.

The little hamlet of Northridge was also home to one of the most legendary horse trainers of our time, Clyde Kennedy. I am sure Clyde could not remember how many stars he taught to ride or the number of films in which he doubled someone. Tab Hunter and Dan Dailey were almost fixtures at his stables, as both actors were professional caliber riders and showed in the jumping horse classes at major shows, and I would often see Pam Powell there, too. She was the daughter of Edward Powell, the fine orchestrator who had more than two hundred musicals to his credit and who worked with musical director Alfred Newman on *April Love*. A fine rider, Pam later married the well-known show horse trainer Mack Lynn.

But the real reason I remember Clyde Kennedy's Northridge stables is because of Don Burt. He was working there before he opened his own training stable in Sylmar. Clyde trained Baldy, who was Pacific Coast Pleasure Horse Champion before the golden palomino jumped flat-footed out of a six-foot corral when frightened by a fire engine and instantly established himself in a new career as a jumping horse! Still, that didn't mean he was an easy horse to ride over jumps. Don's ability to do it led to Baldy winning the Big Jump at the legendary Cow Palace in San Francisco, at that time the biggest jumping competition in the western United States. That win launched Don's career as a major rider and trainer.

Not long before that, I had purchased from stuntman Clint Sharp, a wonderful horse named Jim, with which I had worked on a jumping horse job at Twentieth Century–Fox. As soon as I picked up the reins, I knew I must own this horse; he was so easy to jump that he seemed to float. I bought him that very same day! One weekend soon after, I thought it would be fun to take him to a small schooling show at an outdoor show ring. We entered the arena all spit and polished with me in casual riding attire of brown jodphurs, jodphur boots and blue and white rat-catcher shirt, made our usual circle and headed to the first fence. Whoa! To my utter amazement, the horse slid to a stop! Well, you are given three tries before being "excused" and we were excused. I can still hear that announcer yet, "Thank *you!*"

I was still sitting on him outside the arena, somewhat stunned at what had just happened (or rather not happened), when an Audie Murphy lookalike wearing a white shirt, britches, and custom high-top western boots slowly walked over, looked up at me, introduced himself as Don, and asked where I had bought that horse. I told him that he'd been Clint Sharp's horse, and Don replied, "Well, before that he used to be mine." He'd been at the Caliente track in New Mexico one day and seen Jim, a chestnut thoroughbred of about sixteen hands, tied to a trailer. Liking the look of him, Don had promptly bought the horse for a mere $25 because no one knew much about his history. Eventually Don had traded him to Jimmy Williams, the Hall of Fame jumping horse trainer, who put him through a crash course in jumping. But it was too much too soon for Jim, and after that experience he would never jump inside a show ring. I looked over at where we had just been and I think a light bulb went on over my head. Don eventually became an American Horse Shows Association judge and president of the American Quarterhorse Association. Little did I know just how much my first meeting with that man would impact on my future, and the yellow brick roads down which I would consequently travel.

Some time later, Jim was sold to Clint Sharp, who figured out that he would still jump just as long as it was outside of a ring. So, out in the open on movie sets Jim happily jumped moving cars, burning wagons, through windows and just about anything else they could put in front of or underneath him. He went on to become one of the best movie stunt horses ever, and insiders marveled at his many accomplishments. As talented as he was, though, Jim was really just one among a litany of horses contributing to a film industry that has neither rewarded nor awarded them.

So, there I was at picturesque Devonshire Downs to double for Shirley Jones in *April Love*. In 1943 Helen Dillman, a wealthy Valley resident, and horseman Pete Spears had purchased the 40-acre Devonshire Downs tract near the intersection of present Devonshire and Zelzah Avenue for $80,000. They opened a large part of the property to horsemen and it became a training and boarding center for standardbreds. About two years later, the San Fernando Valley Trotting Association was formed and the Downs started holding harness races on Sunday afternoons in 1946. Weekly quarterhorse races were added the following year, and the Downs quickly became the center of equestrian Northridge. Two years later, the state purchased the land for supplementary use as the home of the San Fernando Valley Fair. Every summer, neighborhood children would show off their prize pet rabbits, sheep and horses. For many years, the Downs also hosted the July 4 fireworks and the Scoutcraft Fair.

Of all the horses that trained at Devonshire Downs, possibly the most famous was Silky Sullivan, often ridden by Willie Shoemaker and trained by West Coast veteran Reggie Cornell, who was Betty Grable's favorite trainer. Silky was famous as the horse who came from behind to win; he once won a race in 1958 by three lengths after starting his run from forty-one lengths back. That same year, he won the Santa Anita Derby from twenty-eight lengths behind. After he was retired to stud, he continued to be paraded each St. Patrick's Day at the Golden Gate Fields track and at every Santa Anita Derby, and when he died in 1977 he was buried under the infield at Golden Gate Fields. He sired a number of winners and his bloodline is continued on in many quarterhorses today. The words "silky sullivan" eventually entered the racing lexicon as a term for holding back before making a huge bid for a win.

For *April Love*, I was at Devonshire Downs to double Shirley Jones riding a trotting horse around the race track bareback at a full extended trot. We finished the lap without any problem but, to my surprise, I then discovered I couldn't pull up my horse. He was a retired harness horse, and he was having such a great time being back on a track that he had absolutely no intention of quitting before he was good and ready. It was the first time I had ever been run off with from a trot, but far from being angry I couldn't stop laughing at this ridiculous situation. Here was I, who had been on horses almost before I walked, and this old horse was not going to let me tell him what to do. Nothing I tried worked. Of course, my uncontrollable laughter didn't help stop the horse either, but it did eventually attract the attention of an outrider who saw my dilemma and came to my rescue.

While we were at the track, I was asked to give Shirley some lessons in driving a trotting horse in a sulky, and I have never met anyone else that took to it so fast and so well. Had she ever been interested, I'm sure she could have driven on the trotting horse circuit with just a little more experience under her belt. A lovely lady and a natural horsewoman, Shirley was a rare person to meet.

There is nothing left of Devonshire Downs today. The track is long gone, as are the stables and corrals. It exists now only in the memories of a few people as a historic feature of Californian horse-training and racing and, of course, as the location of a number of enjoyable films, least of all *April Love*. On the other hand, for another generation the Downs is remembered in an entirely different way. During the three-day weekend of June 20–22, 1969, it was the site of the infamous second Newport Pop Festival. Some 200,000 people packed the area to experience acts such as the Jimi Hendrix Experience, Eric Burdon, Marvin Gaye, Joe Cocker, Creedence Clearwater Revival, Jethro Tull, the Byrds and many others. It all ended in a riot on the Sunday afternoon during which police trying to clear the neighborhood area were struck with rocks and bottles; fifteen police and three hundred people eventually needed medical treatment. Shocked city politicians banned any more concerts. At the time, it was the nation's largest outdoor rock event, but it was overtaken by Woodstock within a few months. By then, however, Devonshire Downs had already been acquired by the expanding San Fernando Valley State College (now CSUN), and its horse days were numbered. The land is currently being developed as a residential community for CSUN faculty and staff. But I will always remember the sounds of the horses there, the rustle of the walnut groves and the smell of the orange blossoms.

The Northridge area itself is now probably best remembered as being close to the epicenter of the devastating earthquake of January 17, 1994. Measured at 6.7 on the Richter scale and occurring along a previously unknown fault line, the earthquake's ground acceleration was the highest ever instrumentally recorded in an urban area in North America. The damage was devastating, and fifty-seven lives were lost.

15

The Big Country

There's no prettier sight in the world than 10,000 head of cattle ...
unless it's 400.
— an adaption of a line spoken by Major Terrill

Right from the beginning, this was a Catch-22 job. The troubles were
not just mine, though, but involved most members of the superb cast of
the 1958 film *The Big Country* and the production team as well. It was as
if the location was jinxed, and I am still in awe as to how so such a fine
film emerged from the tangle of problems that had to be overcome.

On this production, I would be doubling two very fine actors, Jean
Simmons and Carroll Baker. Jean stole your heart in her role and in the
stealing easily maintained her reputation as a beautiful, classic actress who
I found was totally without ego. She was obviously thrilled to be able to
ride her own horse, Harry Boy, in this film and she was quite a good horsewoman in her own right. Carroll was also amazing at handling what turned
out to be a problematic shoot on which she had to endure a difficult director, William Wyler, along with wearing restraining garments to minimize
the show of her four-month pregnancy. On the other hand, her painful
shyness and extreme sensitivity meant she could be a difficult person to
understand. I really don't know how she did it, but Carroll could have you
hating her. Still, that is what the part called for. Personally, I thought that
Wyler was very hard on her; in one scene on the ranch house steps, he had
her on the verge of tears because she could not seem to meet his standards
for a satisfactory take. Finally, as he so often did, he used the first take
anyway, after putting her through total humiliation and hell while making her repeat the take about sixty times under a cruelly hot sun.

I have often laughed at the write-ups and glorified publicity claim-
ing that stars in *The Big Country* did all their own fight scenes. They most

certainly did not. Most of the time, stunts and action shots are done with the second unit and usually another director, allowing the film shoot to roll along faster and freeing up the principals for work on another set. The most famous fight scene was between Jim McKay (Gregory Peck) and Steve Leach (Charlton Heston) but, despite claims to the contrary, two of the best fight stunt men in the business also worked in this scene. Chuck Roberson doubled Greg and Bob Morgan doubled Heston. They worked really hard at that fight, and consequently it has gone down in film history as one of the best ever. Unfortunately Bob Morgan, who was married to Yvonne De Carlo, would later be so severely injured in an accident on the set of *How the West Was Won* that he was no longer able to do stunt work. Both stunt men are gone now, but they are in the Hollywood Stuntman's Hall of Fame and their contributions to western films will long be remembered.

Early in my movie career I quit trying to figure out the continuity of a film while I was working there, and *The Big Country* was no exception. Films are usually shot in a sequence that has little to do with the plot but more to do with actor or location availability, crew availability, economic demands, script demands or sometimes just the whim of the director. I just went where they sent me, and so once again I spent a lot of time during the three months of this long location shoot in "hurry-up-and-wait" mode.

Contrary to how it might seem on award nights, a film production company on location is rarely the "one big happy family" that people might prefer to remember later. More often, it customarily resembles a gathering of tribes that temporarily either resolves or postpones their differences in order to join together and dance. In the film business, you see, the caste system has always been very much alive and breathing on the set and so, as a rule, the stars don't fall as far as the earth on which the lowly stunt person treads now, and they didn't then. After a day's work, they retired to their personalized trailers while we to our scattered motel rooms went. *Yellow Sky* was my sole exception to the rule, one of the rare film shoots on which I was invited to socialize with the stars after work.

Now, because I was from the Stunt Person tribe I was rarely acknowledged for anything I did. We were hired to do the impossible, so compliments were apparently considered redundant. My thanks would be a call from the studio on another day to do more work for them. If they didn't like your work, you didn't get the call. I suppose that, one way or another, news about my merit was passed on by word-of-mouth amongst the casting directors because I kept on receiving those calls. Our closest contacts were usually the wranglers, who fit you to the horse and vice versa. They were the people who had the real power to assess your abilities and to use you or not. Many people in the industry were not aware that a casting director often left the selection of a star's double to the wranglers, who considered all aspects of the work to be done and pretty well knew the capabilities of the doubles and stunt people who were available to do it. The top man was the ramrod wrangler, who had an office at the studio and was furnished a full working script of the film so that he could select the animals and the riders required.

The Big Country is about two families feuding over water rights, yet it is also a tribute to honor and decency and the benefits of diplomacy, rather than the brinkmanship and grudges that can lead to mutual destruction. It was said to be one of President Dwight D. Eisenhower's favorite movies for just that reason. Most of the shooting took place on the Orvis Cattle Company's Snow Ranch, established in 1873 to the west of Farmington, just outside of Stockton, California, where vast, grassy areas substituted for the untamed, unsettled areas of the West. It was also later used as the location for the *Little House on the Prairie* television series. The "desert ranch" scenes used the stark beauty of the towering canyons within Red Rock Canyon State Park, some twenty-five miles northeast of Mojave, California, while some other footage was shot in the legendary Canyon de Chelly National Monument, in Chinle, Arizona. After the shoot was over, most of the buildings constructed for the town were eventually moved to Pollardville, north of Stockton. The Stockton area has, in fact, been the location for over forty movies including *Cool Hand Luke, Fat City, God's Little Acre, Raiders of the Lost Ark* and *Indiana Jones and the Last Crusade,* and the television series *The Big Valley.*

The good days on location were very good and the bad days were very bad, and some days were such a mixture that all you could do was laugh. It was extremely hot weather. Most of us were staying at the wonderful old Stockton Hotel, right in downtown Stockton opposite Hunter Square, and each evening we would congregate in the bar for refreshments to cool down. I am a minimal social drinker but they taught me to drink Heinekens by loading me up on the salty beer nuts. My education was so effective that to this day when I see a Heineken bottle I still think of beer nuts. Then, each morning the limo would pick us up and take us about twenty minutes outside of town into a whole new world where rolling, golden-colored grassland stretched out to the horizon for miles and miles.

Gregory Peck and William Wyler had decided to co-produce *The Big Country*, having persuaded United Artists to fund it with a $2,800,000 budget, and Greg had personally hired me for the job. He and Wyler, who were good friends, had decided to divide up the producing responsibilities on the picture: Wyler as director would be in charge of artistic matters such as shooting and editing, while Peck would have casting and script approval and supervise ranching matters such as hiring the wranglers, horses and cattle. Peck already had a cattle business, leased grazing land and could ride, rope and brand so it was an area with which he was familiar. They wanted a commercial hit, but also realized that the script was nowhere near ready. In the end at least seven writers, including Leon Uris, would try to make it work. James R. Webb and Sy Bartlett were still working on the script when shooting started in July. I ran into Sy one morning at the hotel for breakfast. He had been a very good friend of Carl, my late stepfather, but I had not seen him since I was a child so he was pleasantly surprised to discover that I was working in the industry. He told me no one could agree on the ending yet, which didn't surprise me in the least. It wasn't a good sign.

Some films and locations just have wonderful vibes where you know that cast and crew will all contribute to a smooth production, but there was little of that on the set of *The Big Country*. While this four-month shoot over two major locations, with a few breaks in between and interior shots at the studio, was excellent pay for me, each day's work felt like the sound of fingernails on a blackboard. The tension that prevailed on this set never let up for the duration of the time I was there. Wyler had a reputation as one of the slowest and most meticulous directors in the business. He had been known to shoot as many as sixty retakes of even the simplest scenes in order to get just the take he wanted. Needless to say, his methods infuriated a lot of people. He seemed to believe that he could only get his best performance from an actor after he'd provoked them into walking off the set. He did such an excellent job with angering stubborn Charlie Bickford over a series of retakes, for example, that he had to threaten him with calling the Screen Actors Guild and telling them Charlie wasn't fulfilling the terms of his contract to get him to emerge from his trailer and come back on the set. He periodically reduced Carroll Baker to tears, and Jean Simmons just plain refused to talk about her experience for years. Like just about everyone else, I had my problems with him. However, had I followed my heart and walked off the set I would have never worked for United Artists again and, besides, I thought then that it would not be fair to my mentor, Gregory Peck. So, I tried my best to grin and bear it. Little did I know what would eventually happen.

Location trips are usually graced with marvelous box lunches supplied by local restaurants designated as caterers. One day, when it was about 117 degrees, it came time for lunch and I was desperate to find some shade. There was an old dilapidated farmhouse with no windows or doors that had become incorporated into the set, having been surrounded by a façade representing the massive, rich, ranch home of Ladder Ranch, and right about then it looked pretty inviting. So, I took my box lunch inside and sat down at a table on which a copy of *Life* magazine lay open. Suddenly, I heard, "All quiet on the set!" and I realized that the third assistant director or someone must be shooting right outside the house. I froze as still as a mouse hearing a cat. Right then, a gust of wind blew through the frame structure and flipped open a page of the large magazine. Amplified through the big microphone on the other side of the wall, the sound of that page flutter ruined their shot. Furious, the assistant director stormed into the shack and tore into me for doing it. Of course I knew better than to do any such thing, and I told him so in a few choice words but he wasn't in a mood to listen. From that day forward, I was on his list.

Later that day, doubling for Carroll Baker, I was required to get on a horse outside the local hotel and ride out of the scene. I untied the horse from the hitch rail and mounted up but, before I knew what was happening, that horse proceeded to walk off right out of the shot! No matter what I did, I could not stop that horse until he finally just lost interest. By then, I was sure I was on my way home, whether I wanted to go or not. Wyler's face was as beet-red as the assistant director's. They'd probably been yelling a lot, something Wyler could do very well on occasions, but I'd been kind of busy with that horse and I hadn't heard them. So, I just affected a completely innocent expression as if they should have known this horse always did that, and they gave us one more try. Fortunately, that was all we needed and this time they got the shot just as they wanted it.

But that horse and I hadn't finished being in trouble yet. My next direction was to ride across the top of a nearby hill in a silhouette shot. It sounded simple enough, but evidently no one had actually gone up that hill to check out the ground. When I dutifully rode to the top of the designated hill, I discovered that there was no defined top to ride over. It wasn't really a hill, just a series of rises. I had to ride back and forth for an hour until Wyler was happy with a take. By the end of that day, I could feel the noose tightening around my neck.

It wasn't just stressful on the set. I am sure the Stockton Hotel could tell many stories, and I added at least one. Built in 1910 at a cost of $500,000, this elegant five-story building with its central tower topped with a tall flagpole had over 200 rooms. When I arrived there, stuntman Bob Morgan and his wife Yvonne De Carlo were moved into a larger room while I was given their room. As I was unpacking my things and putting them away in the dresser drawers, I found a great deal of very expensive jewelry tucked into the back of one of the drawers. As she had only just vacated the room, I could only assume it had belonged to Yvonne and of course I immediately went to their room to hand the jewelry back to her. I thought she'd be really happy to have it returned but to my surprise she was furious, so furious that she didn't even thank me. I couldn't believe it. She just snatched it out of my hands and slammed the door! After some thought back in my room that night, I came to the conclusion that I had probably inadvertently stumbled on a ruse that she had been trying to pull with her insurance company, and I had gone and ruined it all. Ironically, we were probably the last film crew to stay at the hotel, as it closed only two years later. Used as county and state government offices for many years, it was converted for apartment and retail use in 2005 and is now on the National Register of Historic Places.

The cast had dinner most every night at a wonderful Italian restaurant called Bruno and Lena's. The food was extraordinary. Over dinner we talked about the food and how Bruno had fed every soldier that walked into his restaurant for free. Years later, when I went in search of this restaurant while passing through Stockton, I was told that Internal Revenue had shut them down. It seems the tax assessors expected Bruno to pay tax on all of those free charitable meals. It must have broken his heart.

I tend to think that stressful behavior is like a contagious disease; people get to treating each other badly because of it and next thing they're beating up on the animals. One morning, I was watching the crew shooting a scene involving a tall, strong major supporting actor sitting on a beautiful, big chestnut horse as he looked down to the river towards where the cattle were crossing. My eyes fell warily on the long, fixed-shank Western bit in his horse's mouth. I had never liked those bits. Suddenly, in an overly dramatic move, Chuck Connors wrenched his mount around to ride away and broke that horse's jaw on the spot with the bit. To my disappointment and sadness, he showed absolutely no remorse whatsoever for what he had just done to an unsuspecting animal that was merely trying to obey instructions. This was a man who was accustomed to working with horses and who eventually starred in his own television Western series. He should have known better.

A few days later, I was sitting in my favorite place atop a ladder, waiting to work. I saw Wyler look at me and then summon an assistant director over to him for some conversation. He pointed at me. "Oh-oh! Here it comes," I thought. "I'm finally fired." It would be a first for me; despite not being shy about expressing my opinion, I'd yet to be actually fired from a job. Nothing happened immediately, but my mind still worked overtime and I fell into a kind of daze until lunch when that assistant finally found me. Instead of bringing bad news, however, he said that Wyler wanted me to take all my meals with Jean Simmons so that she could try and modify her English accent by listening to me and picking up some of my "Western twang." He offered to pay me an extra $100 per week, so Jean and I exchanged glances, shrugged and agreed to talk about it later. It had probably been Greg Peck's idea rather than Wyler's, because we had known each other a long time and he knew my voice. In the end, though, Jean and I never did take too many meals together. She felt her opinion had not been invited about these impromptu lessons and so maintained she had other plans. But, I still got paid. Things were looking up. The pendulum has to swing the other way sooner or later.

I've always thought that the scene I found most entertaining to watch being shot was when Slim Pickens, doubling Gregory Peck, did the bucking horse routine with his trained horses, John and Little John, in the Old Thunder sequence. It might have been fun for me, but I doubt it was a lot of fun for Pickens. Wyler, as usual, had Slim do the bucking horse routine over and over again. His horse, John, was a highly trained Appaloosa that Slim used in his rodeo act. You can only buck these horses on cue so many times and after that, understandably, they tend to get somewhat annoyed. If you persist, they get downright angry and then you don't want to be anywhere near them, believe me. John was no exception, and Slim was being slammed to the ground harder and harder as John became angrier. Now, as I've mentioned before, a stunt such as this was only paid for if it was a "print," so Pickens was only being paid the day rate for each time he was slammed into the ground until the director decided he had a fall fit for a print. Unlike Peck, Wyler had no idea of a horse's capabilities, nor did he seem to care. He just had Slim and John perform repeat takes until it was a coin toss who was angrier. I would say he finally got a print take only just in time before Slim grabbed Wyler and tied him to the horse to see how he liked it! I shared a dressing room on set with Slim, and any other time he was really just a sheer delight to know. I was one of the few people who knew that, as well as working on location during the day, Slim was also clowning the local rodeo at the Stockton fairgrounds at night until exhaustion took its toll one evening and he was nearly killed by a bull. How do I know that? Well, I was also leading the rodeo parade every night.

For me, a real highlight of *The Big Country* shoot was to see Buff Brady and Chuck Hayward's trick riding scenes. Buff rides a running horse, his own trick riding horse, backwards and then flips to the ground and "walks" behind the running horse for a long ways. By this I mean he walks in step with the horse's hind legs while it was in a full run. It was amazing work to see. Chuck Hayward doubled as the Hannassy boy who jumps onto the running team and buckboard with me and Chuck Roberson, doubling Baker and Peck, and rides the team Roman style, standing up with one foot on each saddle. In the movie, Baker has just met Peck at the stage depot and the local roughnecks are going to show this dude from the East a welcome he will not forget. Trying to scare the newcomer, Hayward ducks down as if he has fallen and then comes up again on the horses that, while perhaps not the quickest team in the world, are nevertheless running as flat out. It was something to see and one of the last great riding stunts as far as I know. Chuck Hayward died in 1998, and it was a great loss to the stuntmen fraternity. Jim Burk also did a hilarious stunt by getting on a horse with the wrong foot in the stirrup and getting all tangled up without being hurt. The stunts were slick, expertly done and quite extraordinary when you think about the technique and years of practice involved.

My own *pièce de résistance* came soon enough. Julie's (Jean Simmons) cabin was situated downhill from the main ranch house. I was to run out the door carrying a real rifle, untie my horse, swing up, ride bareback as fast as possible up the hill to the main house and then do a running dismount about ten feet from the camera. At the same time, I had to remember to duck my head so the audience would not see this was really me instead of Jean. The stunt men offered to help by burying a trampoline to help me swing on to my mount, but I declined. After all, I had done something similar to this for that *Have Gun — Will Travel* television episode while carrying a duck as well as the rifle, and that had been a bareback mount.

So, I rehearsed my routine and realized that, once again, the weight of the rifle was actually going to be a help in swinging up onto the bareback horse. Still, I was nervous. There was a lot to remember. The first take worked like a charm. It went so well that I relaxed, took a deep breath and was just starting to sit down as I congratulated myself when I heard those dreaded words, "Now do it again!" Oh no! But I did do it again, and again it worked. For the first time in my career, I received an ovation from the crew as I did the running dismount. I was so thrilled to receive such an accolade from my peers. It was truly the highlight of all the films I worked on.

But for every highlight there's a low point, and I hit one of those in *The Big Country*, too. In the last scene of the movie, I was given an older horse to ride down a very steep hill. For some reason, the director kept insisting we do the shot over and over. I would ride that horse down the hill, then get off and walk him back up the hill until I was the one that eventually collapsed, to resume consciousness much later in the first aid trailer. The horse was just fine. They still use that shot in the trailers for the video version you can see today.

Unfortunately, my misgivings about the vibes on this picture proved right. The relationship between Peck and Wyler steadily deteriorated after an incident involving cattle. Earlier in the shoot, he and Wyler had planned a sweeping panorama of the livestock grazing on the Terrill ranch for which Greg ordered an impressive 4,000 head of cattle, with a price tag of $10 per head per day. On the day of the shot, Peck arrived to see just a few cattle scattered across the range. Wyler had a rare bout of economizing and, without consulting Peck, had changed the order to 400 head. Consequently, what should have been an extraordinary framing of rolling pasture filled with cattle as far as the eye could see, emphasizing the theme of a "big country," was reduced to an average ranch of a few hundred head. Wyler was seldom this wrong, but Peck had been right in his original estimate and he knew it.

However, the final bale of hay that caused this barn to collapse was Wyler's refusal to shoot a retake of a close-up in the buckboard scene early in the movie when the Hannassey boys tie Peck up alongside it. Peck wasn't happy with his take on the scene at the time and wanted to do it again, but Wyler kept postponing any retake until the day before they were leaving the location. Peck saw it still wasn't scheduled and queried Wyler, who flew into a rage and shouted that it wasn't going to happen. By now they were over-schedule and over-budget; the original $2,800,000 had blown out to $4,100,000, and they still didn't have an ending. Peck went to his trailer, got out of his costume and makeup, climbed into his car and drove

The young daughter of Snow Ranch owner Bill Orvis looks out from the hill where, in *The Big Country*, Gregory Peck sits on his horse studying his map, with the same tree and horseshoe creek bend over his shoulder. The ruins in the foreground are all that remain of a famous little house on the prairie (Courtesy Bill Orvis).

home. He and Wyler didn't speak to each other again for three years, even when they were shooting the interiors at the studio the following week and standing on the same set.

Perhaps sensing this wasn't going to be one of his great pictures, Wyler didn't even personally complete work on it, departing for Rome and preparation on *Ben-Hur* five months before *The Big Country* opened in October, 1958. He left his editor Robert Swink, who had been with him on five pictures since 1950, in charge of the post-production scoring, editing, dubbing and cutting, and so it is Swink whom audiences have to thank for shooting the final scene. Even though Wyler praised him for his new ending, *The Big Country* would be the last time they worked together, too.

The Oscar-nominated score by Jerome Moross will live forever. Hardly a day goes by that you don't hear excerpted bits in various commercials. If you close your eyes while you listen, you can almost hear the harness jingling as the magnificent six-horse hitch gallops over the golden hills to pull the stagecoach carrying Gregory Peck into his opening scene.

Film legend Jean Simmons (right) presents the Golden Boot Award in 2005 to Martha (left) at the Beverly Hilton Hotel.

Many consider this one of the top ten pieces of music ever written for films. Franz Planer's cinematography was likewise absolutely stunning. Yet, in all their wisdom, the Academy Award judges that year gave the film's single award to Burl Ives for Best Supporting Actor.

For me, though, working on *The Big Country* was an extraordinary experience. I was thrilled to be chosen as part of Jean Simmons' support team at the time, and I still am today. Many years later, that work led to another highlight of my career when Jean presented my award at the Motion Picture and TV Fund's Golden Boot Award event in the International Ballroom of the Beverly Hilton Hotel in Beverly Hills. Strange as it may seem, although Jean's close friend Jo Jordon was her stand-in for *The Big Country,* Jo and I hadn't met officially until then. Jo was with Jean on that occasion, and as we were chatting over dinner, Jo told me how relieved she was to see me arrive on *The Big Country* set all those years ago. Jean, with a very straight face, had been telling her that being the stand-in also meant she would have to do all the riding and stunts if the stunt double didn't show up. Jo had been mortified until I'd ridden over the hill to her rescue! What a time we had that night rehashing the ups and downs of a movie that almost made it to greatness.

16

The Sheepman

"Was he very bad?"
"Well, let's just say he wasn't in any danger of getting a headache from the weight of all the gold stars on his crown."
— Jason Sweet answering Dell Payton's question
in *The Sheepman*

Some films are such a compilation of talent that it almost takes your breath away, and that is how I think of *The Sheepman*. Of course, just because some people are talented doesn't mean they are easy to work with. This film shoot brought together a group of actors with diverse experience, Glenn Ford, Shirley MacLaine, Leslie Nielsen, Pernell Roberts and Slim Pickens, to play roles in an age-old drama of cattlemen versus sheep herders. The audience knows that before the movie is done there will be some kind of a battle between them and, sure enough, *The Sheepman* doesn't let you down.

Though I had never met Shirley MacLaine until then, it was she who personally asked me to double her for this film. Some time prior to this, I had been in makeup talking with Eleanor Parker when Shirley and Rhonda Fleming both came by at the same time to ask me if I would double them in their movies. Rhonda was about to begin work in *Gun Glory* and Shirley in *Sheepman*. As they arrived, each insisted with a smile on her face that they were there first. I just tried to act like this happened all the time!

I got so many of my jobs because I did not look like anyone's preconceived notion of a stunt girl; I looked more like one of the stars, and that often paid off for me. It sometimes had its funny side, though. I often weighed more than the average female star, for example, because of my muscle tone but my actual measurements would be less when compared to them. I had as good a figure, if not better, than most of those women.

More importantly, when I was younger I had been taught by one of the best modeling agencies in the country how best to walk, sit, stand, get in and out of cars and look good in a reception line. I knew how to use all the grace of my finely tuned body to its best advantage, even while sitting in the saddle. However, as well as learning how to be distinctive I had also learned how to blend into a crowd and, strange as it may seem, that could also work in my favor. I had no outstanding, distinctive physical features, which meant that directors could blend shots of me into a star's scenes so well that an audience would never be shaken from their belief it was the star they were watching do all that physical work.

This, of course, was very appealing to the average female star. As I already closely resembled a number of them, I didn't have to spend hours in the chair being made up to look like them. In no time at all, I could be ready to double *and* do stunts. Not only that, I was perfectly content to let the star be the star. I had no ambitions to replace them as an actor and was just happy being paid to perform my hobby. A star knew that she would have no reason to be watching her back or to be concerned I'd be looking for a chance to upstage them in a scene. Because of my looks and physical training, I could be photographed far closer to the camera lens than the average double and still be absolutely convincing, as I was during the street scene shoots for *The Seventh Sin.* Shooting a double that close was almost unheard-of in those days when our faces were customarily hidden in long shots and our roles went uncredited because studios wanted audiences to believe that the stars could do everything. Today, things are different and the roles of doubles and stunt crew are accepted and recognized, and consequently they are awarded the credit they deserve.

To meet an actress who is multi-talented, an epitome of professionalism, never late on the set, knows her lines and is totally deserving of industry awards was not that unusual. However, to meet someone who is all of these things without ego, who is highly intelligent and has a personality to compete with the brightest star in the heavens — now *that* is rare. I found Shirley MacLaine to be all of these things. Whether it is in film or television, or in person, I have always been impressed with her naturalness and unaffectedness. Shirley MacLaine would be one of the most talented comedians I have ever met, and what makes her so very funny is that it is frequently just Shirley being Shirley. She is never trying to be funny; she just *is*! As they say, she could read you a menu and have you rolling in the aisles, laughing, without any idea of what she had done. She also had a great memory. Months after I doubled her, I was walking in the gate at MGM one morning when a little red sports car came tearing by me. All I heard was, "Hallllllloooooooo, Martha!" It was Shirley.

I was happy to accept the job on *Sheepman* as I would work with one of my favorite movie horses, Ski, the horse that I reared into the "fire" in *Interrupted Melody.* I would also have a chance to work again with Glenn Ford, who I knew was a horse lover, and with my good friend Slim Pickens. Many people forget now that Leslie Nielsen played straight dramatic roles for twenty-five years before turning self-parody into a comedic art form. Although *Sheepman* was early in his career, he was already well known for his appearances in *Forbidden Planet* and *Tammy and the Bachelor.* This movie was also early in the career of handsome Pernell Roberts, who had only just arrived in Hollywood after some very successful years on stage. Fame would be waiting for him the following year when he first appeared as Adam Cartwright in *Bonanza.*

Paradoxical is the only way I could describe my feelings for Glenn Ford, who insisted on riding his own horse in this movie even though it was a pure-bred Tennessee Walking Horse that was out of place in a story set in this era. He had come to me one day on the set of *Interrupted Melody* and congratulated me on the job I was doing and said how he admired my riding ability. He was a softly spoken, educated, delightful gentleman with a reputation for bravery. Already a decorated World War II naval officer, he would later volunteer for active duty with the Marines during the Vietnam War at the age of fifty. I had always admired him for his acting craft, and he seemed to be the consummate professional. By the time we were making *The Sheepman*, he had been in movies for twenty years, and I was looking forward to working with him again. Perhaps my quandary came about from seeing how personable he could be off the set and yet how he could change when performing on the set. On the other hand, perhaps that ability to change when he walked through the gates is what made him such a fine actor. In any case, we all had a job to do, and I have always figured that if we can bring our individual skills to the table and work together, then it is better for everybody.

That was a great dream, it really was. There was just one problem: despite all his politeness and compliments, Ford would not step up to the table and cooperate with me one iota. In the end, I had to make the decision about how to get the best shot for the scene in which we were both appearing, and I had never experienced anything like that before where a major actor was concerned. The stunt was my arena, and most stars were more than pleased for me to make suggestions in which they had confidence because they acknowledged my experience and skill. But for some reason Ford could not bring himself to give me that acknowledgment or that trust.

The particular shot at the center of this power struggle, as I believe this really was, called for me as Shirley's double to drive a buggy fast down the main street just as Glenn, in his role as the newcomer, was walking onto that street. Horse and buggy would seem to be on the verge of running him down as he walks directly into their path. Glenn, of course, would need to react as though he really thought he was about to be trodden underfoot, stepping back and throwing his hands up in shock and surprise as the horse rears. This was a crucial scene because it would bring the characters of Jason Sweet and Dell Payton together for the first time so, one way or the other, it had to be done.

Ski was a highly specialized, trained rearing horse for which the SPCA rules hadn't changed since *Interrupted Melody*. We were still only allowed to rear them eight times in one day, and an SPCA representative was always on the set to ensure those rules were followed. That meant we only had a maximum of eight takes to get the scene "in the can." If that didn't happen, it would all have to be postponed which would add further expense to the budget. For some reason, Glenn was apprehensive about the whole thing, so I explained to him that it is impossible to get a horse to run over someone unless the horse is terrified and running unchecked. There would be no chance of that as I would be in complete control. All Glen had to do was hit the piece of tape that was his mark on the street and stand still; apart from his gesture of shock. I would do the rest.

After three unsatisfactory takes, I could see that Glenn was not standing close enough to Ski when he reared to look convincing. Now we had only five takes left, or we would have to go to all the trouble of finding another space in the schedule when the scene could be shot. It would mean setting up all over again, never something we looked forward to. So I took Glenn aside and asked him if he would step in just a bit closer as I drove up to my pre-arranged spot with the horse and then we would have a believable shot. To my surprise, he just shook his head emphatically, looked away down the street for a few moments and then declared that under no circumstances would he step away from his mark on the road. That was as far as he was going to go and not a toe further! Then, having made his point, he walked off. In desperation I turned to the director, George Marshall, who I knew was no newcomer to working with horses and stunt people during a career as an actor, writer and production supervisor as well as director spanning over 160 films. But he just shrugged and said he'd figured out long ago that the best thing to do was to stay out of disputes such as these. No wonder everyone liked him; they all thought he was on their side.

None of this was much help to me, of course. I was plain mystified, flummoxed even, and to be honest I was a tad angry over Ford's attitude. An avid horseman and ex–polo player who lived on his own cattle ranch, Ford was no stranger to horses or to the Western genre. He'd already appeared in a dozen Westerns, including *The Fastest Gun Alive* and *3:10 to Yuma*. In fact, with a draw timed at 0.4 seconds, Ford had the reputation of really having the fastest gun in the movie West, faster than John Wayne or *Gunsmoke*'s James Arness. This was one man who should have been familiar with the capabilities of trained horses, and here he was refusing to get close to one.

Well, we tried again and then again, and soon we only had one more SPCA-allowed take available to us. By now, I was absolutely tired of all

Doubling for Shirley MacLaine in 1958, Martha encourages Glenn Ford to be surprised in *The Sheepman* (Warner Bros. Entertainment).

this. What was worse, he was making *me* look bad and I was getting angrier by the minute about that. As far as I was concerned, he could do what he liked with his reputation but there was no way he was going to make mine look sorry! I simply refused to let Ford's attitude get the better of me, so rather than put the horse away and subject the company to the extra expense of another day's filming for this all-important scene, I seized the reins in my hands quite literally. Without consulting Ford, I asked Marshall if I could re-organize the shot and because of my experience he gave me the benefit of the doubt. The scene called for that buggy to be coming fast into the scene, so I galloped in as fast as Ski could make the turn into the street and I aimed that horse straight at Ford. I had carefully worked out the distances so that we would all arrive on the mark at the same time and arrive we did, much closer than Ford had expected. He was so shocked when Ski reared right in front of him that he threw his hands up and involuntarily stepped back in totally unfeigned fear. I think I heard a few chuckles from George Marshall, but for sure I heard, "Print that!"

It was obvious from his reaction that Ford had been sure I'd lost it and was going to run over him. While by then that solution had probably become tempting, in the end one's training cuts in and you do your job in a professional manner. Ford was a competent horseman, but he obviously lacked the experience to know that a trained horse like Ski simply would not have harmed him. I couldn't have made Ski run him down even if I'd really wanted to. Ford had failed to give me credit for being the serious perfectionist I was known to be in my field and for being able to make us both look better. Ironically, in the end it was his fear that I worked with to make the shot exactly what the director wanted. Now that I come to think of it, I don't think Glenn ever spoke to me again.

Between scenes, I had the chance to chat briefly with James Edward Grant who was the writer of *The Sheepman* and who had written a quirky, humorously witty screenplay with William Bowers that would be nominated for the 1959 Academy Award for Best Writing, Story and Screenplay. Jimmy had been a close friend of my polo-playing father and he would often come out to the club with John Wayne. We reminisced about those times and shared a lot of memories, although Grant had difficulty with separating the stunt double talking with him from the young horsewoman he had known back then. As well as being a fan of polo, Grant was so passionately fond of bullfighting that he later moved to Spain for a few years. He and Wayne were good friends and collaborated on a number of films, such as *Angel and the Badman* that Grant directed as well as wrote, *Sands of Iwo Jima*, *Flying Leathernecks*, and *Hondo*.

Much of *The Sheepman* was shot on the backlot at my home studio of MGM. Although I often saw it happen, I was always thrilled to see how quickly a new set could materialize from out of nowhere. Walking through it, I would feel transported to another place and time as though I lived within a dream world where anything was possible. Right before my eyes, that quiet little Western street on the backlot would suddenly become alive with a train-car full of real sheep. All of the livestock, including horses, used at both MGM and Fox was supplied by "Fat" Jones who, if he didn't have the required animals readily available, would contract out for them until he had acquired all the stock needed for that particular film. Large herds of animals were handled just as skillfully as small groups on the set. Usually the director would set up a long shot, say in this case the large flock being unloaded from the stock car, and then they would create a matching set inside on a sound stage where they could shoot using just a few animals and get their close-ups under controlled conditions. During editing, they would cut between the two sets and the end product looked totally believable.

The ramrod wrangler for *The Sheepman* was Dick Webb, who had suggested me to the casting offices for many jobs. I first met Dick on *Interrupted Melody* and worked with him often after that. Each studio had their own casting office staff and it was usually from them that I received the call for stunt or doubling work. When I first started seriously in the business, I met with the casting directors at each of the various studios to introduce myself and to show them my picture portfolio, and we discussed my riding experience and the stunts I could do. They in turn filed me in the back of their minds for when a star whom I matched in looks needed a double. Once I was working, though, it was usually the wranglers who would suggest me because they were the people who knew what I could do with horses. Occasionally, by way of supplementing my stunt work, I would get a call to do background work where, for example, I might be just one of a group of riders, wagon drivers, or stagecoach passengers. This wasn't usually regarded as stunt or double work, and so those calls would come from the Screen Extras Guild and the jobs carried on my Extras Guild card, whereas my stunt jobs were carried on my Actors Guild card.

Any acting stars who required a double could, of course, request a particular person for that work unless the casting office was not using them for some reason. If they found they could work well with that double, major actors would then find it easier to always work with the same double, who often not only looked like the star but who would eventually develop the same physical and verbal mannerisms through constant study and imitation. In some cases, they even became personal friends. One of the most famous examples of a close star-double relationship was between Errol Flynn and his stunt double at Warner Brothers, Vernon "Buster" Wiles. They bore such a close resemblance that, with a minimum of clever makeup, Wiles was known to stand in for Flynn at social events as a joke. They remained close friends throughout Flynn's tempestuous life and when he died suddenly in Vancouver, it was Wiles who escorted Flynn's body back to Los Angeles by train.

Sometimes, though, it would be an assistant director or unit manager who might request me, once they got to know me or had previously worked with me. There were only about ten or twelve of us who did horse stunt work, and so hiring frequently came about through word of mouth as to your capabilities because casting directors and ramrod wranglers preferred to work with people they knew. The ramrod wrangler would be given the production script by the studio and he, in turn, would select and acquire the proper horses. He would search for gentle horses for the stars to be on during the close-ups and a matching action horse for the doubles to ride. A double horse might then be touched up with paint to match the star's horse, perhaps creating a white blaze face or white stockings, or perhaps even covering existing markings.

Wranglers were the general horse handlers on set, and they really knew their stuff. They might be on the ground out of camera range holding a horse's foot so as to keep him still during a close-up, or applying a piano wire to an ankle to make a horse limp. They were the "pick-up" men if a double had a runaway chase scene to do in a buckboard, wagon or stagecoach, galloping alongside if necessary after the shot to grab reins or traces and slow speeding horses to a stop. The work that looked easy was often the most dangerous. Watching the wranglers load the horse trucks in the early morning seemed simple enough, but these were not "horse vans"; the trucks had ramps with no sides to them. So many times I have watched a wrangler toss the rope over a seasoned horse's neck to send him up the ramp to take his place alongside the others. However, there were always the new horses that you thought understood the routine until they made a sudden U-turn in the middle of the ramp and came right back over the top of the wrangler who had not had time to get out of the way. I speak from experience because after my retirement I was asked to wrangle on *The Apple Dumpling Gang* and I learned about new horses the hard way. On that occasion, both the new horse and I landed at the bottom of the ramp with me underneath his belly looking up and hoping he wouldn't kill me.

As the wrangling boss, a ramrod wrangler had a great deal of clout with the casting office, and it was one of them who got me the job on *Love Me Tender.* Even stock contractor "Fat" Jones recommended me on occasion. Your reputation was everything. After my work on *Interrupted Melody,* the biggest film set-up that year, news traveled pretty fast about the quality of my horsemanship, and a lot of the subsequent work calls I received were a result of that. It was rather like a young jockey winning his first two races at a new track and finding that from there on, the owners came looking for *him.*

Once I had worked on a few films, there was little doubt in the minds of casting directors that I could do whatever they required. I seemed to get a lot of calls for fast mounts and jumping, work that was not what the average trick rider could do well on command. You only had to be working there a short while to realize that Hollywood was a far closer-knit business community than it first appeared, and that word of mouth carried most of us till we got our foot in the door of a regular studio. Stunt people at that time seemed to stay with the studio where they first worked. I was fortunate to become known for my work at both MGM and Twentieth Century–Fox, two of the biggest and best studios, and consequently spent most of my time between them. Occasionally I might be called by Universal, but only once for Warners. Sometimes I knew I got a call because of personal preference from someone much higher up the food chain. For example, Gregory Peck as producer of *The Big Country* hired me personally for that shoot, having known me and my work from *Yellow Sky.* He also knew my father, and everyone knows those kinds of relationships are also highly significant in Hollywood.

When the call came from the studio for a stunt job, it was usually to tell me I was needed to double a particular actor and that I should report to, say, the Wyler film company at that studio at a certain time on a certain day. The film company was usually labeled with the name of the director. If we were going on location, they might tell me to report to the studio for transportation to Lone Pine or, if it was the Fox Ranch which wasn't far away, to be prepared for the limo to pick me up at my home in the San Fernando Valley at a particular time, usually very early in the morning. Most of the time you had no idea how long you would be gone, and they may or may not be specific about the stunt or stunts they would require me to do, such as stirrup mount, jumping, runaway chase, or buckboard chase. You needed to be ready for anything.

On occasion, if there was a jump to be done such as in *Love Me Tender*, I would ask if I could use my own horse. It was better to work with the animal that you knew for potentially difficult tasks. If he fit the color or could be colored to match the cast horse (the horse the star was riding), then there usually wasn't a problem with using him. However, allowing your own horse to be used could have its down side. I once had a really beautiful Palomino that a film company took on location to Nogales, Arizona, for Jack Carson to ride in *The Bottom of the Bottle*, but while there he was bitten by a rabid skunk. I had to put him down two weeks after he came home. So, I often just arrived at the work place and mounted up on whatever horse had been selected as the cast horse's double.

Charlton Heston once said that Hollywood really only employs about two hundred people; you just keep seeing the same two hundred being used over and over. He could well have been right. Stunt people were certainly a very close-knit group because it was absolutely essential in our line of work to know who we could trust and on whom we could rely. Each studio usually had their favorites or regulars. Word spread fast if you could do the job, and it spread even faster if you could not.

17

The Law and
Jake Wade

"Always know what you are going to do if what you have planned
doesn't work!"

— Joe Yrigoyen

Bishop, California, is a town of about 3,500 at the junction of Highway 395 and Route 6. North is Mammoth Springs, Yosemite and Reno, while south is Lone Pine, Death Valley and eventually Los Angeles; east on 6 is Provo and Salt Lake City. It's a town from where you could go anywhere or nowhere. I always thought it an interesting paradox that though Bishop was only a small town, it had a better class of hotels, motels and restaurants than would usually be expected in a town of this size, and more *of* them. Although these days the town's economy is based on its popularity as a base for rock-climbing and mule riding, in the fifties the Californian towns of Bishop and Lone Pine and St. George, Utah, had long histories as locations for the film industry. Studios contributed in a big way to the economies of these otherwise typical, small desert towns by insisting that their personnel be accommodated in first class conditions. Needless to say, the food was also the best and restaurants would compete to get the contracts for catering the lunches on set.

MGM's *The Law and Jake Wade,* from a novel by seasoned Western writer Marvin Albert and directed by the legendary John Sturges, was shot in 1958 mainly in the Death Valley region between Bishop and Lone Pine, an area that is as close to a natural kaleidoscope as one could experience. It is a riot of intense color encompassing purple mountains peeking through pure white snow, golden sand and white salt flats, trees of bright yellow and orange leaves, sparkling blue streams, and bright evergreen foliage. I don't believe even Metrocolor could truly do it justice, but Robert Surtees' cinematography came close. By the time of his work on this film, he had already won two Academy Awards for the color photography for *King Solomon's Mines* in 1951 and the black and white photography on *The Bad and the Beautiful* in 1953. Seven years after this he would win a third for *Ben-Hur*.

Once again, I was working on a movie that brought together an interesting group of actors. Jake Wade (Robert Taylor) is a former outlaw who has gone straight and is now the marshal of a small town. His past catches up with him when his old partner Clint Hollister (Richard Widmark) comes looking for the money from a bank hold-up they pulled together. He kidnaps Wade and his fiancée Peggy (Patricia Owens) and they all go looking for the old ghost town where Wade has hidden the loot, only to find that the local Indians don't want them leaving alive. I was glad to meet Richard Widmark again. I could always appreciate the honesty of a man who said that although he felt comfortable working in Westerns, he never considered he could actually ride. After our introduction some years earlier on the set of *Yellow Sky,* our friendship had developed and now included his wonderful wife, writer Jean Hazelwood, and their daughter Anne, whom I would later teach how to ride. I still consider that one of the most enjoyable and self-rewarding experiences I ever had in the horse world.

Richard's career had also developed rapidly. Despite appearing in such classic roles as that of Harry Fabian in *Night and the City*, Skip McCoy in *Pickup on South Street*, and Lt. Anderson in *The Halls of Montezuma*, Richard's relationship with Twentieth Century–Fox had deteriorated so badly by 1954 that he had opted not to renew his contract. He had since formed his own production company, Heath Productions, and was now working independently.

For the next two weeks, I would be doubling the lovely, redheaded Patricia Owens, who had only just married noted screenwriter Sy Bartlett, good friend of my father and co-writer on *The Big Country* and *Twelve O'Clock High*. The Canadian-born Owens had been working successfully on stage in England and in films with Gainsborough Pictures when she met Bartlett, who was having problems finding work in the U.S. due to the McCarthy blacklist. Following him back to Hollywood in 1956, she married Bartlett in a Palm Springs wedding at which Gregory Peck was best man. The following year, she appeared in important roles in *Island in the Sun* and *Sayonara* to great acclaim but, in one of those quirks of acting renown, Owens would become best known as the wife of an over-zealous scientist in a science fiction movie. Immediately after being seen as Peggy in *The Law and Jake Wade*, she would take up the role of Helene Delambre in *The Fly* in which she tells the story of her husband Andre's transition into another state of being. It would be difficult to think of two successive roles that could be more different than those.

Even though she must have known who I was and of my connection to her husband, Owens never once acknowledged my presence through-out the entire time I was on the set. Day after day, despite being involved in stunt work that could have had disastrous consequences and having been obviously accepted by her co-stars, I was the stunt double for an actor who never spoke to me. The only explanation I can think of is that perhaps it was Sy who was the problem, not me. Their marriage, his third and her second, had quickly developed problems and as soon as our shoot was done, Owens filed for divorce. I'm reluctant to think she was a snob, so I prefer to think that maybe I just reminded her of something that had become painful right then. That would explain, too, why her heart just did not seem to be in her work on our set; she just seemed to be walking through it.

However, Owens' coolness was more than made up for by DeForest Kelley's warmth. He was always a pleasure to meet, and once again his wry sense of humor cheered my working day. Yes, that's right; I once worked with Dr. Leonard McCoy. Although many people these days tend to think his entire career was about *Star Trek*, Kelley's career in movies had begun with Paramount in 1945, and in 1949 he appeared in the fourth episode of the first *Lone Ranger* series with Clayton Moore and Jay Silver-heels, making him one of the earliest actors I knew who had worked in a television Western. He's outstanding as Widmark's pal in *Warlock*, and just the previous year he'd been directed by John Sturges as Morgan Earp in *Gunfight at the O.K. Corral* with Kirk Douglas and Burt Lancaster. Until *Star Trek* took over his career after 1974, he would continue to add so significantly to the Western genre that he was presented with a Golden Boot Award shortly before his death.

After I had been staying in my motel in Bishop for a few days, I dis-covered that Robert Taylor and his beautiful wife, Ursula, were also there and we eventually came to know each other quite well. They had a suite with a full kitchen and Ursula, being the extraordinary cook she was, cooked breakfasts and dinners for Bob while the rest of us had to eat at the Copper Kettle restaurant. Lunch was catered on the set and I can still

Martha and Robert Taylor's horse Tommy at her stables in California's San Fernando Valley in 1959.

remember those long tables laden with food set out under spreading trees that were changing color. I usually sat between Robert and Richard Widmark, good friends who admired each other's acting skills and who enjoyed working together.

Bob and I would usually talk about either flying or horses and sometimes both. He was a fine pilot, having been a flight instructor for Navy pilots during World War II, and my own flying days were still fresh in my mind. I once confessed I was fascinated by his extraordinary chronograph watch and he showed me how to use it. He was one of the legendary faces in motion picture history, but I knew him as a quiet, shy, educated gentleman whose honesty was reflected in that famous face. Early in his career, he once told me, he had vowed to always appear in movies that the whole family could see and had endeavored to keep that promise. Exquisitely beautiful Ursula, who had been brought out from postwar Germany by Howard Hughes to work at RKO, complemented Robert and they were very happy. Once billed as "The Most Beautiful Girl in the World," Ursula had virtually given up her film career to devote herself to her family, even turning down Clark Gable's personal invitation to appear with him in *The King and Four Queens.*

A gentle human being, Bob loved his horses just as he did his family. He had an extraordinary quarterhorse named Tommy whom I also loved from my first day on the set. Tommy was the perfect horse for this movie; the dapple gray was beautiful against the backdrop of the colorful Bishop and Death Valley scenery. Bob had made arrangements to ride Tommy for this film with ramrod wrangler Dick Webb, who managed his horses. A celebrity in his own right, Tommy had been the last horse trained by the legendary reinsman M.R. Valdez, and such highly trained horses were few and far between then and are especially so now. Valdez trained the thoroughbred Ebony Knight by Flying Ebony out of Vibrant after Ebony Knight's retirement from racing. Consequently, that horse became one of the greatest cow ponies ever shown in the horse show arena, and it was Valdez who put the rein and mouth on him that made him so great.

At Dick Webb's suggestion, Bob sent both Tommy and Ursula's horses to me at my home after we had wrapped on the set, and I looked after both horses for them for some time. Ursula's horse had foundered and I cared for him daily, digging mud holes for him to stand in to draw out the heat and to keep the hoofs as soft as possible. My vet designed a concave shoe for him, and eventually Ursula was able to ride him again. Bob's horse Tommy was a very light gray and required daily care to keep him that way, but Bob knew that and they never came out to visit without calling first. One Christmas when they came to see the horses, Bob arrived with a twenty-pound box of chocolate candy upside-down under his arm!

Soon after my other horses arrived, along came Buck! An older buckskin quarterhorse in his twenties, he had been the horse Bob rode in his first western, *Billy the Kid*. He was a dear, but only a year or so later Buck died with his head on my lap in his stall. By that time, I had moved to the ranch owned by western legend Wild Bill Elliott where I had more stalls and a lighted arena. Buck had been showing signs of colic, and his condition deteriorated rapidly. By the time the vet reached him, Buck was in great pain. He had been walking stiff-legged around the stall with his lips curled back, and my vet said only severe, potentially fatal pain would cause that. He was right; a later autopsy would discover a basketball-sized intestinal tumor. I was absolutely devastated. I sobbed uncontrollably as I agreed that the best thing we could do for him was to put him down.

Bob was stunned when I called him. Telling him that news was one of the hardest things I have ever done. He loved Buck and, even though he had been an old horse, Bob had spared no expense in caring for him all the years Valdez had his horses. Talking through our memories then, we reminisced for a while about *Billy the Kid* in which Bob had starred as Billy Bonney. Right-handed Bob had to practice for weeks so that he could draw a gun left-handed for the role. I was rather partial to this movie because I had more than one connection to it. Although the credited director is David Miller, the original director had been Frank Borzage, a long-time friend of my father because of their shared interest in polo, and his brother Lew was the second unit director. Frank, a high-ranking Mason, had been a successful actor on stage and screen before beginning his directing career in the silent era. He surely must hold some kind of Hollywood record for directing nearly as many films (107) as he appeared in as an actor (115). He was the first to receive an Academy Award for Best Director in 1929 for *Seventh Heaven* and then was honored again in 1932 for *Bad Girl*.

Martha sitting on Tommy while waiting to enter a horse show in the San Fernando Valley.

It was due to a subsequent dinner invitation to the Taylor home in Pacific Palisades that I met their closest friends, future president Ronald Reagan and his wife Nancy. Like myself, they were also there to partake of Ursula's homemade cabbage rolls. Ronnie was my dinner partner and, of course, horses were the talk of the evening. He was fascinated by stunt horses and jumping horses, and we discovered we shared the same blacksmith. Then our conversation moved on to Wild Bill Elliott, my favorite furniture craftsmen and one of only two in films. Although Elliott was a master of his field, many people had never heard of him at that time except as a Western film star. The usual well-known antique dealers could not tell a real Elliott from a copy, but I had spent many hours watching in awe as Bill crafted his pieces of furniture, so I could certainly spot an original. I was there to share his heartbreak after his last four saddles, monogrammed with BE on the saddle horns and steeped in history, were stolen and never recovered.

Even though the Taylors later purchased a six-bedroom home with exceptional stables in Mandeville Canyon, built by Phillips of Phillips 66 Oil, it was their Pacific Palisades home I always loved. It was a typical Californian, two-story white stucco home that was totally unassuming and demonstrated the same simple elegance as Bob and Ursula. When I first visited that house and entered the living room, I was drawn to a lamp table with an unusual finish I had never seen before. It was of pine or perhaps a fruitwood but when you looked down at it, it was like looking into a mountain lake. I had never before seen a finish on furniture like that. The Taylors told me that this was one of the finest examples of furniture made by another Western star, George Montgomery, who had made all the pieces for their house. The round dining room was another delight, with a matching round table in the center of the room that comfortably sat eight to ten people. When I looked up at the ceiling, I saw a large wagon wheel that almost covered the whole area. The hub and spokes were of the same magnificently finished wood as the rest of the furniture.

Montgomery pieces have an American Traditional theme (as do those of Bill Elliott), and many of them can still be seen today on display with some of his fifty bronzes at the Palm Springs Museum. His sculpture of ex-wife Dinah Shore and their two children graces the entrance of the Mission Hills Country Club in Rancho Mirage, California, home to the LPGA Dinah Shore Golf Tournament. As well as being such a great artist and craftsman, and designing a number of homes, Montgomery had a long career as an actor and stuntman in some eighty-seven films for such studios as Republic and Fox as well as working for television. His creative genius will ensure the memory of his name endures.

Other than doubling Patricia Owens in *The Law and Jake Wade*, I begged and pleaded to be given a role as one of the Indians in the movie while we were out on location. Of course, I didn't want to be just *any* Indian; I wanted to be one who was shot so I could do a fall. The incredibly soft ground surface out there was just begging to be rolled on from off the back of a horse! But my repeated requests were stone-walled and, as I look back now, I realize it was perhaps the stunt men themselves that did not want a girl doing the work!

When we got out to the Death Valley location, we worked in an area where the hills had the consistency of flour. I have never seen that anywhere but in this particular place. To get the horses up a hill, the crew had to set up a frame with a pulley attachment on top of the hill, and then they would loop rope from the pulley around the saddle horns so that by hauling on it they could assist the horses to climb. Henry Wills, who was doubling for Robert Taylor, was an incredible stuntman who had performed over 1,500 horse falls. He broke his pelvis doing one particular fall while doubling Marlon Brando in *One-Eyed Jacks*. He was a perfect match for Bob; they were both quiet and fairly shy and perfect gentlemen. "Hank" Wills appeared in at least a hundred films and some, such as *Shane* with Alan Ladd, *The Magnificent Seven* with Yul Brynner, and *Westward the Women* with Robert Taylor became classics of their genre. A lot of Hollywood's top stars including Audie Murphy, Alan Ladd, Dean Martin, Richard Widmark, Roy Rogers and Jerry Lewis all insisted that Hanks double for them in their films. Some actors were so fond of Hank, and so impressed with his ability, that he was written into their contracts. He was one of the nicest people I ever met in the business.

Hank and I ate a lot of dust together in that film working in those canyons under the constant glare of the desert sun and, believe me, those conditions were hard on a woman's hair. I was fortunate that Agnes Flanagan, who had been the hairdresser for Jean Harlow and Marilyn Monroe, was on this shoot keeping our blonde hair looking and feeling like silk. She showed me a trick of the trade that I still use today. Applying a mixture of half olive oil and half castor oil to my hair before she bleached it, Agnes would put the color right on over the mixture. It looked wonderful. After several days in the very hot sun, she would apply this olive oil and castor oil mix again and wrap my hair in hot towels for a minimum of thirty to forty minutes. It would wash out in three shampoos and look like new hair.

I usually tried to have my hair the same color as that of the star I was doubling so I would not have to wear a wig, but I often had to wear one anyway. The set hairdresser would make small pin curls all over my head, fasten them with two crossed bobby pins and then add a tight netting cap over that. Then they fitted a wig band to the edge of your hairline around your forehead and your now-pinned hair. When they put the wig on, they would take two long wig hairpins and stick them under each pin curl to anchor the wig so it would stay in place, no matter how violent my actions. I suffered some serious headaches from those tight bands in the name of having good hair for the camera, but those flattering wigs could make you look so much more glamourous than you really were. You would see yourself on-screen and figure it was worth every bit of the pain.

Those wigs are not like the selection from which you would choose in a store, I might add. The hair piece that traveled with me to Hong Kong was valued at $5,000, and that was just a ponytail hair extension that could be made up into a bun. Full wigs could contain almost half again as much hair as a natural head of hair. If you know what to look for, you can often see that a star's hair in a film might appear to be heavier and fuller than you recall from their last candid magazine photo, in which case the odds are very good they are not wearing their own hair! The three most practical reasons for an actor to carry out this slight deception are that you look better, it is much easier to have ready-to-wear hair for a quick scene change than take time out for a hairdresser, and you look better. Believe me, once you have worn this type of wig, you will never be satisfied with your own hair.

On the other hand, Jean Harlow was at least one classic example of a star who grew tired of being bleached and wearing a wig and reverted to her own hair. Harlow's natural hair color was more of a honey-blonde, somewhat darker and richer than the bleached blonde hair for which she was more famous. Her natural hair caused her face to look softer. She originally took to wearing a wig to preserve her hair from the damaging effects of constant bleaching, and then lobbied to be allowed to appear before the cameras in her natural hair color. In this way, she could leave behind the "blonde bombshell" typecasting to undertake more serious roles. The studio, however, feared losing the audience that wanted to see that very bombshell, and so they resisted the change for many years. In the end, Harlow had her way and they were proved wrong. Audiences loved Harlow for who she was, not just the color of her hair.

Of all the stunt men that I knew personally, Joe Yrigoyen was the finest. He gave me some advice at the beginning of my career that has stayed with me ever since: "*Always know what you are going to do if what you have planned doesn't work!*" Now, as easy and obvious as those words might sound, it is not always possible to follow through with the best-laid plans, and an incident that occurred during this shoot is a great example. We were working at a place in Death Valley known as Bad Water, the lowest geographic point in the United States. Bad Water, at 282 feet *below* sea level, is little more than a salt pond with a touch of arsenic, yet pup fish, a small species of blue fish, has survived in it.

Fortunately, in a place where it can reach 125 degrees in the middle of summer, we were shooting close to Thanksgiving and the weather was relatively comfortable (although, being below sea level, the air seemed heavier). The moderately sized Bad Water pond is surrounded by a huge expanse of salt flats that appear deceptively solid. Instead, they are really just a salt crust over liquid mud of indeterminate depth into which you can sink as if it was quicksand. Every now and then, according to the Park Rangers, a wagon will rise to the surface from the days when the pioneers attempted to cross the flats to the California gold fields. This potential death trap lay on both sides of the narrow foot trail used for the horses, so we received strict instructions from the Park Rangers to stay on the trail and not wander onto the salt flats, at the peril of our lives.

The director was holding us, waiting for just the right cloud formation to drift into place as a backdrop. When it did, the plan was for him to drop a handkerchief instead of calling "Action!" as after a while the horses get wise to the word and begin to anticipate it. Well, it seemed a good idea but this time it didn't work. The really savvy movie horses also pick up on the preceding phrase, "All quiet," learning quickly that "Action!" comes next. So, there we were in an "all quiet" hold when my horse suddenly reared and jumped off the trail as he anticipated the director's action signal. Caught totally unawares, I came off and I think we both hit and broke through the salt crust together. Before I knew it, I found myself floundering in the thick, slippery mud with my long western riding skirt wrapped in a stranglehold around my legs. Alongside, my horse was up to his belly in this totally un-navigable goo. Fortunately, his enormous underside offered us a moment of precious time as it was so buoyant.

I grabbed the stirrup from my side and the wranglers were able to reach the bridle reins from their side of the horse. As he tried really hard to get out, thrusting and lunging and striking with his front legs, I began to fear that once again I'd become a sought-after rock. A horse will try to climb up on you in these circumstances just as if you were both in water, so I made sure I stayed off to one side and slightly behind him while maintaining my hold on the stirrup. At last his flailing hoofs found solid ground, and he pulled us both back onto the trail. Naturally, all this sound and fury had upset the other horses and they all took some calming down. It was small comfort to me to find that mine was the only horse to have jumped the start. It would have been a one-in-a-million usable shot except for the fact that Robert Taylor's double Henry, who had started out with his hands behind his back in handcuff mode, had to quickly bring his hands forward when all the action started to hold onto his agitated horse and that ruined the continuity of the shot. So, despite its dramatic potential, they could not use this spectacular event. I have often wondered if Joe Yrigoyen would have already had a plan worked out while he was sitting there waiting for that handkerchief to fall, just in case.

Some twenty years later, I returned to Bad Water and found the marks of my horse's hoofs still there imprinted in that arid, salt surface. Nothing changes in Death Valley.

During the last two years Frosty, my little Texan that nobody wanted, had been mastering his exercises easily. I could hardly believe he was developing into such a beautiful horse. In 1956, the first Texan to be elected president of the United States, Dwight D. Eisenhower, had been re-elected to a second term while folks were singing along with Doris Day to "Que Sera, Sera." Now folks were whistling Dean Martin's "Memories Are Made of This."

These had been comfortable times for me, but busy and unforgettable times too. I had worked long and irregular hours, waiting and wishing for breaks between casting calls that would allow me to start on Frosty's advanced programs. They had been a while coming. *Love Me Tender, Dakota Incident, My Friend Flicka, Cheyenne, The Killer Is Loose,* and *The King and Four Queens* had all been in production just around 1956 alone, for example, so it was a busy time for those of us involved in the making of western films and television horse operas.

I had little time for anything except my work and my four-legged family, but I'd sometimes wander over to Don Burt's stable where I would enjoy watching him teach Loren Janes to ride. Loren twice qualified for the Olympic trials Pentathlon which consists of five events: pistol shooting, epée fencing, 200-meter freestyle swimming, show jumping, and a 3 km cross-country run. After that, he became one of the all-time top stunt men in Hollywood. On occasion, I'd ride a nice working hunter he had there by the name of Contender that had recently won the Working Hunter championship at the Cow Palace under Don's training and riding. He was for sale very reasonably for a horse that had won several major Championships, but he was very difficult to haul and had to be shipped by himself, instead of on a van with the other show horses. I often wonder if my Achilles heel is horses that have problems.

Eventually, though, there would be some gaps in my schedule and Frosty and I would get right back to training. I knew his exercises could be a tad tedious, and so I frequently encouraged him by whispering his secret word and with generous pats on his neck because his success with this program called for lengthy, extraordinary praise. I would often discuss his progress with Les Hilton, trainer of Flicka and Mr. Ed, and he was most encouraging. The film business could be very stressful. Don't get me wrong, I loved it, but working and teaching this responsive horse was the most relaxing thing I knew. Not only that, I felt I was creating something with Frosty just as, I am sure, an artist feels when they first sketch a drawing to which they will later add detail and color.

One day, after watching Frosty roll and drag his favorite 2 × 4 board around the arena for a while, I had to pry myself away as my enthusiasm was at an all-time high. I went into the house with Sancho on my heels and once again plopped in one of the sugar pine captain's chairs at my kitchen table. Looking at the blueprint I had made all that time ago for Frosty's development, I could see that nearly all the pages were now turned down at the corners. I pillowed my head on my forearm and thought for a long time about what we had accomplished, and about what I had accomplished in my career. It was a good feeling.

Suddenly, my reverie was interrupted as the phone rang. I considered just letting it ring, but I finally picked it up. It could be more work, but to my surprise it was Don Burt! He wanted me to ride Contender in an upcoming Union Oil 76 Sports Club TV show. Don was going to jump Baldy, the Pacific Coast Open jumper champion owned by the Squirt Company. We would be performing with the Onandarka Riders, an impressive group of young riders trained by Harry Symington who performed bareback with only neck straps to control their horses. Jumping Contender and Baldy would demonstrate the difference between performing styles of a hunter and a jumper. Don had no doubt been selected for the show because he was a great rider and women loved his Audie Murphy looks, so I could not deny I was flattered he would ask me to ride in the show with him. Before that, though, there'd be one last ride into a celluloid sunset.

18

Ride a Crooked Trail

> Okay — bring on the empty horses!
> —Director Michael Curtiz while shooting
> *The Charge of the Light Brigade*

Ride a Crooked Trail was the last Western I worked on at Universal Studios and I learned something from my work on it, as I did on all the sets. The extraordinary costume designer Edith Head once said that she looked on her work as a cross between magic and camouflage where she created the illusion of changing actors into what they were not. As a result of her magic, every time the audience saw an actor on the screen, they were expected to believe that here was a different person than the last time. In my own way, I also made a contribution to that illusion. I, too, was involved in the magic and camouflage of turning stars into what they were not. Between the director, the cameraman, the editor and I, we could have had a star ride on water if necessary.

But I also knew what Edith meant about the magic of costumes, even though I rarely wore anything really elaborate. In *Yellow Sky*, for example, I only wore one outfit: a pair of dungarees with rolled-up cuffs and a paisley shirt, for which I'd been fitted in wardrobe at Twentieth Century–Fox before we left for the location at Lone Pine. Even in that simple outfit, though, after a few days I felt like I could have ridden out across the range ready to hold off a whole posse of bad guys single-handed. After a few years, the camouflage of outfits, roles, stunts, horses, actors and crew members formed a kaleidoscope in my memory. All the different things I was asked to do while doubling so many different stars made me question my own identity at times. I started to wonder, could it be possible I was all those different people somewhere inside myself? After all, to be a successful double, you had to convince the audience they were watching the

176

star, and to do that successfully you had to study them and then for a few moments you actually had to believe you were that person. Even though you weren't really that person, and it was all pretending and make-believe, in order to successfully convince the audience you had to convince yourself first. However, I didn't have any problems being able to do that. I so loved working in these Western films that I could easily believe I was living the roles and, in fact, I often looked forward to it.

Make-believe plays a big part in *Ride a Crooked Trail,* which in some places is quite a funny film with lots of byplay on the lead character's last name, Maybe. While on the run, bank robber Joe Maybe (Audie Murphy) sees the pursuing marshall, Noonan, fall to his death from a cliff. Maybe decides to pretend he's Noonan in the next town but local law enforcer Judge Kyle (Walter Matthau) is suspicious, so Maybe and past acquaintance Tessa Millott (Gia Scala) partner up as fake husband and wife to throw him off the scent. But she already has a man, outlaw Sam Teeler (Henry Silva), who has noticed, along with Maybe, how ripe the local bank is for plucking. Audie and Gia are both playing roles within roles here, with a need to be convincing both to the cast of townspeople and to the audience.

However, it was hard for me to believe Audie in any of his parts. He was so good-looking in the flesh with such an infectious personality that, no matter how well he played a role, I could only see the Audie Murphy I knew. When you met him in person, he seemed to possess an intangible beauty that the camera just couldn't capture, and I'd be just mesmerized by him. Only a few other revered stars had that quality. Linda Darnell had an inner beauty that was like an aura enveloping her in its arms, and my friend Clark Gable possessed something similar. It was one thing to see him on the screen, but when you met him you realized how much the camera failed to capture of the man himself. Like Clark, when Audie spoke to you and held your eyes with his, you and he became the only people in the world. And he could just be discussing the weather! I've thought since then that it was a fitting way for me to end my career at Universal, caught up in fantasy just as the studio preferred one to be.

One of the most highly decorated soldiers of World War II, who overcame many years of suffering from post-traumatic stress disorder and addiction to sleeping pills, the slightly built Audie Murphy had embarked on an immediate postwar movie career at the insistence of Jimmy Cagney. However, he had limited success until he appeared in *Bad Boy,* a movie promoting the work of Variety Clubs with disadvantaged and troubled children. As a result, Universal signed him to a seven-year contract during which his most famous role was playing himself in *To Hell and Back*, the 1955 film based on his own life. No other film would be as successful for Universal until *Jaws* in 1975. Yet it was not in war films that Murphy would become most popular, but in Westerns. He would appear in thirty-three of them, and not always as the good guy; in 1959 he played the professional killer in *No Name on the Bullet*. He was also a rancher away from the screen, becoming involved with breeding and raising quarterhorses on a number of ranches in Arizona, California and Texas.

As much as I would like to say that I left the Universal lot after some spectacular piece of horse riding, I have to admit that *Ride a Crooked Trail* was something of an anticlimax. I was not here doubling anyone on this occasion, nor was I racing a buggy down the main street. I was just one of a group of riders that got a little roughed up, rode a few horses and got lost in the background. Most of the shooting was either on the Universal backlot or out on the Conejo Ranch at Thousand Oaks that would later become better known as *Bonanza*'s Ponderosa.

It is for a different reason entirely that I remember this film, something that seemed to emphasise for me the circle I had ridden. When I reported to wardrobe at Universal, I was handed a shirt and long western skirt to wear. The more I looked at that shirt, the more familiar it seemed. The soft paisley material even felt familiar. I looked at the muted colors and saw a collar band with one pearl button and then I knew; I knew! I held my breath. It almost talked to me. I hardly dared look inside. There on the collar, in the shirt I was holding in my hands, was a label that said, "Double — Anne Baxter — *Yellow Sky*." It was the shirt I had worn in my first film so many years and so many miles ago. After a certain number of years, the big studios would assign their Western wardrobes to Western Costume, who would then rent them to the lesser studios. So, my shirt had made its way from Twentieth Century–Fox Studios to Western Costume and then out to Universal so that on this particular day it would be handed back to me. I felt I had indeed come full circle.

When I took off my magic shirt at the end of that day, I held it and examined it for a moment. I couldn't help but wonder what stories it could tell of horses and dust, of main streets and prairies, of stagecoaches and wagons, of gunfights and corrals. As I handed it in for the last time, I knew the curtain was coming down on my beloved career. My trail, too, had been a winding one, twisting and turning between truth and make-believe, reality and pretense. Every now and then I had fallen off my horse, but I had always climbed back in the saddle.

The big-budget, big-screen matinee Westerns were riding into the sunset now for what many people said would be their last fade-out. Westerns were already nine years old on television and were having a noticeable impact at the studios as they brought the same heroes, villains and excitement right into the audience's living room for a fraction of the budget of putting them in the theater. Those expensive trained horses, riders, spectacular stunts and acres of backlot were becoming a liability. You could use half the people for a smaller screen at half the cost.

I was going to miss those movie horses that had become such an integral part of my being. As it turned out, Ski's leap into the fire for *Interrupted Melody* may have marked the beginning of the end of the major studio horse stunts, just as Rex Allen marked the end of the singing cowboys as he rode into the sunset in *The Phantom Stallion* that same year. Ski was a stocky, mixed-breed black gelding that was built like a cinder block (as Laura Hillenbrand, author of *Seabiscuit*, would say) with a marvelously intelligent eye and curious ears. He was a skilled performer and deserving of a special award but most honorary awards went to trick horses, the most easily understood by the public. Many of the more difficult feats went unnoticed by the average movie audience because they looked so ordinary. The true unsung horse heroes were those who ran their hearts out up the hill as cowboys' horses and down the same hill as Indian ponies. They "packed" the actors willingly, bouncing on their kidneys day after day, in spite of bad hands on the reins and harsh bits in their mouths.

Then, there were the falling horses. Prior to the late 1940s and the eagle eye of the SPCA, horses were made to fall by the use of trip wires known as "running W's." While these devices made the fall look dramatically spectacular, they could be quite literally murderously effective. The running horse's front legs were yanked out from underneath it without warning, sometimes causing it to completely somersault, often resulting in a broken neck for the horse and broken limbs for the rider if they didn't roll out of the way. These were quite literally throw-away horses.

Since the fifties, though, "falling horses" have been trained as specialists to be worked by the individual stunt men who own them. Even though horse falls still look nightmarish, these are now carried out by very valuable horses for which extraordinary precautions are taken during training and working them to ensure they will not get hurt. In most cases, two spots are prepared in soft ground or sand for the projected fall: one to aim at and another to hit. Every precaution is taken to prevent their injury, and horses now willingly perform falls on cue. They are trained horses; if a fall has caused them pain or distress, there is little chance these days of a falling horse being pulled down in the traditional mode if they do not want to do it.

Although most movie horses were specialists in a particular area, such as jumping, falling, fighting, and rearing, there were a few that were extraordinarily versatile. Midnight was one such horse. Black and powerful with a tiny white star, he initially became well-known as a cast horse, ridden by many stars (including Clint Eastwood, Henry Fonda, and Audie Murphy) in television series such as *Rawhide* and movies like *Beneath the Planet of the Apes* and *The Cheyenne Social Club*. William H. Robertson in his book *The History of Thoroughbred Racing in America* describes the legendary race horse Native Dancer in words that echo my own thoughts of Midnight: "He was a pro: little or no cliff-hanging excitement. The feeling he inspired was the relative calm, solid satisfaction of seeing a task accomplished with competence by an expert. Confidence that he would get the job done was a large part of his appeal: the pleasure was in observing how smoothly he did it." This memorable horse was also used as a leader with six-up hitches on stagecoaches. Few horses could ever have adjusted to both of these feats on a regular basis, but Midnight had a way of making those who worked with him look better than they were. One day, I would have a chance to find out for myself.

My personal meeting with Midnight came when I was working on the set of *The Apple Dumpling Gang* in early 1975 as the first lady wrangler and "pick-up man." I would ride Midnight to pick up any runaway loose horses, watching carefully for just the right time to jump out there and get alongside because that horse would usually be running flat out. Midnight would invariably put me in the right place at the right time every time. He was so versatile, and I came to like him so much that, when we were done there, I asked Randall Ranch about buying him. They came back with a price of $40,000, a sum I certainly couldn't afford at the time, but I told them that if there ever came a day he couldn't work any more, then I still wanted him. A few years later they did call me to let me know he was about to become pet food.

I lost my temper into the telephone, yelling: "You bastards! You've got an entire ranch you could have retired him to and, after all the money that horse has made for you, that's all you could think of to do with him? How much do you want for him now?"

"Four hundred dollars."

"Right," I replied, gritting my teeth. "I'll be standing in your office in an hour with the $400, and that horse had better still be there!"

So, Midnight was duly retired to our ranch to live out his last few years in the comfort that he had earned. No one ever sat on his back again, and he had ten acres on which to browse. I would often look out and see him way up at the top of the pasture indulging in some delicacy that he had found there. When he passed away five years later I missed him a lot, but I knew that for a while there I'd been able to give him some pleasure that he so richly deserved.

So many horses contributed to a film industry that did not reward them. They were my teachers. Their insight was real and they taught me a valuable lesson, that as we strive to learn the best ways to motivate our horses, they are motivating us to be the best we can be. So much credit for the success of the Westerns belongs to the horses.

19

It's All in the Game

Mister, you can say anything you want about me, but I'm gonna have
to ask you not to talk about my horse that way.
— Frank Hopkins rebuking a disgruntled
competitor in the movie *Hidalgo*

I eventually accepted Don Burt's invitation to appear on the Union
Oil 76 Sports Club TV show. Shot live, it was completely nerve-wrack-
ing. There could be no stopping for a retake if I made a mistake. To my
great relief it went off exactly as planned, but after it was all over we were
exhausted from the stress. On the way home, we stopped to eat at a local
barbecue restaurant, still dressed in our riding clothes with Don once more
wearing his trademark high-top black Western boots cut in a hunt boot
style. This was one of the best barbecue places around, with a juke box
and a small dance floor. Don was a wonderful dancer, and we fell in love
while moving together in time to Johnny Mathis singing "Chances Are."
So, while my film career on the big screen slipped below the horizon, another series of adventures dawned. Nineteen fifty-nine would be a
total change of direction for Frosty and me. A new future with many decisions to be made was ahead for the two of us, and our lives would be pro-
foundly affected. The more I had thought about it, I figured I could parlay
some of the tricks of my movie trade into appearances in promotional
advertising, if I could only find a door open. It was time to climb into a
different saddle where I could still hold my head high and know in my
heart we'd done a job well. Frosty was now sixteen hands and strikingly
beautiful, just as I'd always dreamed he would be. He had learned his lessons well and developed muscles just the way nature had intended them
to be. Right about this time, the #1 song was the Tommy Edwards version of "It's All in the Game." Originally written in 1912 as an instrumen-

tal tune known as *Melody in A Major* by Charles Gates Dawes, who would one day become vice-president of the United States under Calvin Coolidge, it has been covered since then any number of times. I liked to think of this tune, written by a young man before he became famous later in his life, as a theme song for my beloved Frosty. My beautiful butterfly was out of his cocoon and ready to fly.

Don and I were married not long after that dance around the floor in the restaurant. We loaded up our four best horses, Frosty, my movie horse Jim, my latest acquisition Contender, and the open jumper Baldy that had been given to Don by the Squirt Company and we headed out, leaving a tall plume of dust behind us as we drove towards our dream of a new training stable. As a spot to settle down we had chosen Northern California, where Don's reputation preceded him from his three championships at the Cow Palace in San Francisco.

Frosty was now almost six years old and his professional career started with a bang. Immediately after we arrived in San Rafael I sadly traded my adored, but flashy, baby-blue Thunderbird for the practicalities of a new red and white Ford station wagon. While at the dealership waiting for the car to be readied, I told all who would listen about my horse Frosty and my desire to do promotional publicity. As I sat waiting for the paperwork, chatting away about my ideas, I noticed a door into an adjoining office was ajar. Suddenly, it opened with a rush as a man hurried out dressed in a dark blue hopsack jacket with gleaming brass buttons, tan slacks and polo shirt. I assumed he was the owner of the dealership. He wore a look on his smiling face that suggested he had just discovered gold. Throwing himself into a chair opposite me behind a leather-topped desk, he asked me to run those ideas through for him again and tapped his fingers on the desk as he eagerly listened. Before the day was over, he had sold me a car and I had sold him on the idea of doing an advertising promotion with my miracle horse as the star.

Frosty's first paid appearance in a new car promotion at that Ford dealership in San Rafael drew horsemen and families from all over Northern California. I had been thinking of various things Frosty could do with a little movie spin and making use of Don's background, and I had come up with a great idea. If you took a ride in a new car, you would be given a ticket allowing you to submit a guess for Frosty's weight, and the closest one to the right answer (1100 pounds) would win a registered quarterhorse weanling. While I handled Frosty at the dealers, Don's job would be to find, buy and deliver the quarterhorse weanling. He duly found a gorgeous one, all chestnut with a white face and white stockings. Well, children arrived at the dealership by the car loads, pushing, pulling and dragging their parents by their hands as they insisted the family take a demo ride in the new cars. The children squealed and clapped their hands as Frosty did his Spanish Walk, Passage and Piaffe variations of a trot in place. There were several tricks thrown in, designed especially for the children, such as counting and bowing and untying knots. Frosty entertained them with his repertoire, and then as a finale Don jumped Jim over a convertible. It was a first for car promotions as far as I know, and as a result Frosty became a veritable Pied Piper (although this time the children got to go home again). It was a dream come true for me that will always be there in my memory, and it was a huge success.

Soon after that, Frosty was hired to be the sidekick for a cowboy in TV commercials for another Ford dealer in Sacramento. The announcer wore a black western suit, black boots and hat and a black mask, *à la* Black Bart, so at our suggestion Frosty wore a black mask as well. I thought it was such a distinctive look for him that it should become his trademark, and so he was known for the rest of his career as "The Masked Horse."

In no time at all, our live commercials became amazingly popular. Our secret word guided Frosty through routines that we worked out ahead of time, and I would usually sit on a high stool or stand just out of camera range at the Sacramento studio so Frosty could hear me. No one ever really understood how I directed him, as so much of what he had learned was due to a combination of my body language and my voice. One day, during a rehearsal of a live promo, the backdrop for the set fell over on him. Everyone expected him to panic and demolish the set. His eyes were the size of saucers, but I talked to him by alternating our secret word with the command to "stay." His ears were pointed directly at me and they remained so as he stayed absolutely still, much to the surprise of everyone. The crew cleared the debris from his back and from where part of the set lay crumpled around his feet. It took all my courage to give an impression of composure, though I knew Frosty had it under control. He just loved to please me and never stopped trying.

In rather an indirect way, one of Frosty's best compliments came from American equestrian legend Gene Lewis, who would later be awarded the prestigious Pegasus Medal of Honor at the 2002 U.S.A. Equestrian Annual Convention and the American Horse Shows Association Medal of Honor. Living and training at the time in the Roseville area, within range of the television programs aired from Sacramento, Gene was shocked when he eventually discovered that Frosty was a real horse. His poor TV reception and the remarkable things the horse did had led him to believe he was a puppet or a mannequin of some kind. I always considered it a privilege to have flummoxed someone like Gene Lewis.

The commercials, though intended to be a serious sales pitch, enthralled the viewers who wrote letters to the station with comments such as: "At last, you have a better commercial than your program." In one commercial, Black Bart tells Frosty they are going to sell a particular used car on the set for a certain amount. Frosty shakes his head no! Black Bart tells Frosty the car wholesales for almost the asking price. To prove his point, he takes out an auto sales Blue Book, opens it and points to a page that Frosty seems to stare at eagerly.

Though all the commercials were scripted by me, it was Frosty's ad-libbing that constantly stole the show, such as the time he ripped the Blue Book from the hand of the car salesman and threw it off-stage when the salesman told him the price of the car. The dealer loved that one so much he took out a full-page advertisement in the paper the next day: "We're throwing away the Blue Book!" They sold 200 new and used cars off their lot that day to parents of children who had come to the dealership to see Frosty in person. The national TV magazine wrote up the story of Frosty and this extraordinarily successful commercial as "Kiddy Show Sells Cars," and it wasn't long before job offers were coming in from all over, including Las Vegas.

Due to the popularity of the TV commercials in the Bay area, Frosty was the unanimous choice to be the official horse of the Pony Express Centennial. We were asked to re-enact the original mail-carrying trip from Sacramento, California, to Carson City, Nevada, with extensive TV coverage. Don, though he had never ridden Frosty, was chosen to be the Pony Express rider. This invitation piqued Don's interest in Frosty that had been seriously lacking. Although Don had a photographic memory, he had never bothered to watch me work with Frosty, an action he would soon have cause to regret. He was consumed instead with his own interest in hunters, jumpers and western horses and there had been no room for Frosty.

But first, some pre–Centennial promotions were set up for live television. I wrote the promo in which the announcer, a local television celebrity dressed as a Pony Express rider, would turn away from the camera and run into the western store for his hat. Then, he would appear to come running out, leap onto Frosty and ride away. Of course, it would

Frosty disguised as "The Masked Horse" in a publicity photo (with Martha) for Frosty's résumé in the early 1960s. Yes, even horses have to have them.

be a double leaping into the saddle and in this case that would be Don. The local TV celebrity just loved that idea because people would think he was the actual Pony Express rider for the news feature. This was old movie savvy, much as I had done with the stars in films such as *Interrupted Melody*, *The Big Country* and *Texas Lady* where the switch happened so fast the fans were fooled into thinking it was the star who was actually involved in the action. Unlike on the movie set, however, this would happen live and there would be no second take if something didn't go according to plan.

So there we were on the day, outside the store with the announcer dressed in the proper outfit for the time. But somewhere, somehow, on his own initiative he had managed to acquire a set of big rowel cowboy spurs. I just silently shook my head. Those spurs were just asking to be tripped over but there was no telling some people and, anyway, I wasn't overly concerned because he wasn't going to be riding Frosty. Just as I had scripted, he duly finished his interview, turned away and ran into the store for his hat without falling over. I breathed out and relaxed. But to my horror, when the door to the western store burst open again it was the announcer who came running out instead of Don! Without telling me, those two had made a deal to let him (the announcer) do the riding. Well, he managed to get into the saddle while the cameras kept turning but then, as he leaned forward to ride his required thirty feet out of camera view, he made the fatal mistake of jabbing Frosty in the ribs with those big spurs. Now what this wannabe hero had no way of knowing was that, as part of his rump development exercises, Frosty had been taught to back up when touched with spurs. That's right, this horse wasn't spurred forwards, he went backwards! The "Pony Express rider" grabbed for the saddle horn yelling, "Whoa — whoa!" Right there on live television, they backed all the way out of sight. Incidents like that, of course, were the very reason why big stars of that era would usually refuse to do live television, but that was the first big laugh Frosty and I had working together and I think we were laughing for days over that one. I heard that guy never did ride another horse.

The following day, Don was scheduled to start the official Pony Express ride from Sacramento to Carson City. A very fine rider, he was quite the local horse show personality by now and, naturally, he would be riding Frosty. Now, this particular event demanded a true Pony Express mount, which means that the rider stands beside the horse with both hands on the saddle horn. As the horse takes off running, the rider springs up to rest his hips on the horse's shoulder and then drops his feet in front of him to touch the ground, using the momentum to vault up into the saddle. It is almost a trademark mount of Western movies but, naturally, you can't do it unless your horse is running.

The big day and the designated time arrived. Once again, live cameras were rolling as the signal was given for Don to gallop off. He was in position alongside Frosty, both hands on the saddle horn, hat pulled down squarely on his head as he stared fearlessly into the distance. He was polished, primed and primped for the cameras. I could see Frosty's ears going back and forth, seeking the familiar voice that usually guided him through this sort of thing, but the silence was deafening. Then, Don started clucking to Frosty which in standard horse language signaled him to gallop off. Oh, dear. This was fatal error number two. Once again, Don hadn't told me what he intended to do and, to compound the situation, he also hadn't bothered to watch me work with Frosty. When I was exercising him to develop his loin muscles, I used clucking as a cue for Frosty to dance. So when Don clucked, Frosty the obedient horse promptly started to dance while standing in place, just as I had taught him to do. The louder Don clucked, the faster Frosty danced while the sun reflected off the gold in his coat and the plain silver ferrules on his head stall and off Don's increasingly red face.

The crowd roared; they thought it was all part of the act. Don became angrier; Frosty became confused. Don impatiently scanned the area as though he was going to walk away and just as quickly returned to position. There were too many people involved now, and he'd just look silly on camera. Not used to being on the sidelines, I had squeezed in amongst the crowd and found a place in the front row to watch the show. Quickly analyzing the situation, I could not contain myself. I yelled over the riotous noise of the laughing crowd, "Don! Just call 'Haaaaaa!'" It was the old traditional cowboy yell and I figured Frosty would instantly know what that meant. Well, Don didn't seem to hear me but Frosty did and I was right. The next second, he took off down the street in a haze of dust, the cheers of the crowd lifting Don onto Frosty's shoulder and into the saddle as they headed for Carson City. Just before I called out, though, I was sure I'd seen a twinkle in Frosty's eye and perhaps a sly hint of a "gotcha" smile.

Frosty and I made many personal appearances, commercials and business promotions throughout the years and they all led to more and more education for him. The tricks I learned in the film business were a never-ending part of it. I refused to ask him to do anything for his personal appearances, advertising promotions or live television that he could not do. We trusted each other so closely that all I had to do was come up with the routines and leave the rest to him. All of these routines were directly related to the basic exercises he learned as a young horse to develop his body. The confidence he gained in his secret word remained with him forever and became an ever more important key in the more challenging routines that lay ahead. This simple learning pattern that we developed would one day guide him to perform in what was considered an event so special that only one in ten thousand horses could accomplish it.

20

Las Vegas

> I know a cool place in the desert.
> — From the movie *Leaving Las Vegas*

Frosty's fan base in the Bay Area continued to grow. His fame spread into neighboring Nevada and eventually Don and I thought it would be worthwhile making a trip to Las Vegas. At that time, the city had a permanent population of only about 60,000, although that swelled enormously at the height of the tourist season when it became one of the great entertainment capitals of the world. Las Vegas beckoned to us, and with Frosty's zooming popularity we felt on top of our little world.

As was my custom whenever I traveled with horses, I called ahead and asked permission to stable at the local fairgrounds. They told me we were welcome to stay as long as we liked at the stable area of the former racetrack for ten dollars per stall per month. It was just two blocks off the famed Las Vegas Strip near the Convention Center and behind the Thunderbird Hotel and Casino.

Frosty and I promptly started doing promotional publicity for more car dealers. Then he was invited by the owner of the nearby Henderson Telephone Company to perform for a staff anniversary party held at the owner's home. Frosty actually went inside the house to perform, and he did so well that the owner of the phone company quickly became one of his biggest fans. By now, Frosty had worked inside so much it was no problem for him to go anywhere. After all, he had spent a substantial amount of time peering into my kitchen on numerous occasions. He knew when action was coming, and so he made all his necessary "pit stops" as soon as I applied his colorful leg wraps. I always did this when he was going to dance because it is such a major strain on a horse's back legs. Then, I would re-set the wraps after the performance and leave them on for just two hours to prevent any wind puffs from appearing above his ankles.

During our time off, Don and I would go to Joe's Oyster Bar at the Thunderbird Hotel, named after the hotel's executive director Joe Wells. Absolutely vintage Vegas, the Thunderbird was a reflection of the town's glamourous early Western-era atmosphere. Developed by Cliff Jones and Nevada gambling pioneer Marion Hicks, the Thunderbird had opened September 2, 1948, on the other side of the Strip from El Rancho Vegas. Its broad, sloping gable roof, heavy wooden ceiling trusses and white rail fence all gave it the look of an old Western bunkhouse. The Thunderbird's Lounge was the famous intimate Pow Wow Room with Navajo-style décor, a small stage (by Vegas standards), bar and fireplace. One day, while savoring every spoonful of a delicious bowl of oyster stew made with pure cream, I found a pearl. A real pearl! Even the chef came from the kitchen to see it. I could not help but feel it was a sign of good fortune to come to us in this city. Although our jobs so far had been great fun and paid well, I secretly wanted something more challenging for Frosty to do if I could think of it or, better yet, if he could lead me to it. I had absolutely no doubts he could do it however it came about.

The Silver Slipper, just across the street from the Desert Inn, was another favorite eating place. Just as the Thunderbird was recognized by its famous neon Thunderbirds, the Silver Slipper was well-known for its giant, rotating high-heeled silver shoe above the building. At the time we were there, it was reputedly the largest gambling casino in Vegas. There was no adjoining hotel or motel, just the casino and its restaurant designed to make you feel as though you were in a Pullman Car on an early train. We often went for their famous 98 Cent Chuck Wagon breakfast, lunch, or dinners. Winter was fading but business was still slow, as often happened that time of year, and I enjoyed having time to learn the history of the Silver Slipper from the pictures that decorated their walls. When the Slipper first opened in 1950, it was on the grounds of the Hotel Last Frontier and its Last Frontier Village and shared property with their livery stable. Its original name was the Golden Slipper Saloon and Gambling Hall, and for the highly promoted opening they had a barbecue complete with a circle of covered wagons and a cowboy band and all the Western atmosphere imaginable. If you bought anything in the Frontier Village, you were given a key and if this key opened a designated lock, you would win $500 in silver dollars.

Now, thirteen years later, the present owner of the Slipper had race horses in California and would often join us at our table to talk about his horse First Balcony, the slow winter business and who were the big winners in town, but best of all he would comp the bill. Eventually, all this conversation got me thinking and I suggested to Bob that Frosty and I could do a promotion for him to boost business. While there was no shortage of celebrities around the casino's gambling tables, relaxing where they could be seen between engagements, Bob needed some actual paying patrons. So, I proposed positioning Frosty outside the main entrance next to the western saloon, which boasted swinging doors, sawdust on the floors, rose-patterned carpets, heavy gold brocade drapes, crystal chandeliers and mahogany bars. Needless to say, it attracted fans of the Old West like a magnet. Though the Silver Slipper was located on the Strip, its main entrance faced a semi-authentic Western street. A constant flow of western music and Tin Pan Alley tunes drifted out the saloon doors, and it certainly appeared to be tailor-made for cowboys and horse lovers of all kinds. It was a natural setting for a beautiful horse trimmed with his own sparkling gold.

I figured we could do a similar promo that we did for the Ford dealer in San Rafael, California. Folks could come and make a written guess of Frosty's weight and the winner would win a registered quarterhorse weanling. The hook was that they had to deposit their guess in a box inside the casino near the restaurant, which meant that they would have to walk past the gaming tables, wheel of fortune, the bar, a sea of slot machines and the famous 98 Cent Buffet radiating enticing aromas from all that quality food. Then, of course, they had to walk by all that again on their way out. It would be a spin-off from that earlier key-and-lock scenario back when the Slipper first opened. Bob loved my idea, and the very next day we signed to do the promotion.

When we arrived alongside the door on the advertised day, I was outfitted in a light-tan suede riding skirt and vest adorned with silver conchos over a blouse with huge puffed sleeves of white organdy. My white hat allowed a bit of my strawberry blonde hair to show. I had tried to match Frosty's colors as closely as I could and also be in keeping with the ladies' styles of the Old West. Just as in California, in no time at all that Western street was full of children and horse lovers who, once again, pushed and shoved to get a ticket and guess Frosty's weight. They completely surrounded the small corral that had been built for the bright chestnut stocking-legged weanling who took it all in stride being the Grand Prize. His new buck stitched halter was the finishing touch.

Martha jumping Baldy on exhibition in Las Vegas in 1963.

I let Frosty entertain the crowd royally: I turned his rear to the cowboys and he danced when I asked him what the showgirls in Vegas had taught him, and he would stick up his head with his lips curled at those who did not go to the Silver Slipper. He side-passed up and down the street, looking in the saloon and bowing when the folks showed him their tickets. He was in his glory in the ambience of the Old West, and for me it was just like the thrill I'd had every time I worked on a Western street in my film career.

All in all, it was a great success and it wasn't long before Frosty was a well-known fixture among the regulars in Las Vegas. The local newspaper even had me on the front page in a photograph that had been shot so I appeared to be jumping Contender over the grandstand at the old race track. Then Arden Farms Dairy asked me if Frosty and I could do some promotional work for them during the summer when their sales usually dropped off. They dearly wanted Frosty to become their "spokeshorse," and so he did. That summer Frosty visited elementary schools that were running a summer schedule, promoted Arden products at stores, and had his own hour-long live television show for children on Saturday mornings *Frosty's Farm Club.* The show would feature him in a "situation" and describe how he handled it. Every Saturday morning, the red light would come on the camera and Frosty would open his television show outside the studio by dancing to his theme song of "Hey Look Me Over." It was one of the few times he knew that he had permission to pre-empt me. As soon as he heard the music he would begin his *passage* or *piaffe,* whatever he was in the mood to do that day. Then he and the cameras would either move inside to the set or, once in a while, continue on outside. I had the crew construct a bar as a prop behind which Frosty and I could stand so that we could interact with each other for many of the "situations."

People often used to ask me whether a horse is color blind. Well, I know that Frosty would always react when the red light came on atop the camera that indicated they were filming, and he would relax when it was off. At his birthday party, he had packages piled up on the bar in front of him to open. As soon as the camera's red light came on, Frosty pulled the ribbons on each and every package, without prompting of any kind, till he had them all open. I could hardly stop myself from laughing until they broke for commercial. Another time, we were standing behind his bar making candied apples for Halloween, and as soon as the red light came on he took hold of the stick and held an apple above a bowl of melted caramel and, either accidentally or on purpose, dunked it in the caramel sauce totally on his own. He was always the pre-eminent ad-libber.

Frosty quickly became a favorite with the crew of his television show. One day, in preparation for a party that was to come later in the show, the cameras rolled while he was being given a bubble bath outside the studio! Imagine my difficulty just trying to stay serious. I so wanted to reward him. There he was, Frosty the Masked Horse, the ultimate car salesman, the Pony Express horse, wearing a shower cap and covered with bubbles! I am sure he thought it would never end, and he probably felt just a tad silly in his own horse way. Luckily, our secret word got him through our first and last bubble bath on live television.

Our trips to the schools were always fun. The children loved to have him do the math problems. I would ask him to pick a number like twenty, and to multiply it by two and then subtract 35 and give us the answer. The children held their breath while he counted out the answer of five, and then broke out into cheering. No one picked up on the fact that he stopped counting when I brushed the hair from my face. The children giggled and cheered and laughed and clapped till they were worn out, and many cried when they had to return to the schoolroom and hugged Frosty on his leg. The teachers grinned from ear to ear, not sure themselves how it was done. They in turn called the other schools and told them to be sure and call Arden Farms so they too could see this horse! He was very busy. And very popular! The requests he had for 30,000 pictures that summer contributed substantially to doubling Arden business from the summer before.

As part of his work for Arden, Frosty appeared in the annual Helldorado Days parade that year. I made a milkman's suit for him, using my shotgun chaps for a leg pattern of heavy khaki material that I thought looked suitable for a milkman's uniform, and I manufactured a vest that lay over his withers and came down over his shoulders to button in the front of his neck and cover the strap that held his milkman's pants up. To top off the outfit, he wore a real milkman's cap. Well, Frosty got more applause from the crowd, especially from the children, than anybody else in the parade. He did not mind wearing the uniform, but sweated profusely at the noise from the brass band in front of us. He wasn't used to that at all, and I think it might have reminded him of his days in San Antonio when the brass bands would march on the parade grounds at Fort Sam Houston directly across the wash from his stall. Perhaps he feared he would have to return to being a pumpkin after being a Cinderella horse for so long.

Due to Frosty's popularity in Vegas, we were asked to stable him at a much better address at a swanky master-planned real estate community near Wayne Newton's Arabian horse ranch. The individual houses were on lots of a half-acre or more, and the home owners were permitted to stable their own horses at the beautiful colonial-style stables belonging to the development. The whole project was encircled by a fully maintained fenced riding trail complete with show ring. It wasn't long till the real estate promoters would bring a prospective buyer to see Frosty, and it was not unusual for the odd visitor to ask if Frosty still wore his shower cap when he had a bath. Frosty had fans of all ages. He would draw quite a crowd on Sundays when he would perform in the show ring for the visitors and Don or I would jump Baldy. By this time, Jim had developed an irregular heartbeat, sad to say, so I made arrangements to donate him to the LARC foundation. LARC was the 65-acre Los Angeles Retarded Children's Foundation located in Saugus, just slightly north east of LA. They actually cared for the less mentally able of all ages, and Jim was so kind to work with from the ground that those people there could crawl under him, brush his tail, trim his mane with scissors (a no-no everywhere else) and take care of him day in and day out. He thrived on it, as did the residents at the Foundation. They had a nice pasture and stall there for Jim and even bought him a retired gray mare for company. It could not have worked out better for such a loved horse.

One day the other Sancho, our faithful cocker spaniel playmate and friend, was buried (wrapped in one of Frosty's blankets) under a huge tree

The Thunderbird Hotel in Las Vegas as it looked when Martha and Frosty were there (UNLV Special Collections).

at the new stables. Frosty stood alongside us with his head lowered, seeming to understand the gravity of the situation. The beautiful horse was reluctant to walk away when it was over, as was I, and we stood there together for some time. Sancho had been more than a companion for both of us and he didn't lie there alone, for part of us was there with him.

The Thunderbird is one of the signature icons of Native American legends. In the fall of 1963, a giant multi-colored neon thunderbird sat atop a pedestal five stories high to mark the location of one of the most famous and luxurious hotels on the Las Vegas strip, the Thunderbird Hotel and Casino. As I drove by it every day, I would often take the time to look up and admire it, but maybe all that time it was looking down on Frosty and me.

21

Thunderbird

If I had the ability to foretell the future, perhaps I would have bet
on a painted horse.
> — Sheik Riyadh to Frank Hopkins in the movie *Hidalgo*

The Thunderbird Hotel's name was derived from the legendary,
supernatural creature that appears in the history and culture of many North
American indigenous peoples as a spiritual messenger of power and
strength. The beating of its wings could stir the wind and bring on thunder and rain. It was said around Vegas that in Navajo legend, the bird was
the "sacred bearer of happiness unlimited." The giant, multi-colored thunderbirds that crouched above and at the front of the hotel were copied from
Navajo totem poles and designed in 1949 by Loyde Lowe, chief engineer
for the hotel's construction, and had then been constructed as neon signs
by the Graham Neon Sign Company. Looking up at them, I often used
to wonder if my personal sacred bearer of happiness was Frosty.

As Nat King Cole, who performed regularly at the Thunderbird, sang
"Those Lazy Hazy Crazy Days of Summer," I sang along with him as the
season faded into fall. With the cooler weather came the opening for which
I had hoped, to give my miracle horse an extraordinary career opportunity. The Thunderbird had quickly become my personal favorite place.
After all, it wasn't every hotel that was about to have its own track. Right
behind the Thunderbird, Joe Wells, the president of the Nevada Racing
Association (and the executive director of the hotel) had just organized
the building of the ⅝-mile Thunderbird Downs racetrack hosting thoroughbreds and quarterhorses. I soon heard that he was looking for a one-
of-a-kind act to perform in the casino and banquet room for the official
opening of his dream track.

Given Wells' position, he was drawing a lot of publicity for this event and so the opening was to be *grand* as only Las Vegas can do *grand*, including an extravaganza dinner. His reputation as an entrepreneur preceded him, and a veritable "who's who" of Vegas rang the phones to be invited. It was announced that the Honorable Sam Steiger, a Senator from Arizona, would be there to announce the first race meet on opening day. An extensive entertainment package was being meticulously planned, and Wells was applying considerable pressure to have a true attention-grabbing "show stopper" be the focal point of the evening, "stopper" being the crucial word. Wells wanted an act that would be so unforgettable that it would stop everyone in their tracks. However, though many ideas had been presented to him by the seven carefully appointed "entertainment directors" for the hotel, he had yet to hear one that really grabbed his imagination. Nothing had "clicked" with him. Frosty, as a local horse with his own one-hour live TV show, had naturally been one of those ideas, but many on the board thought it just wasn't feasible to bring a horse into the casino itself. He could perhaps perform on the show room stage alone (as had Rex Allen and his horse Coco several years before), but they couldn't see their way to having Frosty actually on the crowded casino gambling floor. Many of them could still remember that good old Coco had one night spectacularly disgraced himself all over the stage, which was at table-top height, giving new meaning to the hotel's slogan, "You saw it first at the Thunderbird!"

Still, Joe's curiosity had been piqued. His intuition had just guided him into Las Vegas history when, with producer Monte Proser, he had brought to the Thunderbird stage the first abridged Rodgers and Hammerstein Broadway show, *Flower Drum Song*, starring Jack Soo. It was so successful that they would later follow it with Mitzi Gaynor in *South Pacific*. So Joe decided to play another hunch and see for himself just what the local TV horse could do because this was, after all, a major horse-related event. Sure, it was a gamble, but that was the name of their business. He figured that Frosty's reputation for live performances might just prove his hunch to be right. If Frosty was a hit, true to their slogan, they would be able to say that people had seen it first right there.

Wells called me in to his office in the casino for a personal interview. He suggested I come early, which for him meant three or four in the morning, to see the floor when it was quiet but, instead, I preferred to look at the room when it was most active, as it would actually be during the performance. After all, I was quite familiar with the Thunderbird as a gathering place for horsemen. The concrete block walls with weeping mortar, adorned with murals of cowboys, chuck wagons and saguaro cactus, gave it the atmosphere of an adobe ranch house. It was the ideal background for a horse-related event.

Arriving at the hotel, I was shown to Joe's office. He came to the door, quickly scanned my best Hollywood look of perfectly coiffed reddish-blonde hair teamed with my Chanel suit and stole and, of course, my trademark Delman pumps, and then he politely offered me a seat, saying he was waiting for the horse trainer. After a chuckle or two, we left to make our way through the slot players and gambling tables to get an idea of the room boundaries. I hesitated in the southwest corner of the casino for another peek into Joe's Oyster Bar with its tufted leather booths, crisp white tablecloths and fine china that made up the warm ambience of the famed room. It opened into the casino and I took a deep breath to savor the aromas that beckoned me in. I told Joe that my good fortune in Vegas had started the night I found a pearl in my oyster stew at *his* Oyster Bar.

Our walking tour soon took us into the center area of the floor reserved for dealers and other casino employees. I met the pit boss, who oversees the pit, and the pit manager who deals with problems and enforces the casino rules. I was puzzled at their cool reception but I was too deeply involved in my thoughts to be overly concerned. I'd been stunned by the visible challenges the huge room presented; it was awash in unseen risks.

Flipping through the pages of Frosty's résumé, Joe stole a sideways glance at the stairway behind the slot machines. "Do you think Frosty could possibly climb those stairs?" he asked.

"Would the stairs hold an 1100 pound horse?" I queried in reply.

He thought about that for a few seconds, and then began talking about the room's layout. He explained that there would be several rows of long banquet tables decorated with flowers for special guests, adding with a laugh that the neon sign makers and florists made all the money in Vegas.

Together, our eyes swept the room once again and skimmed the smaller gaming tables and the slot machines. As I focused fleetingly on one of the large craps tables, I remembered that Frosty would have to arrive via the side entrance to the grounds and walk around the narrow flagstone walkway that circled the pool to come in the poolside entrance to the casino. Surrounded by palms and lawn, the Thunderbird's 360,000-gallon pool was at the time considered the largest in Nevada. I suggested that Joe and I walk the narrow flagstone path around the pool to check that it would be feasible for Frosty to also walk along it that night. I could tell, as we strolled along, that he'd be able to do it but he'd need to wear borium parade shoes to insure he would not slip. One misstep and Frosty would be swimming, probably taking a few flagstones with him.

Not only that, the impact on Frosty of distractions such as crowd noise, flashing lights, and slots with sirens and bells was a lot harder to gauge than the narrow walkway around the pool. Fully aware that my possible choices varied between non-existent and not easy, my enthusiasm was nevertheless almost running away with me. I had to keep bringing myself back to earth by remembering that things such as walkways and floors and stairs had only been designed to bear the weight of people weighing between one and two hundred pounds, not large horses! With a sigh, I began to discard one idea after another.

Joe suggested we sit down and talk over coffee at a table in the nearby lounge area. He was telling me again of his desire to *dramatize* the event of the race track opening as he pulled out the chair for me to sit down. He wanted something special that would be remembered for years afterwards! The curved-backed chair looked comfortable and inviting, and I sighed as I slid onto the leather seat. I removed my tortoise-shell glasses and polished them slowly with a napkin from the table to give myself time to think.

Never in our lives had I put Frosty in a position where both he and I were not in control. Consequently, there had been no failures throughout his long career, and I did not want to leave us open to one now. I did not want to agree to some exotic event where there was a chance things could go wrong. The palms of my hands were sweaty as Wells pressed me for an answer. Frosty and I would have only ten days to prepare, and this made it very difficult to perfect a new, foolproof routine to be performed in a totally foreign atmosphere. He and I would have to do it ourselves, too. This type of training was totally out of the scope of Don's horse training world, and his lack of interest in Frosty had been a major disappointment to me from the moment we got married. Frosty was my world and something I thought we could share together, but it did not seem that would happen. There would be a lot staked on this performance. Frosty's reputation would be forever tarnished should we fail in front of the Las Vegas elite. Although I had often profited from failure in my life, I felt suddenly overwhelmed with the possibility of embarrassing Joe Wells and putting Frosty in a position of ridicule. It was all too reminiscent of my experience in the movie business where if you didn't get it right, you weren't called again. If he made a mistake, Frosty's career could be over. I felt under pressure and not comfortable at all. I knew that my old friend Joe Yrigoyen, with his motto about knowing what you would do in case what you planned to do didn't work out, would have had a Plan B ready but I couldn't see a Plan B for this setup no matter how hard I tried. My breathing became a tad ragged as my thoughts desperately rattled around in my brain.

Knowing Joe would not play a waiting game, I was preparing myself to announce one of the most heartbreaking decisions of my life, to turn the offer down, when the answer to my quandary suddenly came to me like a bolt from the blue. I realized that I could parlay one of Frosty's early "tricks" into this extraordinary opportunity. He would be totally comfortable with what would be a familiar routine for him, and so would I. It would be *dramatic* enough to please Joe, and Frosty would indeed bring to them something they would remember for a long, long time.

I put my glasses back on, set my napkin on the table and presented Joe with a proposition that I'd be prepared to bet was unlike any heard before by a Vegas hotel director.

"You know," I said, "Frosty can stand at a craps table and roll the dice. Not only that, he could go upstairs to your banquet room, canter sideways and dance between the long tables for your guests, if you can arrange for your strolling guitar player to be available to play for him. The only thing I'd need is for your hotel engineer to guarantee the stairs are strong enough to carry Frosty's weight."

I watched Joe carefully, trying not to let the sparkle of anticipation in my brown eyes grow too bright. He held his coffee cup with both hands at his lips for a second as he looked squarely at me over the rim, then slowly raised his eyebrows as a glimmer of excitement flitted across his face. Lowering the cup thoughtfully into the saucer, Joe glanced at the pit area, then back at me. With a tiny twitch, the corner of his mouth began to lift with the beginnings of a grin, and my heart leaped as I knew he could see it. Right before his mind's eye, Frosty was rolling that dice and he knew just what this unique event could do for the Thunderbird. Even though some small doubts may have persisted for him, our eyes held for a moment and it was a deal.

I settled down to explain my idea in more detail. Frosty would walk up to one of the craps tables and take his place between the shooters. He would then take the dice one at a time from my outstretched hand and throw them on to the table. Years ago, I had taught him by using my body position to take something from my hand and then hold it in his mouth without eating it. Joe, who knew a great deal more about horse than his hotel associates, understood just how special it was for a horse to be able to do this and nodded as he listened, taking it all in. He agreed to see to it that colored spotlights followed Frosty the whole time he was in the casino.

We left the table and walked through the casino again to choose the right craps table for the event. Joe gave a rundown of our plan to the pit manager, who did not warm in the slightest to the idea. When he realized we were serious, I thought he was going to faint! Apparently, my rather polished appearance confused the pit bosses. I did not meet their stereotyped perception of a horse trainer at all, and I was sure the pit manager doubted I could handle a horse in the manner we were suggesting. It felt like my first cattle call at MGM as, cool and suspicious, the pit manager called Joe aside and animatedly whispered to him. Joe had the final word, though, and evidently told him in no uncertain terms that the horse was in! With a sigh, the pit manager reluctantly selected a table for us near their surveillance camera, known as the "eye in the sky." It was settled that he would advise the dealers and crew what would happen. Perhaps he feared Frosty would be the getaway vehicle for a heist, because he was still shaking his head with his arms folded over his chest as we walked away.

Well, it was a deal, but we would have only ten days to perfect the act. When I happily told Don, he was very quiet. He hadn't followed what I was doing with Frosty anyway, so this was out of his league. Frosty was my horse, so he just didn't understand why this was so important to me. Still, when he talked about this in years to come, I would hear him constantly refer to "his horse Frosty."

Many horses have performed stage acts, but usually on a stage. Frosty and I would be performing in the midst of a room packed with enthusiastic, loud and boisterous gamblers. An act like this would require a highly trained and skilled horse that could be trusted not to kick or scare any of those 1,500 people fighting to spend their money, but to entertain them.

The room and its potential problems were overwhelming but exciting. This was the chance of a lifetime I had been waiting for! My biggest fear would still be those hundreds of four-legged metal stools placed in the aisles in front of the slot machines. We would have to walk by many of them on our approach to the craps table. A frightened horse who accidentally stepped through the metal legs on the stools was more than my imagination could handle.

The date for Frosty's appearance was finally set for the night before the official opening of the new Thunderbird Downs track. Wells had taken the old Joe W. Brown track and replaced it with a smaller track, refurbishing the original grandstand and stable area. Many of the country's top quarterhorses and thoroughbreds traditionally qualified here to run in the stake races at Los Alamitos in the Los Angeles area. The famed Gill Cattle Company had several among them, and one belonged to the owner of the Henderson Telephone Company who would no doubt be at the casino cheering us on. Many big name riders, owners and trainers were being flown in to enjoy the grand opening festivities.

I knew that success or failure would depend on Frosty's trust in me and I kept reminding myself how I had eventually succeeded in mounting a horse carrying a duck and a rifle. I'd thought I wouldn't be able to do that but it had worked out and, instead, become a true asset. We practiced at home with the dice and in just a few minutes Frosty understood what was wanted and could throw the dice to a makeshift table. It was old hat to him and he picked up the same cues he had for the "Throwing Away the Blue Book at Black Bart Motors" television commercial. In no time at all, it became so much fun for him that it was obvious he would need the built-in back-stop on the dice table in the casino to catch the dice he was inclined to roll with such enthusiasm.

I made an appointment with Frosty's blacksmith to come mid-afternoon of the big day to put his parade shoes on him. These are iron shoes that have dots of borium applied to them. Borium is one of the hardest known metals and when it is applied in dots to a shoe, it will actually cut into the surface and allow a tractable footing on a slippery surface such as ice, or cement or flagstone. His bath came after the shoes and, as this was such a special occasion, I rubbed him dry with my hands in a paddlewheel motion. I had learned this from the gauchos who flew with the polo horses for the U.S. vs. Argentine International polo games. They brought about fifty horses with them, and each horse had his own gaucho (groom). I had never before seen horses shine like theirs, so they taught me how they used their hands to dry them, thus transferring the oil from your skin to their coats.

Frosty glowed like a newly minted coin, his pure white mane and tail a perfect compliment. I had made him a new mask of gold brocade with matching leg wraps, and once he was dressed I could hardly take my eyes off of him. Still, I reminded myself that it was my judgment and our experience that the Thunderbird was hiring, the kind you often learn the hard way, and whether success or failure was the outcome we were totally dependent on each other. It had been that way from the beginning when he believed that there was someone who could see the magic waiting in him. I was that someone, and that magic was called Desire.

We had been preparing for an opportunity such as this for a very long time and so we eagerly accepted the challenge before us. The Bright Light City had reached out to Frosty.

22

The Horse of
Many Miracles

He touched the imagination of men, and they saw different things in
him. But one they all remember is that he brought exaltation into
their hearts.
— Walter Farley, writing about the great horse Man o' War.

It was not quite dark, and each and every neon wonder of Las Vegas
was illuminating the approaching darkness. Frosty and I stood together
on the flagstones outside of the highly reflective glass entry that led from
the pool area to the interior of the Thunderbird Casino. The atmosphere
was somewhat surreal, and the spellbinding allure was beckoning everyone to share the magic. As I leaned against Frosty's left shoulder, I felt his
heart beating at a faster pace as he stared in amazement at his surroundings, though it could have been my own heart.

Waiting, I gazed into the reflections of the glass. In my mind's eye,
I saw myself peering into that empty stall in Texas and then walking in to
see the young foal. It had all started there when I saw his belief in wishes
and the impossible in his eyes. I could hear again the snickers and comments from the swells at the Biltmore in Phoenix as the "grubby little
misfit" and I walked their promenade. I thought of the promises we had
made, and kept, since his early life when no one wanted him and referred
to him as a disappointment and a runt.

I looked up at Frosty's strong profile that I knew so well now. His
deep brown eyes shared such noble intelligence. The hint of tightness
around his mouth indicated a glimmer of anticipation. I could not help
but wonder about the road we had traveled, Frosty and I, to find ourselves
reflected now in the windows of this world-class hotel.

It was a special night and all of Las Vegas, the invited and the uninvited, had streamed into the casino. Though only a few were prepared to see a live horse walking through the crowd, word of the horse waiting at the door spread like wildfire. As we stood listening for his theme song, "Hey Look Me Over," to signal his entrance, I knew that Frosty's reflection mirrored in all that glass presented an unlikely sight for a horse to see. There were a thousand faces looking back at him. He was lost in the gaze of these smiling people with their inquiring eyes, but he did not realize they had come to see him. They were no different from a thousand other people who had surrounded him before, really. This night, though, would be different.

Leaning against his left shoulder, I felt his skin tighten in anticipation even though he had no idea of what lay ahead of him tonight. He lowered his head and tucked one highly polished foot under him for a closer look. His long white mane fell every which way as he shook his head in wonder. Framing himself in the glass, he could see an outline of a sign that said, "Thunderbird Hotel, Las Vegas, Nevada." There was a challenge in his eyes, and I was afraid to breathe lest I destroy the magic.

Standing there, he listened for my voice that was now his lifeline. I saw his ears searching, and I knew he wanted to hear our reassuring secret word. Waiting was hard. I was nervous, too, hoping my trembling legs would carry me forward when I heard our cue. I slipped my hand under the girth to make sure his saddle was good and tight, straightened his finely braided red split-ear show halter, and made sure his gold brocade mask was comfortable and straight on his head. The matching brocade leg wraps accentuated his slender legs. Don, my Audie Murphy look-a-like husband, would have to carry his bridle for the upstairs dancing event. Many, I was sure, would take a second look assuming it was Audie!

Darkness had fallen and, dazzled by the splendor of the setting and the lights blinding our eyes, we heard our music. I heard a faint clicking sound from the immense glass doors, indicating they were going to open. As they slid apart, our reflection disappeared with them. I nervously touched the high choker collar of my silk shirt with my fingers and reached to smooth my riding pants with my hands. I had selected them because they were the exact color of the palomino hairs in Frosty's sleek coat. I felt him take a fast breath and hold it, as the first sounds of his theme song drifted through the doors onto the flagstone patio.

I paused, slowly letting out a long breath to release the tensions churning in my stomach, and then I hesitated for a few more seconds so that Frosty could hear his secret word and take in the sight of the people awaiting his arrival. I caught a glimpse of my diamond tiara sparkling in the lights of the disappearing glass as I looked up at him to whisper that word.

It was a pressure-filled moment. This experience would be the pinnacle of his achievements, and yet I found myself fighting my own nerves. I trusted Frosty implicitly, but I remembered how stunned I had been when a few well-rehearsed stunts went wrong in my film days as they flashed before me now. I mentally whispered to Joe that there could be no Plan B this time. This would have to work the first time!

As soon as we set foot inside the door, the lighting engineers showed their enthusiasm for Frosty by cradling him with spotlights of all different colors. They meticulously followed him and allowed the colorful lights to bounce off the golden hairs in his coat, his pure white mane, and my blonde hair topped with the rhinestone tiara. A palomino horse, wearing the best coat in the room, was about to snatch the attention from the celebrity-packed marquees on the Las Vegas strip.

I walked beside Frosty with all the style I had learned in my high school modeling course years before, hoping my demeanor masked my inner turmoil. Frosty stayed right beside me exhibiting his usual *savoir faire*. Standing on tip-toe every few steps to locate our pre-selected table, I could see that a horse walking through this sea of people certainly stopped all the action. We slowly picked our way through the maze of guests that swarmed around us; the sea parted as it must have for Moses. Don, in his red velvet vest that I had made for him with the black file lapels and black string tie, gave me moral support as he carried Frosty's bridle and walked on his right side to buffer the slot machines and the dreaded four-legged stools.

We made our way to the table that Joe and I had selected. The pit manager had explained what was going to take place to the stick man, so he would know what to expect. No one was really prepared for what was to come, though; explanations often blur the magic. Standing behind the green felt table, dressed in a plaid western snap button shirt that still showed the folds of being new, the stick man greeted us by grinning from ear to ear. A nervous Joe Wells, in his blue business suit befitting the position of executive director, was leaning on the highly polished wooden edge of the crap table as he watched Frosty approach. Anxiety and hope, mingled with just a trace of disbelief, was written all over his face.

The table was surrounded by unsuspecting gamblers. Frosty gently but firmly nudged two of them aside as he pushed his head over the edge of the table between the stunned patrons. He was just as cool as could be, standing directly opposite Joe, who now had beads of sweat appearing on his forehead. Watching intently as the croupier cleared the dice from the previous game with his stick, Frosty appeared to analyze the situation. Then he gave a deep sigh, and I knew he had decided to accept the job.

The pit bosses, still unsure and suspicious, walked around with their arms folded across their chests and scanned the entire area with guarded expressions. They hovered warily near the table as they kept a disapproving eye on us and another on an impassioned Joe Wells. Frosty's presence sent out a demand to be noticed, though he himself was oblivious to his

Frosty at the dice table in the casino of the Thunderbird Hotel in 1963. From left to right: unidentified patrons, Don Burt holding money, Frosty, Martha and Johnny the hotel guitarist. The dark-suited gentleman in the foreground with his back to the camera is Joe Wells, CEO of the Thunderbird Hotel.

stately image in the hotel that night. He had a way about him that reached out to an audience and held their attention, whether they were seeing him in person or just watching him through the impersonal medium of television.

Frosty, all sixteen hands (64 inches from floor to top of his shoulders) and 1100 pounds of him, took his place at the table with authority between the two displaced gamblers. I was to his left and Don squeezed in on his right side. To my left stood the hotel guitarist, decked out in blue western regalia with generous white fringe, *à la* Roy Rogers, complete with white Stetson. Frosty stood patiently as if using his vast knowledge to guide me! The whole crowd was now aware of the show at the dice table. They watched, mesmerized, as his golden ears flipped back and forth to decipher the meaning of sounds he had never heard before; then his left ear was directed my way, listening for our secret word. The once-noisy casino fell eerily quiet. A slight smile curved across Joe's mouth as he nodded his head to me for the show to begin.

On cue, Frosty took the first cube from my outstretched hand. With a confident flip of his nose, he threw it into the middle of the green felt table where it rolled noiselessly and eventually tumbled to a stop. It was a three. Still the only sound in the room was a collective gasp from those clustered around the table. With an almost arrogant toss of his head, Frosty gleefully removed the second cube from my hand and sent it on its way. It ripped across the table and hit the back stop before slowly tumbling to a stop. It was a four!

There was an instant of stunned silence before the crowd roared! Their cries of praise and wonder bounced off the walls and up the stairwells. Not only is a seven on the first roll a big winner in craps, but it was a horse that had rolled the seven! It was big news when Frosty strolled into the casino, but now he had walked into the record books as the only horse ever to win at a table in Vegas.

The crowd closed in and settled around the table like a giant cloud of dust. For publicity purposes, someone handed Don a large fake bill to present the horse for his win. Typical of Frosty's show-stealing, ad-libbing reputation, he took the money into his mouth and ate it. Then my golden horse raised his head, shook it back and forth and up and down till his long white mane fell every which-way, and he whinnied. The sound traveled to every corner of the huge room as if to mock those who had doubted him.

I stole a quick look at Joe, whose smile of relief was worth a thousand words. Even the pit manager had unfolded his arms, and I heard a whistle of wonder and approval coming from him before the guitarist broke into "Frosty the Snowman." The casino gamblers continued to shout their approval, and rushed in to touch Frosty for luck. He lowered his head and reached out to touch some of them for the special occasion. Photographers clicked away; chefs came running from the Oyster Bar clutching their white hats. I had the pearl I found in my oyster stew tucked safely in my pocket, and it had indeed brought me luck.

Soon it was time for the next event, and I led Frosty up the twenty-one stairs to the banquet room for the "who's-who" of Vegas. Mounting up, I rode him at a cantering side-pass between the flower-bedecked tables. The bartender had a bottle of orange soda ready for Frosty, and he held it in his mouth and drank it gratefully. When Frosty was done, Don and I led him, against all odds, back down those twenty-one stairs without a hitch to riotous clapping from the guests. He did not offer to jump as Montie Montana had warned that he might, but then Monty didn't know Frosty.

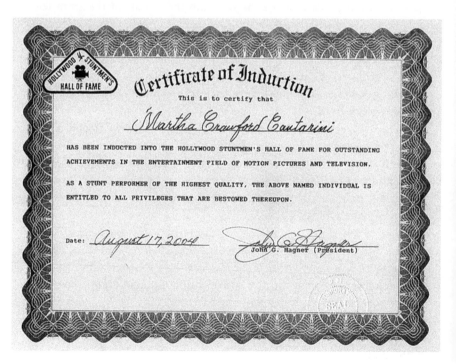

The Stuntman's Hall of Fame Certificate presented to Martha in 2004.

This time, instead of laughing as the people at the Arizona Biltmore had at the "too small" misfit, these people were cheering! Chappy, who by now had gained international fame by training Cass Ole for the movie *The Black Stallion*, said that only one in 10,000 horses could have done what Frosty did that night. What Frosty accomplished was more than I could ever dream of, yet I knew that he did it not only for me but for the vow he made to himself to be somebody.

My ears were ringing with all the noise in that casino, yet I am sure I heard just the whisper of a nicker from Frosty. I know he would have hoped his beautiful mother heard it, wherever she was, because deep down inside him there would always be the hope that she had given him.

And so it was. Lives so extraordinary they would one day read like a book. I would one day be recognized for my work in films and Frosty became big and beautiful, just like his brother, with the white mane and tail of his dreams.

Perhaps the magic was, after all, within both of us.

Epilogue

In the early 1980s, veteran movie sidekick Pat Buttram conceived the Golden Boot Award as a way to recognize the achievements of cowboy film heroes and heroines, as well as writers, directors, stunt people and character actors who had significant involvement in the film and television western.

I stood for a moment, stunned, looking at myself in the reflection of the glass entry to the luxury hotel. Now I knew how Frosty must have felt when he saw his reflection in the glass doors at the Thunderbird Hotel the night he rolled the dice. But this was 2005, Frosty was long gone, and I had never thought to see myself quite like this. It had been many adventures ago since I worked on my last film and rode my last movie horse. I took a step closer and I asked myself, "Is that really me?" As I stood there holding my white Stetson hat, I gripped my blue-beaded Indian prayer shawl with a tightly clenched fist.

I could see the faces of people passing behind me, looking at me, wondering who I was, assuming I must be somebody important. They did not recognize me then, and probably wouldn't have recognized me years ago even if they had just seen me up on the big screen. It was not common knowledge back then that glamourous stars had doubles to do riding stunts for them. Lost in my gaze of the smiling people with inquiring eyes, I momentarily forgot they had come to see me along with five other celebrities who would receive Golden Boots tonight: Debbie Reynolds, Mark Harmon, Wilfred Brimley, James Caan and Ben Cooper. Receiving those awards, we would be joining such stars of the past as Clark Gable, Gene Autry, Roy and Dale Rogers, and Fess Parker. Perhaps the biggest thrill for the audience would be to see legendary film icon Jean Simmons, who would later present my Golden Boot, and Tom Selleck who was scheduled to present one to Mark Harmon.

Looking back at my reflection, I could only shake my head in disbelief at the image of the expert makeup job looking back at me; it took so many years off the face I had come to know so well. I remembered how the stars and I had just taken for granted the talent of the makeup people we worked with back in those studio days and the miracles they performed on us. They were true artists of color contouring. All this reminiscing was getting me a tad edgy, so to calm my nerves I quickly thought about a few highlights of my film career that had brought me to this night, as one of only three stunt girls in the 25-year history of the Golden Boot to ever receive this prestigious award. I should have been accustomed to being part of a small group; when I started my career, I was one of only twelve women who actually did horse work for the glamourous ladies of the screen.

I thought back to *Interrupted Melody*, the true story nominated for an Academy Award that was one of MGM's biggest productions at the time, when I doubled the studio's premier star, Eleanor Parker, rearing a horse into flames for a live opera sequence. Well, they looked enough like real flames to get the whole scene featured in a spectacular color spread in *Life* magazine. Chuckling to myself, I remembered Eleanor insisting that MGM charter an entire United Airlines plane just to take me to St. George, Utah, to double her while she costarred with Clark Gable in *The King and Four Queens*. I shivered a little thinking of how cold that water was when, substituting for Debra Paget, I jumped my horse off a bridge into a lake in Elvis' *Love Me Tender*. I could still hear his voice as we sat and talked on those ladders. And doing that bareback mount for *Have Gun Will Travel* while holding that "duck" in one hand and a rifle in the other felt like a piece of cake compared to this!

Still, I could remember at least one other blond nervously waiting to walk onto a stage who became way more famous than I did. Even though I hadn't succeeded in that long-ago audition at Twentieth Century–Fox, at least I could always say it had taken Marilyn Monroe to beat me. Really, in the end she had done me a favor. It was because of my non–success as an actor that I was able to follow my dream and have a stunt career doubling for the stars. Looking back on it, that's what I had wanted to do all along. I have never feared failure since.

Now, squinting my eyes and peering through the glass into the hotel lobby, I could see an outline of a small neon sign that said, "Beverly Hilton Hotel, Beverly Hills, California," just as Frosty had seen the sign that said Thunderbird Hotel back there in Las Vegas. I took it as an omen. So, taking a deep breath, I held my head high and walked through those glass

Martha (left foreground) and Debbie Reynolds in the Hilton Hotel lobby in Beverly Hills before entering the International Ballroom for the presentation of their Golden Boot Awards for 2005 (courtesy Debbie Reynolds).

doors that the doorman held open for me and I left my reflection behind in the past.

A few short hours later, I was walking down the legendary red carpet with my personal escort dressed in Western regalia into the International Ballroom where, by invitation only, 1500 actors, directors, producers, family, friends, and fans of the golden age of Western films had paid $500 each to attend the Golden Boot Awards. That red carpet was lined on both sides with fans, held back by red velvet ropes. I had tried desperately to get a quick glimpse of my reflection in the glass doors as I left the lobby but, as I knew it would be, my reflection was gone. Then those eight-foot-high, solid mahogany doors to the International Ballroom swung open for me, and I could only marvel at my fortune in having my name become a permanent part of movie history.

As I look at my Golden Boot award sitting in my home, I think of all the things it represents. With great fondness, I remember each and every horse with which I worked. I remember, too, the stars I doubled: Claudette Colbert, Rhonda Fleming, Annie Baxter, Linda Darnell, Debra Paget, Eleanor Parker, Jean Simmons, Caroll Baker, Shirley MacLaine, and Martha Hyer. But, it's the horses that will always be my favorites.

My journey that began as the daughter of a professional polo player invited to ride in the Olympics, and that had then taken me to a screen test as a pretty, vain young girl in the wide open spaces of

Golden Boot Award 2005 trophy awarded to Martha from the Motion Picture and Television Fund.

Martha today with beloved companion Mae (*Beyond 50* Magazine)

Hollywood, eventually took me down another path entirely. I will always think of myself as so fortunate in being able to work with and develop relationships with all those horses. My horses were my teachers. As I strove to learn the best ways to motivate them, they motivated me to be the best I could be. While many of the other "horse girls" I knew were focused on their trick riding and performing in rodeos, I was one of the chosen few able to travel much further in life than being just a female imitation of a cowboy, and for that I will always consider myself blessed.

Once upon a time, a girl stepped out of a stereotype and reached for a dream.

Index

Milton Keynes UK
Ingram Content Group UK Ltd.
UKHW041830121124
451104UK00012B/87